Damn This War!

Damn This War!

Between the Blitz and the Desert, a Story of War-Crossed Love

Julie Hankey

ICON

Published in the UK in 2023 by
Icon Books Ltd, Omnibus Business Centre,
39–41 North Road, London N7 9DP
email: info@iconbooks.com
www.iconbooks.com

ISBN: 978-183773-036-0

Typeset in Berling by Marie Doherty

Printed and bound in the UK

Contents

For Rosalind

Prologue

Zippa & Tony

It has taken almost a lifetime to be able to stand back from my parents, Zippa and Tony, and to see them as a story. It seems peculiar even to explain my mother's name – a corruption of Philippa. They were themselves, not 'characters' to be interpreted. There were no inverted commas round them. As for their being part of any context, that too feels faintly treacherous. These two were as real and unique to me as the shape of their hands and faces. How could I think of them in relation to history?

But the decades have passed, and the edge has worn off. I've opened their letters, mulled them over, and I now surprise myself thinking of them as figures in a frame. Death has helped. They are completed, with a beginning, a middle and an end. But what has tied them off more completely than death is just that overwhelming sense of their context – namely the war. The years from 1939 to 1945 made their story, the whole arc of it. The war introduced them – they met as blackout wardens in London. It gave them darkened streets to wander in, hand in hand, as they searched for chinks of light in the windows. Then, by sending Tony away to officer training camps across England, it sharpened their hunger for each other. It cast a glow over his comings and goings. It turned them into schemers and wanglers against fate and army regulations. It pressed them into marriage, and when the war decided to deploy him to North Africa, it whispered the urgent question of a baby. To which Tony, thinking of the war, replied maybe not; and Zippa, thinking of the war, said yes.

And so to the long separation, he in Egypt, Libya, Tunis and Algeria, she in London and, when the bombing was bad, in Derbyshire where her cousin Betty lived. In spite of themselves, experience was changing them both, and yet both were hanging on, looking back, suspended in memory and time, and living from letter to letter.

~

When I and my sister were growing up, my mother would tell us stories about the people on her side of the family. We grew up with them, dead or alive, Edwardians and Victorians all jumbled up alongside the moderns. They were like people in a play. We even had some of their clothes in our dressing-up box. We knew too that this family had written to each other constantly, and that our mother had boxes and bags of their letters going back well into the 19th century, stuffed away in drawers and cupboards. When in her last years she became very frail and left her home to come and live with us each in turn (luckily we lived not far from one another), it became a question in our minds – what to do with the letters?

As it happened, I had already by then become interested in my mother's father, an Egyptological archaeologist well-known in his day. This had been at the prompting, not so much of my mother, as of my mother-in-law, Vronwy Hankey, who was herself a distinguished archaeologist and had come across him quite independently. My mother had therefore given me every-thing relevant to him and I had used those letters as the basis for a biography. But the question remained – what about the rest, dauntingly untidy and unsorted? Unless we made a bonfire of them, there was nothing for it but to carry them off to my house – my penalty for writing about the archaeologist! – and stuff them away there. Over the coming years, there they sat, a growing reproach, until I turned them into a second book – this time, largely about the women my mother had so often talked of. Then I put everything away and stopped thinking about them.

But there remained at the back of my mind one stubborn and silent bundle. These were the letters that my father had written to my mother during the war. My reaction to them when I had first found them in one of her drawers is perhaps difficult to understand now. My heart had not leapt. The Second World War, the experiences of those who lived through it, the vanishing number of its veterans, are now subjects of great interest. But we as children, born in and soon after the war, had not been brought up to think in this way. It was not that the war was unmentionable. It was just that our parents didn't speak of it much. My father hardly ever. My mother would tell us a few things, but between themselves they didn't reminisce. Those who did were called 'war bores'. So I had not pounced on Tony's wartime letters with a sense of excitement and discovery. In fact I had given an inward groan. I was reluctant to embark on yet another journey. I took them home and half-forgot them.

My parents died within a few years of each other around the millennium, and a decade or so later, when my sister was approaching her 70th birthday, I wanted to write something for her about her birth and early childhood. I turned to my father's bundle to see what I could find, opening the letters at about the right dates, dipping and skipping, and not always understanding what I was reading. Still, I found myself more interested, more moved even, than I had expected. The letters were a surprise. I realised that I hadn't really known my father.

Time passed. I thought I had done with family history. But it wasn't so easy. There were obstinate things among those wartime letters that wouldn't lie down – and among other wartime letters too, the ones my mother wrote to her brother. In them, she had spoken of my father, and of their courtship and marriage in a way that had surprised me. Perhaps, after all, I hadn't really known her either.

It was no good – this stuffing away and half-forgetting. I fished them out, and Tony's too, and began reading. This time I was caught – and having already pushed the door ajar for my sister, I couldn't resist giving it a proper shove and walking through.

Chapter 1

'Those golden autumn days'

When my parents first met in the autumn of 1939, Zippa was 25 and Tony was 21, fresh out of King's College, Cambridge that very summer. For him, Zippa was simply the most beautiful, graceful, poetic thing that had ever happened to him. It was a *coup de foudre*, overwhelming for them both: 'He is a most passionate boy', Zippa told her brother Alured, then with his regiment in India, 'so vital and young', and 'he loves me so generously that I sometimes wonder whether women can ever know anything about love at all'. In fact, it made her nervous: 'I feel very tenderly towards him and so hope I never hurt him'.

Tony was a surprise. He stopped her in her tracks. As it happened, he was very good-looking – fine-featured, athletic. But he didn't invade her heart. Not at first. They had met at Chelsea Town Hall on the King's Road, just around the corner from where they both lived – she in Oakley Street, and he in Oakley Gardens. They might have passed each other in the street a hundred times already and never known it. Now they were at the Town Hall to volunteer as blackout wardens. With the declaration of war came the immediate fear of night-time bombing. Everyone had to put up black curtains and, at lighting-up time, wardens were sent about the streets in pairs to make sure no chink of light escaped. Somehow Tony and Zippa found each other and set off into the

1

night. More than three years later and thousands of miles away, in the midst of the war in North Africa, Tony could still recall the moment: 'Do you know Dearest,' he wrote, 'almost the first lovely thing that thrilled my senses in you was the smell from your hair those first days I ever knew you in the Town Hall.'

I try to imagine them. Would they have made for the little streets to the north of the King's Road, up Dovehouse Street, down Sydney Street, house after terraced house, each full of windows and curtains? Or would they have been drawn the other way, towards the Embankment, to lean together on one of the windy bridges over the Thames? During a spell of clear cold nights a few months later, my mother again wrote to her brother in India, describing for him the strangeness of the city he had left behind – the blackout and the barrage balloons that people were just getting used to. 'London is still astonishing in the black-out,' she wrote:

> *Last night there was a curious effect. The new crescent moon was brilliant in a blue sky at dusk and just beside it, one above it and one below, were two black balloons, and a little to the left another stood beside a star. They looked like guardian dragons, or great insects hovering before they pounced – but mostly they looked on guard. And when you turned your head around, other balloons in a darker sky still caught the sun.*

It doesn't sound as though she was looking closely at curtains.

During those early months, before the bombs began to drop, the London blackout felt both sinister and romantic: 'verdurous and gloomy', wrote Virginia Woolf on a visit to London, 'one half expects a badger or a fox to prowl along the pavement'. Country and city drew close, like a 'reversion to the middle ages' she thought, 'with all the space and the silence of the country set in this forest of black houses.'[1] On a cheerier note, Londoners took a liking to their new barrage balloons and gave them nicknames: Flossie and Blossom were Chelsea's two.[2] Zippa told Alured about a show that was running that winter which included a sketch about a barrage balloon man, played by a popular comedian of the day, Bobby Howes. He's 'very sentimental about his balloon', she wrote, 'the great silver thing, with Fred Emney's head and hands sticking out in front' – Fred Emney being another much-loved comedian:

> *Then he says what it's like up there, and talks of the birds and the clouds and the stillness, and all the time the light is fading and you get the feeling of a clear winter's evening, and then the balloon begins to swing from one side of the stage to the other, while Bobby Howes croons it to sleep, and the effect is both funny and absolutely charming.*

~

This was the poetry of wartime London, something that Zippa would have seized on to put in a letter to her brother. She never wrote of the other London, which he would have known anyway, the London of sandbags and barbed wire and gas masks – snouted goggles, issued at the time of the Munich crisis the September before. The authorities had long been preparing for war. That very summer, in June 1939, a full-scale civil defence exercise had happened all over Chelsea. The scenario had been high-explosive bombs dropped on nine different places, and all the emergency services had been mobilised. A contemporary historian wrote:

> Prompt at 12:30 the sirens sounded over Sloane Square, the traffic stopped, the public moved obligingly into

roped-off enclosures to represent the as-yet-unbuilt shelters, and loudspeakers warned that bombers would arrive in eight minutes.

Four hundred air raid wardens were on duty that day. Five thousand children were taken from their schools to railway stations so as to test the evacuation plans. And 200 people from across the country observed the whole performance from the roof of the Peter Jones department store.[3]

One of those who took part was Frances Faviell, an artist who lived in Cheyne Place, a few minutes' walk from Oakley Street and Oakley Gardens. In her memoir of the Blitz, she describes lying within chalked lines on the pavement, pretending to be a casualty, while 'ambulance bells clanged, whistles blew, fire engines raced, rattles sounded'.[4] In fact, by her account, the whole thing was a bit of a lark. None of the ordinary residents really believed in it, and there was laughter and jeering among the 'casualties' on the pavements. But a little over two months later, at the end of August, she describes another exercise, at night this time – more difficult and dangerous in the blackout. Now it was taken for real. People by then were speaking of war as a certainty. They were stocking up on food. Those who could were leaving town, or sending their children away. Faviell watched them: 'carloads could be seen, toys, perambulators, dogs, cats, and birds all piled in with them or balanced on top of them'.[5] And the railway stations were full of other children, government-organised children, half a million of them from nearly a thousand London schools: 'weeping children, wailing children, laughing children and bravely smiling white-faced children'.[6]

There were no children in Zippa's or Tony's households, but there were old people. At least, in Zippa's. In 1939, she was living with her mother, a sister, Veronica, and two ancient ladies, both of them bedridden: a great-aunt Katharine who was confused and senile, and the family's old nurse Nonie, who had been with them since 1910. How to manage the old ladies in an air raid? It was an impossible thought. Best to leave London altogether, find somewhere to rent in the country, and sublet Oakley Street to friends. At some point that autumn, the five of them moved to an old mill-house in Essex – Watermill House, outside the village of Stansted,* near Bishop's Stortford. It was farming country, something that Veronica in particular had become interested in. So as soon as they were settled, she enrolled on the local farm as a land girl.

The idea of land girls sounds quaint now, like the old 'Dig for Victory' posters – a period touch. But it was serious work. Britain was importing 70 per cent of its food, much of it across the Atlantic where it was at risk of being sunk by German submarines. By the end of 1940, 728,000 tons of it had been lost.[7]

Old Mill, Stansted.

The mill house at Stansted

---

* Not yet an air base. RAF Stansted was officially opened in 1943.

A Ministry of Food was therefore created whose object was both to ration food, and to increase its production at home. Tens of thousands of acres of grassland were to be ploughed up for crops, and tens of thousands more labourers recruited for the work. But how, when the extra men were joining up? Women were the answer. They had worked as agricultural labourers in 1917, towards the end of the First World War, and so they would in this one. They were issued with uniforms as though they were soldiers – there are lists and illustrations in the Land Girl's manual:[8] breeches, boots, khaki overcoats, brown felt hats, ties in Land Army colours, badges and armlets. Lady Denman, honorary secretary of the Women's Land Army, even borrowed a Churchillian phrase to make the point: 'The Land Army fights in the fields. It is in the fields of Britain that the most critical battle of the present war may well be fought and won.'[9] Not that Veronica would have felt especially military. In fact the reverse.

Veronica and Zippa were incurable romantics. They had always had a dreamy hankering for the country and its ways. Woods and fields fill Veronica's childhood diaries and it would have been the same for Zippa had she kept one. The sisters were very close, only a year apart, and almost twin-like in their sympathies. Years before, in the summer of 1934, when they were nineteen and twenty, the family had been lent a farmhouse in Dorset by an old painter friend – Gilbert Spencer, the brother of Stanley – and they had helped on the local farm, working side by side with the men to bring in the harvest. It had made a deep impression on them, and had sowed the idea in Veronica's mind of one day becoming a farmer, or at least a farmer's wife.

Zippa, by contrast, had no such thoughts. Her first love lay elsewhere, in the theatre, acting and dancing, and in a small way she had already made a start. She was a student at the Old Vic for that 1933–34 season and had taken tiny parts in the great

Veronica (left) and Zippa

Shakespeare productions of the day. She had stood in the wings watching actors such as Edith Evans and Charles Laughton, and had silently prayed, so she told me, for a smile from James Mason. She had been invited back for the following season, but there hadn't been enough money for the student fees. And so she was now scraping along in a semi-professional way, training herself, taking dance classes, performing in small productions and hoping for work. I have an envelope of references from actors and producers who saw her: 'she is a person of talent and dramatic promise' says one; 'I was carried away by the sincerity of her acting' says another; 'how well she interpreted the music … as a dancer on that little stage'. So now from the Stansted mill-house, while Veronica set off for the farm, Zippa would catch the train from Bishop's Stortford for classes and rehearsals in London, stay with friends, sometimes at Oakley Street itself, and come back every few days.

And Tony? At the beginning of the war, Tony was a pacifist. Politically, he was of the left. He was not, however, a Communist, which at that time he might easily have been – especially as a Cambridge man. The Marxist historian, Eric Hobsbawm, had been an exact contemporary of his at King's. Tony knew him a little, and admired him greatly.* But he didn't agree with him altogether, particularly over Russia. He didn't see why socialism should be identified with Russia – why, as he put it, it should be 'Russia's private property': 'Russia as a result of her history must be a socialist dictatorship. I believe that we can be a socialist democracy.'

It was a compromise characteristic of him. By the same token, he wasn't the kind of pacifist who refused absolutely to take part in the war effort. He joined the Friends' Ambulance Unit in Birmingham, to start training there in January 1940. Meanwhile, that autumn, he filled in the time working on a local newspaper in east London, *The Hackney Post*. But really, whatever else he was doing, Tony's main object in life was Zippa – in London, at Stansted, wherever, whenever.

It happened that Stansted was particularly beautiful during the freezing winter of 1939–40 – clear skies, frost-furred fields, the grass hung white with spiders' webs and the sun a red ball sitting low on the horizon. That's how Zippa described it for her brother in India. Tony stayed there for the whole of the week before Christmas and as they all scoured the fields for holly and ivy, and the house filled up with family and friends, the place began to work on him like a kind of magic theatre. In fact, Zippa's letter to Alured describes the house that Christmas very much like that, as though it were a stage set:

---

* Tony once reminded Zippa that she had met him too, early on in the war, in a cafe in Bloomsbury: that 'odd young man', he wrote, 'a sjt in the Education Corps … Eric Hobsbawm was his name'.

8

All the holly trees were so thick with berries that we could pick as much as we wanted, and we stuck it up all along the beams and over the arch in the dining room ... I sat for hours staring at the little tree when I'd finished decorating it ... the old feeling of magic came over me – it's like being touched with a wand ... Joyce [a painter friend] had made a great garland of ivy which hung diagonally across the ceiling, and another looped across the wall in the alcove ... and the archway was picked out with trailing ivy and holly, and all the time we had a huge fire going ... well, somehow, what with the holly and the table at an angle with a white cloth and 6 brass candlesticks ... and the firelight and the dresser – there was something almost extraordinarily bewitching about the room ...

And for Tony, it wasn't just the room. It was the whole cast. Families, let alone large ones, were a foreign land to him: 'so new to me', he remembered later, 'to be in a house with crowds of people'.

Tony and Zippa with a dog at Stansted

Tony was an only child. Not only that, but he had also experienced little family life beyond his parents. There were uncles and aunts and cousins, at least on his father's side, but he hardly knew them, nor the grandparents on either side – apart from one very old lady, his mother's mother, in Heathfield, East Sussex. This absence of family was nothing surprising. Tony's parents had lived abroad for years both before and after he was born. When he was very little, in the early 1920s, they had been in Tehran where his father, Arthur Moore, was the resident correspondent for *The Times*. They had then moved to Calcutta (Kolkata) where he became assistant editor and later editor of the most prestigious English-language newspaper in India, the *Statesman* – a post he held until 1942, when he was eased out for advocating independence and Dominion status for India.

Tony's father was a brilliant, quarrelsome, and philandering Irishman, enormously vital and attractive. He had made his mark early, as an undergraduate in 1904, when he was elected president of the Oxford Union, and he had done it without being an old Etonian or the son of anyone but an obscure Protestant clergyman, and an Irish one at that. He had then thrown himself into the radical circles of his day, living at Toynbee Hall in the east end of London,* 'in the company of Oxford friends Beveridge and Tawney'.† At the same time he had been employed as secretary to the Balkan Committee – a body that lobbied the government on the plight of the Christians of Macedonia and other Balkan countries then under Turkish rule.

---

* A charity established in 1884 by Christian socialist reformers, Samuel and Henrietta Barnett, to provide welfare assistance and education to the poor. It also offered accommodation to graduate volunteers.

† As he wrote in his (unpublished) *Memoirs*. William Beveridge, author of the Beveridge Report 1942; R.H. Tawney, social and economic historian and reformer.

Arthur Moore, editor of the Statesman *(India)*

Arthur had a taste for adventure, and in the following years, armed with letters from the British authorities, he travelled the Balkans, riding on horseback through the lawless mountains of Albania where few Europeans had ever penetrated. Albanian brigands, Macedonian village headmen, Turkish administrators, an Orthodox bishop or two, Muslims and Christians – Arthur had sat and smoked and feasted with them all. And all the while, both in the Balkans and, from 1908, in Persia, he had written articles for the press at home about these places and their politics.

Nothing in all this suggests a man ready to fall in love, marry and settle. But in 1913 *The Times* sent him as their special correspondent to St Petersburg, and there he met Eileen Maillet, secretary to one of the other correspondents. With the kind of timing that their son was to repeat in the next generation, Arthur and Eileen married in 1914, and true to the same pattern, the war sent them in different directions: Arthur to the Balkans again and Salonika, and Eileen to Belgrade as a hospital administrator with a British medical team – where she had her own adventure. When enemy bombs dropped on Belgrade, she joined a column of refugees and walked 400 miles in freezing temperatures over the mountains of Albania to the sea. From there she made her way to Italy and at some point – where and how I don't know – she and Arthur met again. In May 1918, their son Tony was born in Naples.

Tony once admitted to Zippa that he was 'no good at families', and the same could have been said of his parents. Even their little threesome couldn't be made to stick together for long. In 1925, when Tony was seven, Eileen did what all English families of their class did. She took him to England to start his schooling. But she never went back. Perhaps it was the Calcutta climate. More likely, the marriage. It had not been a success. Eileen was quite unlike her flamboyant husband – a reserved, even withdrawn figure, not unkindly, but rigid and humourless. She was also inclined to depression, and would console herself discreetly (so my mother told me) with a bottle of gin in her bedroom.* She doted on her son.

Tony rarely spoke of his childhood and was always loyal to his mother – 'such a very good person' he once wrote to his father, 'that sometimes I feel guilty that I don't do more to make her happier'. But he did occasionally let slip a remark which gave the

---

* I remember her when I was about five and six in the 50s – a little red in the face with wild grey hair, but more openly affectionate than this picture suggests. Perhaps time and the drink had mellowed her. I remember the Victoria Wine Company shop she would visit on the corner of Oakley Gardens; also, and improbably, accompanying her to the Chelsea Classic cinema to see the latest Gina Lollobrigida films. We must have made an odd couple.

game away. 'You my darling,' he once told Zippa, 'will teach me an awful lot about being happy that I missed when I was young.' When Zippa met Eileen and observed them together, she saw at once how matters stood. It was simple. 'He doesn't love her', she told Alured.

By contrast, Tony was exhilarated by his father. He didn't see him often, but when he did, it was a treat. Once, when he was eleven, Arthur took him to Venice – perhaps in the gap between prep school and his next school, Rugby. When, in 1941, Tony heard that his father would be visiting England for a few months, the schoolboy in him burst out: 'DADDY is coming home', he told Zippa, 'I am so thrilled, I know you will like him ... he really is awfully nice and tremendous fun'.

Arthur was a natural *bon viveur*, sociable, generous, extravagant. So was Tony, at least by temperament. But it wasn't until Cambridge, Zippa told me, that he discovered it in himself. Cambridge was a revelation to him, a breath of freedom, an escape from the gloom and guilt of Eileen. It was talk, ideas, friendship. It was also fun, and a taste of the good things of life: skiing (one winter holiday), 18th-century glass (an early taste), silk shirts and handmade shoes (a generous parental allowance).

And now, Christmas 1939, here he was, landed in the middle of this big, young, attractive family. He 'adores Veronica' Zippa told Alured (not, I think, with any anxiety), and Veronica returned the compliment. 'Beautiful', was her verdict in her own letter to Alured from Stansted, 'and he moves gracefully' – always a plus with my mother's family. 'Most awfully nice,' she went on, 'just like one of the family. He gets on famously with Denny [the other brother] and makes a fuss of Geraldine [the other sister] and brings out the best in her. Also good with Mother.'

Over the coming years, from wherever he was – in barracks somewhere doing his officer training, or in the desert, Stansted

Zippa and her brother Denny

lay like a warm jewel to be turned over and over in his mind. Do you remember, he would ask,

> *those golden autumn days the first autumn of the war, when I used to come down from London by the early train and do you remember the time I arrived by bicycle for breakfast … All my hundred thousand memories of it are so happy and all because of you, our walks in the evening coming home from harvest, and winter evenings that first winter, and Christmas with you, the happiest I have ever had.*

That Christmas, before he left for his ambulance training in Birmingham, Zippa and Tony became lovers. 'I have lived with him', wrote Zippa to her brother, using the euphemism of the period. It was inevitable, she said, 'the most natural thing in the world'.

Tony and Zippa were now a couple. And yet, in spite of themselves, this 'living' together shifted the pieces a little. For the first time, they looked at the future. Might she become pregnant? Though they snapped their fingers at convention and respectability, still, unmarried motherhood was a strong taboo. Neither of them knew much about precautions. She consulted a friend. He sent off for a brochure. The question of marriage arose. Their fairy tale began to shade into the ordinary world. As it happened, the whole subject was alive, not to say electric, in the family just then. It was to do with Veronica.

Veronica was a faithful diarist, and had been since her early teens. Her entries for 1938 often mention Jewish refugees among their friends, young men, mostly Austrian, fleeing the Nazi persecutions. One of these was a fiery young Zionist called Israel and her diary records many meals and walks and conversations with him. Halfway through 1938, Veronica's little exercise book which

Veronica

she used as a diary reaches its last page – and the whole row of little exercise books comes to a stop. The diarist, always so full of description and reflection, even after midnight with eyelids dropping and pencil wandering, falls abruptly silent. Perhaps she gave up keeping a diary. More likely, she destroyed what followed.

Zippa told me something, however, though only the barest outline. I understood that the young Zionist and Veronica became lovers, and that she conceived a child by him. He begged her to marry him, to have the child, to adopt the Jewish faith and lead a pioneering life with him in Palestine, as it then was. It was an agonising choice, but in the end, she couldn't do it. His heart was broken, he left for Palestine and Veronica had an abortion secretly in Paris. The secret was kept even from parts of the family.

So perhaps, after all, the Stansted move was more than an escape from bombs. Perhaps it was a place that gave Veronica peace, away from prying questions. In fact it was soon after, in November 1939, that Zippa reported to Alured that Veronica was well again: 'It is wonderful to see her looking happy and laughing like her old self.' But the shadow of her story remained, and it lay across Tony and Zippa now: 'If I get myself into the same trouble as Baby,' Zippa wrote again to Alured, using the name the family gave to Veronica, 'then My God! I don't know – but fear of that has seemed wrong as a reason to hold back.'*

Reading them now, Zippa's letters to Alured about herself and Tony are surprising, uncomfortable even. Why tell him about 'living with' Tony? She hadn't known whether to say, she writes, but 'it makes me much happier to tell you'. Why happier? Was she confessing? Did she want her brother's approval? Did

---

* In a sign of how strong the taboo was, Alured blacked out the words 'the same' and 'as Baby'. But his prying niece has managed to make out the words beneath.

she need to say, as she does, that it was 'vastly satisfying'? That Tony looked lovely naked? And that he thought she did too? On the face of it, it seems too much, too intimate, vaguely incestuous even.

Much lies behind Zippa's letters, a history that she, Veronica and Alured shared and carried with them, one way and another, all their lives. To understand it means going back a bit.

~

The pool that Tony dived into when he fell in love with Zippa and her family was deeper and more strewn with hidden rocks than he could have known. The family was not only large but complicated in ways that had drawn all the siblings – five altogether, two brothers, and three sisters* – into a tight, almost tribal, circle. And within that circle, there had been – and still was – another one, even closer, consisting of Veronica, Zippa and Alured. This drawing together was the consequence of a precarious and chaotic upbringing by parents who had been too distracted by dramas of their own to notice their children much.

At the heart of it lay Hortense, their beautiful American mother. She was a mystery to her children, as they were to her. Her real companions were books. In every other area she was distant and vague, a graceful drifting figure catastrophically at sea in all practical matters. Her weakest point was money. She spent without a thought. She would sign cheques as though they created the money she filled them in for; and she would borrow as though there were no day of reckoning. Dud cheques and furious tradesmen never ruffled her composure. If her debts became overwhelming, she would smile and even, like the Cheshire cat, disappear. When Veronica and Zippa were seven and eight, she

---

* The brothers were born in 1907 and 1910; the sisters in 1913, '14, and '15.

fell into serious debt – hundreds of thousands of pounds in modern money – and sailed for America to visit her family. The visit was meant to be for a few months. But, except for a brief return to collect her eldest daughter, Geraldine, Hortense was gone for two years.

As for their father, another Arthur,* the children hardly knew him. He spent his time tearing his hair out, trying to stave off financial ruin in London where Hortense refused to live, preferring places in and around Oxford. He visited when he could, but otherwise his nose was to the grindstone and what consolation he found was with other women. The marriage staggered on for two decades, during which the children were saved from falling between the cracks only by the energy and devotion of three women: their nurse, Nonie, their paternal grandmother, Mimi and Mimi's daughter, Geanie, always known to the younger generation as Aunt Jane. These women did what they could, according to their lights, to love, train and civilise the children. But in 1924, when the brothers and sisters were aged between eleven and seventeen, the long, slow car crash came to a juddering stop. Arthur pressed for a divorce and Hortense reluctantly agreed. It took another three years, as was usual then, to reach the conclusion of a decree nisi.†

During the divorce years, Hortense took the children to live in an old mill-house (another mill-house) in Mitcham, just south of London, at that time still a country village. Except for the second son, Denny, whose school and university fees were paid by their grandmother Mimi's second husband‡ – always known

---

* Arthur Weigall. Both Tony's and Zippa's fathers were called Arthur, a popular Tennysonian name in the 1880s when they were born.

† I tell the full story in *Kisses & Ink* (FeedARead, 2018).

‡ An Anglican clergyman. Mimi's first husband had been a soldier, who had died in the 1880 war with Afghanistan.

as Uncle Tony – very little was done to educate them. Alured had received some schooling, but nothing formal after sixteen. As for the girls, only the youngest, Veronica, was given any serious education at all. Of the three, she showed the greatest academic promise, and when she was sixteen or so, a godmother paid for her to attend a school in Paris which had connections to the Sorbonne. There she applied herself in earnest to learning the language and its literature, and to using her diary as a writer herself. But no one thought much about the future of any of the girls, and never spoke to them about university or careers. It was assumed they would be vaguely artistic and – like all girls – get married.

But, out of their parents' neglect the sisters snatched a semi-wild freedom. The Mitcham mill-house was surrounded by a large garden with a stream running through it. For Veronica, Geraldine and Zippa, this became their world. The boys made them a tree house and they would disappear up into it and read, sometimes forbidden books. They roamed the countryside, took picnics into the woods and, on fine summer nights, slept under the stars. They collected an alternative and multiplying family of animals – dogs, cats, rabbits, mice and a goat called Anne – which they loved with intensity, and buried with ceremony. Their closest ally in some of this was Alured.

~

Of all the brothers and sisters, Alured had perhaps suffered most from the mess of his parents' marriage, particularly in relation to his father. Arthur Weigall had originally been an archaeologist living and working in Egypt before the First World War. When that dried up in 1914, he had exploited an extraordinary versatility, turning his hand to all kinds of literary and artistic work. He had designed scenery and composed song lyrics for the London theatres. He had written popular historical biographies, best-selling novels and mass circulation journalism. He had even become involved in early film production. Anything to keep the family afloat.

When Alured was about eight, his father had taken him back-stage, and the boy had been smitten: the scenery, the lights, the make-up, the actors, musicians and dancers. In due course, the boy had himself begun to paint and write and show some promise as an actor and dancer. It's a long story,* but when Alured was about thirteen, he tried to run away to sea and did actually accomplish the first stage of his adventure. His wild plan had been to work his way to India where he would live like Kipling's Kim and write a great work. The attempt failed, the family was thrown into convulsions, and in the aftermath, Arthur persuaded himself that his son was some kind of a genius. He took the boy out of school, devised a special curriculum, and hired a tutor. It's hard not to see that, just at the moment when the marriage was foundering, the drowning Arthur clutched at his son as a promise of hope.

For Alured the consequences were disastrous. He spent his youth trying and failing to live up to his father's expectations. In fact, he never fully recovered from the whole crippling epi-sode. His father died in 1934, bitterly disappointed in him. But at least at Mitcham, with his sisters, Alured found a role. Seven and eight years older than them, he became their idol, their touchstone. There was a hint of the magician about him. He was a storyteller, a spell-binder. He read poetry aloud to them, they read Shakespeare together, he made model theatres and devised dramas. Even his failure was a part of his charm. He was both an odd kind of parent to them and, like them, a child. His kingdom in the attic of the Mitcham house – as far from the adult world below as possible – became a magic place for them.

---

* I tell it in *Kisses & Ink*, Chapter 21.

Fourteen-year-old Veronica described in her diary its hypnotic atmosphere:

> *Up in the loft with Alured's stove giving off glowing heat ...*
> *just in a sleepy heat we'd sit ... perhaps doing quite nothing*
> *or sewing or reading, or Alured reading to us, and the dogs*
> *snoring, cats purring. ... content is a funny feeling. It starts*
> *with a tingling feeling in the chest, which gradually goes to*
> *the head, as though it were wine, and the head tingles till it*
> *nearly bursts ... and you come to yourself with a start when*
> *someone's voice parts, not harshly, the silence. ... Silence, in*
> *the soft heat and light of the stove, then a voice and the dogs*
> *raise their heads, and then let them flop back with a deep*
> *outlet of breath. The cat's purring ceases with a little rumble,*
> *and the yellow eyes open, so sleepy that they are watering,*
> *and then they close and the faint purring starts, and becomes*
> *louder and louder until it alone rules the renewed silence.*

The Mitcham years cast a spell on the children. When, as adults, they looked back on them, they remembered chaos and neglect, but also a paradise. The family left in 1930, and not long afterwards, the village was engulfed by London, the mill-house was pulled down and in the garden a factory was built. 'All over the countryside,' wrote Veronica in her diary, 'soon it will be the City of England'. England obliterated; paradise lost. It was the lament of their times – a cry against the 'red rust', as E.M. Forster called it, of new brick spreading across the land.*

∽

---

* See the last pages of *Howards End* (1910).

By the time Tony came on the scene, the relationship between Alured and his sisters had developed and matured. He was still revered by them, but they were also colleagues – he and Zippa particularly. The two of them were now trying to make their way in the world of dance and drama. Alured had performed at the recently established Dartington Festival and in several early television films for the BBC: mime-dance versions of *Acis and Galatea* (to Handel's music), *Hansel and Gretel* and *The Pilgrims Progress*.* Both had been members of a small troupe run by an Australian dancer and teacher called Margaret Barr, a pupil of the American dancer and choreographer, Martha Graham. Veronica's 1938 diary frequently records them rushing off to class, rehearsing all evening, and coming home exhausted. As performers and dancers they were equals, watching, judging and analysing each other with sometimes ruthless honesty. Nothing escaped them, either physically or emotionally. In the circumstances, and given their particular and peculiar history, Zippa's confiding words about her lover were perhaps not so surprising.

But there's something more. Zippa had, in a sense, been rushed by Tony, and it had frightened her a little. She was fearful that the great hurricane of his love would sweep her from her moorings. Alured and Veronica moored her, Alured in particular, who kept her steady in the work she loved best. Talking to him about Tony as she did was perhaps a way of 'placing' him, of cutting him down to size. She was spinning into Tony's vortex faster than she quite wanted, and she needed to recover herself – her self. As she put it to Alured:

---

* However, when war broke out, he refused to join ENSA (the Entertainments National Service Association), fearing the family would think he couldn't even be a proper soldier.

Alured performing with a fellow dancer, Margaret Dale

Last week-end … [Tony] came up here [from his ambulance unit in Birmingham]. He was speechless when he saw me and then he cried. Sometimes I just don't understand. I love him in a way myself, but it's not like that … I wonder whether I am a very very selfish person – I suppose it's really that you and Baby are the only ones that really matter to me. Sometimes I think I could quite easily marry and live in the country and be happy ever after – I could too – then comes something in dancing, in poetry or trying a part that gives me such joy, that is more vital to me than anything else, and I know I shall have to do it.

The Margaret Barr Dance Drama Group.
Zippa is in the front row, second left.

Chapter 2

'Damn this war'

In Birmingham, Tony was heartsick – though he was also in luck. The Friends' Ambulance Unit was set up in the grounds of a mock-Tudor mansion belonging to a Birmingham Quaker family – the Cadburys, philanthropic cocoa and chocolate magnates. As it happened, a godfather of his knew the Cadburys and had written to say Tony was coming. So when the lady of the house, Dame Elizabeth Cadbury, invited the camp commandant to lunch, Tony was included in the party: 'rather an honour', he told Zippa, 'as everyone here seems to worship her.'

> *She really is perfect, a pile of white hair, thin, erect, with an ebony stick … She has a hand in everything and rules them all. Lunch was good, a great patriarchal table, adoring middle-aged nieces, their husbands and children. She informed me there were 37 grandchildren and four great-grandchildren.*

After that, he was invited to tea by one of the sons, the current managing director of the factory, and had a lovely time at that house too – 'bristling with every possible luxury', including a proper bath which they offered him, with bath salts. Tony made friends with his host's children, two boys of twelve and thirteen, 'so natural and friendly', and 'two sweet little girls, 7 and 3'. The five of them got on famously and Tony was asked to come again the following Sunday.

Now he was back in his hut, lying on his bunk bed, and had decided to cut both supper and prayers so as to use the quiet of his dormitory to write Zippa a long letter. A good fire was roaring in the stove (it was early January) and the few other men around him were also writing. He wanted her to know not only that he loved her, but how he loved her, and all the things she meant to him – her 'gaiety and courage', her 'perfect taste', and her 'sense of rightness in things and the proportion of things': 'I do really get a feeling of strength and help from you … You are something of which I am absolutely and utterly certain, and I know so surely that you could never be different.'

But then comes this: 'I don't think I have ever before in my life had any person except Mummy I suppose, in some ways, from whom I got help. I have been very fond of people and felt that I cared for them and would do a great deal for them, but never that they could really help me.' He sounds very young – as indeed he was, still only 21. But Zippa might have paused a moment over his remark about 'Mummy'. Was Tony really looking for a mother, another, better mother? Tony's 'I suppose, in some ways' is rather grudging. Much more fun to have Zippa, with all her gaiety and strength. In fact, Tony himself might have been a little uncomfortable – putting Zippa and his mother into the same sentence. For he quickly goes on to hope that she, in turn, will let him help her:

Darling do let me, because it is never really any good if it is one sided … I am so frightened sometimes of your self reliant side … you make me so happy and I rely on you so much and care so terribly terribly that it should be alright and that I should be able to do and be the things you want.

What exactly he thought she wanted him to do and be, let alone what he himself wanted to do and be, is left hanging. The truth was, he had no idea. The war had claimed him before he had experienced anything much beyond university. All through the war years he would wonder what he was good at. He had no particular wish (or so he said) for much more than a 'sufficiency' of money – just 'an opportunity to have some little influence on things for good rather than ill'. At different times he thought he might be a journalist (like his father), or a teacher, a farmer maybe (like Veronica?), a businessman (not often), something in politics. Thinking perhaps of Zippa and Alured and the people they knew, he once warned her that he didn't think he was an artist of any kind.

In one of Elizabeth Bowen's novels, set in London during the war, there is a character, Roderick, a young soldier of about Tony's age. He too has little idea of what else he might do: 'since he was seventeen,' she says, 'war had laid a negative finger on alternatives; he had expected, neutrally, to become a soldier; he was a soldier now ... Everybody was undergoing the same thing.'[1] Something like that had been at work in Tony. He once told Zippa that he had known there would be war 'ever since I was about 15' – since 1933, that is, and Hitler's rise to power. That conviction had been at the root of his pacifism. He had always been sure, he said, that the next war would have 'no rules, no limits, that there would be mass bombing'. Events, of course, were to bear him out. When, much later on, in mid-August 1943, Zippa wrote of her dismay at the bombing of Italy,* he replied with a weary shrug: 'What will you?' he asked. What did she expect? 'It was all implicit in '39, and that was why I was a pacifist.'

---

* The Allies had recently dropped bombs on Milan, Turin, Genoa and, on 13 August, on Rome.

That generation was acquainted with war. The First World War was there, just behind them, over their shoulders. If they didn't remember it directly as small children, they knew it from their parents, their teachers, their older contemporaries. Alured was old enough to have memories of newly maimed men – soldiers he had seen at close quarters in a nursing home run by a great-aunt. Such men remained scarred. In 1928, a decade after the end of that war, when he was 21, he saw something that he put in a letter to his grandmother Mimi. He was on a walking tour in northern England, staying in hostels and sharing washrooms. In one of these, a man

showed me a gash down his whole back and thigh from a shell during the war, that had blown all the flesh away, and had battered his head against a tree so that his scalp was skinned and hung over one ear. You could see the great weals round his head – and his arm, which was such a funny shape and had a dent in the middle like a bite out of it, had been cut in two; and a skilful doctor had fixed it together, and had patched and sewn him up into shape out of a muddle covering several square yards of ground. It was amazing. His whole battalion had been wiped out, and he was the only survivor of the lot.

The odd thing about this description is not so much the horror (though there is that) as the cool curiosity of it – as though it were an interesting and rather extreme example of something he and Mimi both knew about. Whether Alured told his sisters, who would have been thirteen, fourteen and fifteen at the time, I don't know. But a few years later, with Hitler's rise and with the Balkans, Greece and Spain all engulfed in revolution and civil war, they began to get the horrors themselves. Veronica's diary tells of the 'dreadful dreams about war' that she and Zippa were having as early as 1934. In 1935, she talks of gas masks and trenches and hideous death:

> *When I think to myself of any one member of my family dying, and I see all through the night, visions of them lying in many twisted and contorted positions, my mind is hollow and full of knocks and my heart swells so it goes right up into my head … It must be the same with everyone.*

In 1938, with Hitler's coup and the Anschluss and the Jewish persecutions, the thing crept closer still. It was on the doorstep. Veronica listened to the refugees she came to know and especially to her friend Israel, until she wanted, she said, to 'weep with him for the Jews in Austria'.

What distinguished Tony from Elizabeth Bowen's young Roderick, was that he wasn't neutral about being a soldier. Soldiering, in his view, put a block on real life. It was an interruption, a hiatus. Life proper, whatever that was, could start only on the far side of it. 'Damn this war Darling,' he once wrote, 'I do so want to get on and start living.'

That was in 1942, but the feeling was already there in his first months in Birmingham. Almost from the beginning, he felt restless and impatient. It was something they both felt, Zippa too – 'restless as the Devil', she told Alured, 'I have the feeling of no time to be lost'. Tony told her about the things they had to do at the camp, about orderly duties, a route march, night ops and all the 'boy scoutery'* of training generally. He wrote about a revue they were getting up and a dance he was going to: 'all

---

* The expression is Alan Moorehead's. 'There is something … childish about army field exercises, a boy scoutery that sits oddly upon grown men'. *The Desert War* (Hamish Hamilton 1944; pbk Aurum press, 2009), p. 453.

very well' he said, 'but damn silly and I don't want to be in Birmingham. I want to be in London, do some work, marry you at once and not waste silly time.'

The worst of it – though it was odd to say so – was that nothing much seemed to be happening. People put up their blackout curtains, but no bombs dropped. The guardian dragons swung in the sky, but no planes flew over. Men joined up, but there were no active fronts. Evacuated children were even trickling back. For a moment Tony thought there was a chance for diplomacy. In March 1940, he wrote to his father in India:

> *I wish we would take some diplomatic initiative and be more precise about the kind of world we want to create. I wish we would mention a few sacrifices we would be prepared to make ... we might remove the suspicion that still exists everywhere that all we want is a return to the British Imperialism of 1912.*

He hated the smugness and hypocrisy, as he saw it, of the press and politicians. He winced at the self-congratulation in the common remark: 'we're damn slow to start, but when we do—!':

> *For the last 5 years we have not resisted Hitler diplomatically or otherwise – now because there is a war, any mention of peace of any kind is at once damned by the press and labelled Peace Intrigue ... now everyone is getting bored and forgets that war is horrible, it seems alright so far, and is demanding more action, 'Better get on with it'.* *

---

* One diarist of the period wrote: 'Our newspapers and statesmen are all trying, by diplomatic and "wrapped-up" phrases, to be saying "garn, come out and fight, you big bully".'[2]

Of course, he himself was getting bored too. There was a rumour that his ambulance unit might be sent to Finland* – 'I was very excited at the idea', he told his father – but it turned out that they had enough ambulance people there anyway:

> *At the moment, like everybody else we are completely hung up. With no active war anywhere, there is no work for the R.A.M.C. [Royal Army Medical Corps], let alone extras like us ... As far as I can see, there may well be a long period of this kind of war; I imagine Hitler will leave the initiative to us, and I fail to see where we can take it.*

In the end, for want of anything else, his unit was packed off for more training at the London Hospital in Hackney.

Tony's letter to his father was written on Easter Monday, 25 March 1940. He couldn't have been more wrong about Hitler. That April, Germany invaded Denmark and Norway, and in May, Belgium, Holland and Luxemburg. By 23 May, it had reached the Channel ports and the British Expeditionary Force was in retreat towards Dunkirk. On 10 June, Italy declared war on France. Four days later, German tanks entered Paris, and on the 18th, France surrendered. Of all the defeats in this terrifying sweep, the fall of France was the most shocking. A popular novelist of the day, Mollie Panter-Downes, who sent reports for the *New Yorker* from London throughout the war, described the city as the news came through:

> *You could have heard a pin drop in the curious watchful hush. People stood about reading the papers ... the boy who*

---

* In the early part of 1940, Finland's enemy would have been the Russians rather than the Germans.

sold you the fateful paper did it in silence; the bus conductor punched your ticket in silence. The public seemed to react to the staggering news like people in a dream ... there was little discussion of events ... With the house next door well ablaze and the flames coming closer, it was no time to discuss who or what was the cause ...[3]

Like many other pacifists at the time, Tony gave it up and enlisted.

~

Meanwhile, Zippa was suffering an emergency of her own. In early June, just as the last British troops were being taken off the Dunkirk beaches, she came down with an infection of the kidneys and was admitted to the Charing Cross Hospital. There she remained for three weeks, while the German army continued on to Paris, and England looked like being next. That hospital has since moved, but at the time it was just off Trafalgar Square. From the window at the end of her ward, she told Alured, she could see the back of the Coliseum theatre and the barrage balloon in the square which went up every evening and came down each morning. No doubt it was some comfort to the patients to have their own guardian so close.

As she lay in the heart of London, not far from the Houses of Parliament at the bottom of Whitehall, she listened to the war news on the wireless 'getting steadily worse' she says. Perhaps – though she doesn't mention it – she heard the broadcast of Churchill's speech to the chamber on 18 June. There he spoke of the end of the Battle of France, and the beginning of the Battle of Britain; of an 'abyss of a new Dark Age' and of the distant promise of 'broad sunlit uplands'. If she did hear it, it was the abyss and not the uplands that struck home. 'I feel awfully depressed', she wrote to Veronica: 'The future is a blank – a big, big BLANK –

I feel discouraged and nothing presents itself to me with joy … I think this war will be the end of the world – THE END OF THE WORLD – like that – and nothing will have been of any use.' Nor did she think there was much point in trying to escape it. Those who could were making for the hills, but 'if England is invaded,' she wrote to Alured, 'I'm sure we'd better stay where we are and not start trekking off to Wales with bundles on our backs. The Govt is urging people to stay put because refugees get machine-gunned.'

One good thing was Tony. She was thankful, she said, that he had stopped being a pacifist. It wasn't, I think, that she herself was against pacifism. She may have been thinking of the awkwardness of it for him. Pacifists, conscientious objectors, were not popular: people called them 'conchies' and 'quitters'.* She may have been thinking too of her father who, in 1916, was presented by a stranger in the street with a white feather, the symbol of cowardice. (He was not in uniform, having been declared medically unfit.) Whatever the reason, Zippa was relieved to know that while Tony was waiting to start his officer training, he had found himself a job on a farm near Stansted. It would do him good, she told Alured, and at least keep him out of London 'if there should be air raids or an invasion'.

Now there was nothing to be done but to wait and hope. Since the beginning of the year their horizons had been shrinking. They had been living from leave to leave. They had counted the weeks and planned their meetings, and worked their way round last-minute hitches. It was an exasperating, infantilising life – like boarding school, ticking off the days until the end of term. A longed-for Saturday might be sabotaged by an unexpected

---

* As one wartime diarist wrote: '… we none of us like conchies. We all of us have someone in the Services and look on them as quitters', *The Diaries of Nella Last: Writing in War & Peace* (Profile Books, 2012) p. 135.

rehearsal of Zippa's. Hortense coming to town and staying the night at Oakley Street could spoil a precious evening. How to get her to go back to Stansted the same day? Could so-and-so ask her? Whole pages are taken up with these manoeuvrings. There was a moment for Tony between the Birmingham ambulance unit and Hackney Hospital when it looked as though he might get leave for 'probably a FORTNIGHT', he writes: 'I'm so excited ... I wonder if we could go away somewhere lovely during it.' But the old nurse, Nonie, who had moved with them to Stansted, was close to death just then, and Zippa was looking after her. Tony hadn't realised. Well, she must do whatever she must, he wrote. He was 'aching' to see her, 'as soon as soon as can be'.

September brought what everyone had been dreading – air raids. It was the beginning of what came to be known as the Blitz, a new kind of bombing where wave after wave of bombers would fly for hours over particular areas until they were flattened. Chelsea, where Zippa often stayed the night, was the third most heavily bombed borough in London. Roughly one in fourteen of its inhabitants was killed or injured in these bombings.[4] Battersea Power Station and the Royal Hospital were targets, as were the bridges – Chelsea, Albert, Battersea and Battersea Railway bridges – all quite close together. The Blitz memoir by Frances Faviell, mentioned earlier, is in fact about Chelsea's Blitz – she called it *A Chelsea Concerto* – and it's one of the most vividly horrifying accounts of those months. On 9 September, in one of the first raids – in daylight – the author describes walking from her house in Cheyne Place near the river, towards the Chelsea Town Hall, and seeing a plane 'very low indeed, being chased by a Spitfire and as it was chased it was unloading its bombs at regular intervals above the King's Road ...'

She heard one bomb falling on Cheyne Walk, round the corner from her house in Cheyne Place, and learned later where the others fell, all in nearby streets – Bramerton Street, Swan Walk, Smith Street and St Leonard's Terrace. Oakley Street itself escaped but the noise would have been terrifying. There's no knowing whether Zippa was there that day, but she would certainly have seen the aftermath. 'The whole of one side of Swan Court was blown out,' wrote Faviell, 'leaving the flats exposed like a doll's house which opens on hinges, and there were all the rooms on display to the public eye like the Ideal Home's Exhibition shows them!'[5]

Zippa rarely went into detail. She never dwelt. The people she wrote to, Tony, Alured, the rest of the family, all knew anyway. When she allowed herself a description or two, she gave them an edge of defiance, of bravado even. She was in London a month later, on the night of 9 October, arriving, she says, just before the sirens went:

> And we had a rousing hour or two with plenty of guns and three bombs which felt pretty close – they were too – Danvers Street and Paultons Square – 2 houses down ... [friends of theirs] were in a house in Paultons Square, they told me next day, two doors away – they never heard the bomb whistle, but suddenly the floor seemed to leap up and all windows in the house were smashed ... we didn't go to the shelter and the All Clear went before midnight. And I had a lovely bath.

Bombs and shelters be damned.

Zippa was lucky another time that autumn when the railway line to Stansted was bombed at Bethnal Green just after her train had left the station. Now, a few days later, she was writing from Stansted to Tony in London, with 'the brightest moon you ever saw and a huge wind'. A full moon meant a good night for bombers, and she had gone outside and leant on the bridge and looked at the water, 'and thought you just ought to have been there, and now I think it a little more'. She could hear 'some nasty German buzzing going on': 'I saw shells bursting in the sky in the London direction and imagine you must be having a bad time on a night like this.' Goodnight, she writes, she does so wish he was with her at that moment, and she hopes she will see him on Sunday.

Little by little, Tony was becoming necessary to Zippa. The tenderness she spoke of at the beginning was becoming an ache. In letter after letter, she missed him, thought of him, wished he were there. She began doing wifely things, washed his socks, knitted gloves for him – though she was no knitter and it made her laugh to do it: 'I got them finished so pooh! Such big flapping things.'

That December of 1940, Tony started his officer training at Winchester Barracks, and there was to be no Christmas leave at all. They were both wretched. Memories of the previous year crowded in and he decided to take a chance. 'I had a magnificent idea,' he told her:

> *I discovered I was unlikely to be missed if I cleared off at 6 o'clock on Christmas Eve till tonight midnight, so I borrowed a motor bike and some petrol and set off at 7 in the evening for Stansted and you. However driving was practically impossible. I was frozen, bad lamp and no goggles. I got to Basingstoke, 20 miles, tried to catch a train, but discovered I could not take a bike on with petrol, also the place was full of military police and I was afraid of being pinched for a deserter. So I pushed on and after a further five miles the damned motor bike broke down. Eventually I got put up at a labourer's cottage.*

Next morning, they gave him bacon and eggs and wouldn't accept payment. There was nothing for it but to thank them warmly, mend the bike and trail forlornly back – 'so my darling I could not get to you after all'. She could have cried, she wrote back. To think he might have been there on Christmas Eve: 'Sweet, I thought about you so much on Christmas and missed you and longed for you. When will you have leave?'

Tony as a new recruit

~

For all Tony's impatience with everything, Winchester turned out to be interesting. More interesting than Birmingham. The army was still stiff with snobbery, but the training system did now require prospective officers to serve in the ranks for a period before joining their Officer Cadet Training Units (O.C.T.U.s).[6] In effect, this Winchester period was a pre-O.C.T.U. interlude.

It meant that he got to know people he would not normally have encountered. There were plenty of young men from the big public schools and universities – Eton and Winchester, Oxford and Cambridge – but there were also state-educated men, some of whom were also applying for commissions. 'The more I come across people here,' he told Zippa, 'the more interesting they are.' There was the man who had run a dress designing business until he was bombed out of London; there was 'a solid quiet P.T. instructor from Jersey who speaks French perfectly'; there was Philip, an ex-butler who read the *Tatler*; there was an actor-dancer-acrobat who had performed all over Europe. And there was George, an ex-miner from Durham:

> *Really a remarkable man, keenly interested in politics, bursting with knowledge and will cite examples from last century's history usually quite correctly. He feels strongly the upper classes are keeping the working classes down, that they made Hitler, as they were afraid of Russia, is on the whole thoroughly suspicious of anything 'they' do.*

'He is of course quite right,' Tony adds, 'but mistakes the part for the whole, and makes what is a contributory reason the prime cause.' If George wrote letters home, it would be interesting to know what he made of this engaging but slightly superior young man.

At the same time, just as in Birmingham, Tony was being taken up by people at the other end of the social scale. Someone wangled him a ticket to a grand regimental ball, for which he was only meant to be on car-parking duty: 'It was a magnificent show, complete with champagne bar, supper, regimental band, about 6–700 people, bristling with generals, medals, men in uniform etc. … behind the bar were my sergeant and sergeant major serving one drinks and calling me sir!' At first he was a bit lost, but he soon ran into men he had known at school and Cambridge and in no time was being introduced to pretty girls. From this flowed further invitations. Even as he was writing, there came another from a lady who was waiting in her car for his reply: 'a "proper smasher she looked"', said the messenger.

So now Tony found himself lunching and dining with the seriously rich – the Guinness brewing and banking family for example – and, just as in Birmingham with the Cadburys, he accepted their kind offers of hot baths in their nice bathrooms. Whenever you like, said one hostess, 'your towel will always be ready':

> *Yesterday, I had an astonishing day. I went out to lunch with Mr Guinness's friend. A lovely house, clipped box hedges, greenhouses, a swimming pool, and a couple of thousand acres of farmland, let out. The house was stuffed with lovely furniture. Roast beef lunch, a butler and very good brandy. Inside was Mr Ffennel, Sam Guinness's banking partner, spats, spectacles and a soft white handshake. He must be about sixty, obviously very rich, and still gets up to catch the 7:30 from Winchester every morning … also present a brother and sister, he 38 business rich, she 34 unmarried, hard, slick, amusing, dour, hunting. Altogether they were the typical parasite rich lot, witty, outrageous, unprincipled … I endeavoured to keep up with them, got asked again and also taken back in the brother's car …*

George from Durham and Mr Ffennel. Chalk – or rather coal – and soft white cheese. It was an education.

∼

At some point that winter of 1940, Tony bought a ring and he and Zippa became engaged. Time was running out. For all its boy scoutery and incidental interest, officer training was a serious business which, sooner or later, would land Tony on some front somewhere. There was no point in waiting. The wedding day depended on when he could get leave, but they hoped for May 1941, before he was due to move from Winchester to his main training course at a military camp on the edge of Salisbury Plain. At the same time there was talk of Zippa getting a job. In the spring of 1941, all women, married or single, were required to register for war work. Someone offered to help find her something in 'the censorship'; someone else had an idea about a job in Cambridge. Zippa thought she would prefer to join Veronica on the farm. They needed someone to do the milk round.

At which point, tempers began to fray a little. Tony said something snappy about the milk round and apologised. No he quite understands that she might prefer it. Doesn't want her to get too tired, though. Thought the Cambridge job might be useful in getting her theatre contacts. He's fed up, misses her so much, wants to feel her 'actually, physically there'. There may be a leave in three weeks' time – 'if nothing odd happens'. He could never be sure until the last minute. She sounded so miserable in her last letter:

> *Please please know that I love you and long for you … don't ever be miserable through thinking of me, because Darling all I want in the world for you is to be happy and do all the things you can do and are so good at.*

Something was up.

None of Zippa's letters have survived for these weeks, but Tony mentions Alured's return from India and it's clear she was trying to choreograph a dance. 'Please will you show me your dance when I come?' Tony says. Had Alured stirred old ambitions in Zippa? Perhaps he stirred anxieties in Tony. At some point, and it may have been at about this time, Zippa had a conversation with him about Alured in which (so he reminds her later) she tried to explain that there was 'a bit of you that belonged particularly and separately to Alured'. The subject would come up in time, but for the moment the thought of Alured may well have knocked Tony off balance.

Not that Alured is mentioned in what happened next. It was usual at the time for people of Zippa and Tony's background to announce engagements in the columns of *The Times*. Zippa waited. Tony delayed. She was puzzled. What should she say to her friends? Then, at the end of January 1941, came a letter from Tony which threw everything into the air. It wasn't that he didn't want to marry her – 'in fact, if by a miracle I were left £300 a year I would like to get married next week'. But getting married was a responsibility. The prayer book says it should be undertaken 'soberly and discreetly'. Not that he was religious. It was just that, on a sober view of things, he doubted his chances of earning enough money after the war to keep them both:

After all, my sweet, I have no qualifications whatever ... I have always had a deep-seated, almost superstitious distrust of my capacities ... I have always been very lucky, passed exams and things much better than I deserved; my friends have always said 'Oh, you'll be alright, you always are', but I have always been very much afraid that when it came to earning money and making a position for myself by sheer merit, I might be a comparative failure. I am reasonably intelligent, but was always conscious at Cambridge that my brain is not really first class ... I am I suppose quite good

41

at people and therefore seem older and more competent and assured than I am …

He goes on to call himself lazy and second rate, not really fit to be married at all; or if married, she would have to push and pull him into shape. Really and truly, she deserved someone more established and fulfilled than he was, with more to give. As for her, he felt as he always had. He would never find anyone to match her:

You are so perfect a whole, consistent all through you, so many people are charming, or kind or clever over most things, and suddenly you find that on some subjects or in some aspects, they are really horrid. My Darling, there is no 'But' about you.

Then towards the end of his letter, come these rather ill-written and confusing sentences:

If we are ever going to be married, there is no point in waiting till after the war because of material conditions. It would not be till after the war we would have to wait, but till two or three years after, before things were any better.

He ends by begging her to confide in him, to forgive him for being snappish the other day, and to believe him when he says that his ill-temper is never caused by her. 'I have never known anyone so patient with me,' he tells her, 'Zippa I love you so so much.'

The whole letter is extraordinary. Why this deep-seated lack of confidence, this sense of being peculiarly undeserving and unqualified? Surely, as a reasonably successful exam-passing product of an elite educational system, he stood as much chance as anyone. His brain was good enough. Who was he comparing himself to? Eric Hobsbawm, who took a double-starred first in 1939? Tony took a perfectly respectable 2:1 in that year. Mediocre by comparison, perhaps, but not many were in Hobsbawm's league.

Tony's self-doubt is mysterious. It had 'always' been there, he says, an almost 'superstitious' distrust, something beyond reason. Speculation is tempting. He rarely spoke of his childhood, which is itself significant. There was the separation at the age of seven from home, from his father, from a loved ayah perhaps (children in families like Tony's were usually cared for by a local nurse or ayah). Then, when he was sent aged seven to prep school, came a second separation, this time from his mother. His time at boarding school, both there and later at Rugby, was lonely and unhappy, possibly even traumatising. From one or two things he hinted at in later life, there was trouble of some kind – bullying, no doubt – which was not handled well. On top of everything, was his mother's depression.

Whatever the underlying causes, it does sound from his letters to Zippa, as though Tony was suffering from some fundamental lack, a need for reassurance, love, or – not to beat about the bush – a mother. He had sounded like that before, in January 1940, when he had written from Birmingham to say how much help and strength Zippa had given him. Only one other person had ever done that, he had said, and that (he grudgingly supposed) had been 'mummy'.

Not that Zippa, with his letter in her hand, would have been thinking about Tony's childhood trauma. The pressing question for her just then would have been – 'what does he mean?' Was he breaking it off? Or postponing it? Was he leaving it to her to decide? When he spoke of waiting until several years after the end of the war, what was he thinking? Did he mean that it would be worth the wait? Or that they couldn't wait so long?

Was he saying they should marry now? Or not at all? After all, who knew how long the war would last, let alone how 'things' would look in the aftermath. 'Material conditions', he says. What? The whole economic, social, and political landscape? Maybe he was half hoping she would decide for him, cut the Gordian knot and say: 'Nonsense! How long is a piece of string?'

Of course, a smart retort like that would have been unlike Zippa. Her side of the correspondence is missing, but she seems to have been badly shaken. One letter she definitely wrote was to her aunt, who was very ill with cancer at the time. Aunt Jane had long stood in as a mother to Zippa and her sisters in place of the unreachable Hortense. Zippa loved her and turned naturally to her for advice. Her letter is lost but from her aunt's reply, she was clearly in a miserable quandary, crying herself to sleep, half thinking of breaking everything off herself and convinced that Alured disliked Tony. Aunt Jane was baffled by Alured. She had met Tony and had been charmed. Alured was probably jealous, she decided. Her advice to Zippa was to be patient. Any young man reading the marriage service might quake in his shoes. If she loved him and he loved her, her best bet in wartime was to keep the whole thing on track.*

Tony also mentions sad letters from Zippa. She was exhausted by her milk round, now in the cold and snow. He wanted to help, but he was useless to her, stuck in the army. The conversation reverted to the question of theatre work. He desperately wanted her to make a success of it. She must concentrate on her Shakespeare; she must follow up an introduction to an agent that Alured knew; she must push herself. She mustn't be lost and

---

* Aunt Jane's advice would have been coloured by her experience of the First World War, which had decimated a generation of eligible young men. See *Kisses & Ink*, p. 312.

wasted. She had so much to give, she was so lovely. He says he wants to marry and keep her, and 'nothing in the world would make me so happy as you getting on':

As you say, what you are afraid of is stagnation and your real work is the theatre ... as you say, we are both lazy. We must not either of us go on satisfying ourselves with the shadow of doing something.

The odd thing about all this is that Tony seems to have forgotten. He talks as though he had never questioned their wedding plans. If there were doubts, they seemed now to have come from Zippa. Her phrases – 'fearful of stagnation', 'the shadow of doing something' – echo her old fears about the clash between marriage and work. Again, Alured hovers somewhere near. In fact it was about now that Tony reminded her of what she had told him – about belonging partly to Alured. He turned it tactfully into her feeling for family in general, which he feared might tug against him. Of course he understood, he says, and he hoped it would never come to it. But surely, surely, she should belong more to him than to them. He didn't mean that in any possessive sense, he says, but if he could just be certain of that, he would never feel jealous.

At the beginning of March 1941 Tony went into the hospital in Winchester to have an operation on his knee. It would be a month before they could see each other, but after that he would have three weeks' sick leave. He now had plenty of time to think and it's clear from his letters that he no longer wanted to postpone, let alone break off, the marriage. It's almost as though he had got something off his chest. He warns her again and again that he is 'weak and ineffectual', and he wonders whether she will find him 'vital enough, with great enough ideas and ambitions'.

He begs her to think of him 'critically and carefully' and to make sure of herself. But he no longer says he's not fit to marry her. The one thing he's sure of is that he will love her with all his heart and he ends by proposing that they get married next month – April – a whole month earlier: 'What do you think? It would be exciting and a lovely spring-like thing to do.' Well! Zippa must have swallowed hard. What had it all been about?

It was during his sick leave, while she was actually with him rather than reading his letters, when she could see his face, listen to his voice, and observe his moods, that she began to understand. Something was seriously wrong. Alured's regiment had by that time moved to Hereford, but the two of them must have talked together, for Zippa's letter to her brother opens mid-conversation:

> *Well yes. 'To be or not to be' is just how it is – I feel just like Hamlet and in the same torment. At least sometimes torment and sometimes nothing at all, but not happy any more.*

The whole question was open. To marry or not to marry. It was 15 April, with the wedding due – still due – in the middle of May.

Chapter 3

'Better not think'

The problem was that Tony was also a Hamlet. Now that she was with him and picking up the signs, Zippa could see clearly that he had 'quite definitely and quite suddenly gone through a period of doubt'. 'It has never happened before,' she told Alured, 'and I feel most wounded.' She didn't know the cause exactly, and she makes no mention of his earlier letter about employment prospects and future earnings. It's as though that were no longer the point. The point was that from 'little tiny things, from his expression and what he didn't talk of', she could tell plainly that he was afraid. The thought of the wedding sent him into a panic. It made her sick to do it – desolate and blank – but she decided to call it off.

She did it, she says, 'not angrily but I thought finally'. Tony's reaction, however, only confused the situation further. He was devastated. He begged her not to. He was desperate, imploring, so miserable that she hadn't the heart to insist. His father, Arthur Moore, was visiting from India at the time,* and Tony wanted her to come up to London from Stansted for a grand celebratory dinner somewhere with both parents: 'He was so terrified I wouldn't come,' she says, 'that he hired a car and came and fetched me

---

* The visit that so thrilled Tony, see p. 13.

himself, at terrific expense!' So they all met, the parents, the couple, and raised a glass as though nothing had happened.

When Arthur returned to India in August of that year, he wrote a series of articles about wartime London and other English cities for his *Statesman* readership. In one of these he seems to describe this very dinner. He says it was at the Berkeley, and in 'celebration of something', although he doesn't say who or what. But the date he gives is about right – halfway through March. The Berkeley at that time was on Piccadilly* – just opposite the Ritz – a place that must have seemed wildly reckless just then. Only a few days before, two bombs had dropped down the ventilation shaft into the Café de Paris, just the other side of Piccadilly Circus – 34 dead and 80 injured.[†] But at the time, people simply shrugged. If a bomb had your name on it, it would get you, they said. If not, not.[1] The Berkeley was packed, Arthur said, everything in full swing, the band playing that year's favourite, 'a jiggy Fox Trot called "The Last Time I saw Paris"'.

After dinner, Zippa and Tony took to the dance floor, as did 'more people than there was room for', wrote Arthur, 'on a tiny platform about the size of a Union Jack'. A romantic moment? Not according to Zippa. As she tells Alured, Tony spoilt it all by suddenly turning to her and saying 'in a matter of fact voice, "Well, is it fixed now, we must make up our minds"'. It took her aback: 'I felt wounded to death and said it wasn't fixed at all'. The band played on, writes Arthur, raising such 'a fearful din' nobody heard the sirens. 'It was not until we set about going home that we knew that a raid was on', he wrote.[2] Altogether, outside and in, it was a disastrous evening – with worse to come. Zippa's

---

* It moved to Knightsbridge in 1972.

† According to Wikipedia. The description of the incident in *A Chelsea Concerto* gives 84 dead. See pp. 192–4.

letter to Alured takes up the story. When she and Tony got back to Oakley Street, one of the tenants was still up and they met. As an old friend of Zippa's, she shook Tony warmly by the hand and congratulated him on his forthcoming marriage. Whereupon, Zippa saw his face blench. Nothing could have been clearer.

Zippa was furious. It was cowardly of him, she wrote. She was filled 'with contempt, rage, disgust and a most terrible unhappiness'. Her despair at the thought of a break surprised her: 'I suppose it means that I love him', she told her brother. But 'I still feel that I could take any blow even with all the desolation and blankness'. Next day, she decided again to break it off, this time by letter: 'I told him that a complete break now and no thought of marrying would be a great thing for him – and I could have borne it if he'd agreed. But anything I say makes him miserable and come rushing back to me – and every time I give him up forever I become desperate and blank.' She hardly knew what to think or do:

> I was only marrying him because of his love – and he held me because of his love. Indeed I didn't want to marry him if he was doubtful. ... It would have been perfectly alright if I had never doubted him. I don't think he realises in the least how hurt I've been.

Wounded as she was, it was perhaps difficult for Zippa to remember how young Tony was – not yet 23. From everything he had been saying for the previous few weeks, it was obvious that he didn't feel ready for marriage. At the same time, he didn't dare let her go. He couldn't imagine finding anyone else. She was his ideal for his future self; she was his insurance. It was just that he couldn't make the down payment now. He was stuck. He could neither marry nor not marry. He had met her too soon.

Tony's sick leave came to an end, and he went back to

Winchester with a bleak goodbye at Waterloo station. In the train back to Stansted, Zippa cried herself sick. But nothing was ever certain either way. Just this last weekend, she told Alured, Tony 'managed to wangle a pass and arrived here [Stansted] for Easter, and he seemed so devoted and urging me to get on with announcements etc. But I don't know what I feel. It's all arranged. The banns are being called for the first time on Sunday – May 17th is the probable date.'

Little by little, as she wrote, Zippa began to cheer up. Or rather to cheer herself up. It was a trick of hers. Just writing about a thing, making a story of it, following its twists and turns, however awful, became a comfort in itself. There were interruptions, she picked her pen up and put it down. Tony rang up from Winchester. The cat had kittens: 'Do you know, all the time I've been writing this letter, Pixie has been having kittens – she's just had the sixth … a most devastating performance as she's tried to have them on my lap … I suppose I shall have to strangle them all except two tomorrow.'* A paragraph or two later she even says:

I feel happier all of a sudden … you'll think I'm crazy to get married. But it has come to the point, break or marry. I couldn't just go on having him for a lover now. I feel somewhere in me that getting married will make things better – the thing is now, Tony, having gone through his period of doubt and agitation, now appears to be completely his old self again.

But she wasn't her old self: 'one moment of doubting his love for me has shattered my confidence in him. And yet I don't seem to be able to do without his love. So I'd better not think

---

* All in a day's work then, before female cats were routinely spayed. The family were animal lovers, but they were practical and unsentimental.

any more and enjoy the wedding.' The rest of the letter is almost gay, a canter through family doings: her mother-in-law ('a deadly bore'), her mother-in-law's hat ('an inverted bowl'), her dance, an audition ('I feel ill at the thought'), wedding dates, getting closer now, 10 May, to fit in with Tony's leave dates. After which she brings the whole performance to a close with a devastating flourish: 'My love to you – I half wish I were dead, Zippa.'

Tucked into the same envelope is a quick note, sent from Stansted the next day, to say she hopes he's got her telegram. It's not 10 May, but 3 May, 4pm!* Tony can't get away until mid-day on the day itself. Please do try and get leave for it. She's much happier. Tired though. A terrible night last night, 'bombs dropped wholesale and landmines without a break. We thought the house was coming down – but all dropped in fields. Mother says Chelsea Old Church is completely down and one side of Leicester Square – you can see straight through to Soho Square.'

That was the night of 16 April, 'the Wednesday' as it came to be known, one of the worst of the Blitz, eight solid hours of bombing all over London – Chelsea along with everywhere else. Frances Faviell's house, 33 Cheyne Place, was one of the many hit that night. By then pregnant with her first child, she was trapped under masonry, with the ceiling and roof blown in and everyone in the flats above killed. Her description of that raid and of the morning after is one of the most harrowing of her book.[3]

$$\sim$$

London was bombed almost every night during the spring of 1941. In his articles for the *Statesman,* Tony's father described the 'banshee wail' of the sirens 'rising and falling in waves of agony'

---

* The night of 10 May was one of the worst nights of the Blitz, so they were lucky.

and the 'methodical' raids 'going on for hours over a given area' night after night. He stood in horrified wonder at the 'capriciousness' of the explosions: 'You see a house cut clean in two. The surviving half stands open to all beholders, and you will see a dressing table on the very edge of the precipice with every trifling ornament on it unbroken and unmoved.' He mourned the 'heap of rubble' that was 'lovely Chelsea Old Church, scene of so many weddings'; and he told of the incendiary bomb which landed on the roof of his own house in Oakley Gardens. It dropped clean through to the kitchen in the basement and 'rolled under a table' – without exploding. The next morning 'a warden came and took the unexploded bomb away in a bucket'.[4]

Luckily, Tony and Zippa hadn't chosen Chelsea Old Church for their wedding, nor anywhere else in Chelsea. It was to be at the church in Heston, just west of London, where Uncle Tony, Zippa's step-grandfather, was vicar. Not that Heston was any safer than Chelsea. In fact, being so close to the aerodrome at Heathrow, it was probably more dangerous. The church windows had already been blown out once in a raid the autumn before. The gardener's cottage had taken a direct hit, and the nearby streets had been smashed. It was a miracle the vicarage was still standing.

These last days before the wedding were fraught. If it wasn't bombs, it was rationing and shortages and not much money. What drinks could they afford? Sherry, Tony's mother suggested. Dull, thought Zippa. Could they afford 'a sort of butler man'? You could get one for about a pound, Tony thought. Wedding cheques helped, but to Zippa's disappointment, people who might have given money, sent her things like hairbrushes instead. Or underwear, or a 'not very nice' nightgown. To everyone's joy, Tony's father waved a wand and a dozen bottles of champagne arrived at the vicarage, plus a bottle of brandy, and something for a champagne cup. 'I'm so thrilled and surprised,' wrote Zippa, 'How wonderful of him.

Oh Tony darling, we shall have a lovely party – he writes "I am so happy about my new daughter. I have always wanted one."' Another joy was Aunt Jane – she would come, cancer or no cancer. She would arrive a few days early, get the musty old vicarage cleaned, supervise the arrangements, and fill the place with flowers.

Tony and Zippa's letters were now breathless with excitement. Tony couldn't help feeling a little nervous about his leave, but really 'I don't think anything bar invasion could stop my getting off on Saturday to marry you.' He would have another ten days' leave soon after the wedding (not immediately though) and they could hardly wait: 'do you realize,' he wrote, 'we have never really had a holiday alone at all … I just live for it now.' They wanted to borrow a car and drive down to Dorset, but petrol was rationed and none of their friends could spare them any coupons. Zippa asked the farmer at Stansted but he said they had tightened up the rules and he couldn't help them either.

As for her wedding dress, two weeks before the day she hadn't found one. She was exhausted – still doing the Stansted milk round, bombs dropping every night even there, and she hadn't the time to go searching. Tony urged her to go to 'Marcel', never mind the cost. So she did. They had just the thing, she said, and would make it for her – but 'oh my God! at a price! 14 guineas!!':

> *It will be in a very pale blue – charming, simple, with a little coat of matching material. They will also make me a little hat to go with it … I shall go for a fitting next Tuesday afternoon and it will be ready on Thursday or Friday. If they are bombed meantime – well – !*

Money, bombs, invasion – to hell with it all, Tony said: 'My Darling Darling one, don't fuss or bother about anything. Honestly and truly it doesn't matter a tiny little damn, any of it.'

The wedding: Tony, Zippa, Alured and Hortense

The Luftwaffe spared the dress, the church, the vicarage and the wedding party. And the Dorset honeymoon had about it a 'touch of wonder', wrote Tony afterwards. He had managed to borrow a car after all, and to scrounge enough petrol. The weather had been perfect, and they had found a couple of horses so they could go riding – a thing Tony always loved.

Soon, too soon, he was back in Winchester barracks – 'sitting up in bed after lights out 10:30 writing by a torch', and telling her how much it hurt to leave her. 'I felt like crying. You gave me the happiest time I have ever had … it is as if the Gods were smiling on us. … Goodbye my treasure, my torch is dim.'

Everything now was dim – for Zippa too. Her 'flat little note', wrote Tony, received just as he was going on parade, left him 'sick at heart'. He could think only of his next leave, a long weekend five weeks away – 'though of course one cannot swear'. What will they do, where will they go? Dorset again? Or on the river at Oxford? He was about to start a course. It was on 'Driving and Maintenance', which he was terrified of, 'with all sorts of engines and models cut in half'.

And so they picked up their old life, counting the days between leaves, at the mercy of cancellations, and occasionally risking an illicit rendezvous. 'I got back quite cleverly' says Tony after one of these, 'train arrived by 10:45 and safe in bed by 11.15 ... nobody has asked any questions so all was well. I am glad I upped and came ... I wanted to see you very very much.'

~

The bride

Tony was now starting his main officer training at a camp on Perham Down on the edge of Salisbury Plain. For the next year his regiment – the King's Royal Rifle Corps – would be moved from camp to camp, from Norfolk, to Hampshire, to Wiltshire, Wales and Scotland. Leaves were few and far between and sometimes so short that Zippa would have to travel to him. At the same time, her life was changing too. In the summer of 1941, the tenancy at Watermill House came to an unexpected end. The landlady wanted it back. It was a shock for everyone, but especially for Tony, who remembered 'oh such terribly happy times there with you, I always think of it as our house'. Veronica too was upset. She had wanted to finish her two years as a land girl, which would have given her a qualification.

Stansted had been very cheap, so it was a worry. One thing was easier, though. Both the old ladies, Aunt Katherine and Nonie, had died during the Stansted years, so they could now get by in a smaller place. Hortense fancied a £20-a-year cottage in Dorset, but in the end she and Veronica settled in Hertfordshire, in the village of Chipperfield, where Veronica continued her agricultural training. As for Zippa, she scrambled for herself in London. From the late summer of 1941 until the spring of 1942, she seems to have lived on the fly, sometimes at a studio flat in South Kensington, sometimes at another in Fulham, sometimes sharing with friends and sometimes at the vicarage in Heston. Her letters are full of talk about dancing, choreographing and auditioning.

But then, out of the blue, comes this:

Mrs Eden is in bed with 'flu and Mrs Buchan and I have been running back and forth with messages and data etc. There has been a pile of work for me over Civil Defence programmes, and I couldn't get away this afternoon, and I've got the Youth at 7:30 tonight and then have to see the

*Shelter Marshall at St Martins in the Fields at 9. Tomorrow
I take a show somewhere. Luckily Mrs E won't be there –
Mrs Buchan says it's most unlikely that she'll stay – she
can't bear Mrs Eden!*

Mrs Eden? Mrs Buchan? Data? the Youth and the Shelter
Marshall? This was a whole new world, and for the next nine
months or so, her letters describe it – days in an office and evenings entertaining people who were sheltering in the underground
stations.

~

Since the late summer of 1940 when the bombings first started –
even before the real onslaught of the blitz – Londoners had been
defying the government ban on using the underground stations
as bomb shelters. The official recommendation was for cellars
and basements, above-ground brick-built communal shelters,
reinforced trenches in parks and public squares or, if you had a
garden, Anderson shelters. But not every house had a cellar or a
garden, and the above-ground shelters were unpopular – smelly,
cold, damp and, above all, not safe.

On the evening of 7 September 1940, a huge bombing raid
hit London, targeting Woolwich Arsenal, the East India Docks,
the Surrey Docks, Tower Bridge, Poplar, Bermondsey and West
Ham. The whole of the East End was on fire and that night,
instead of darkness, 'a curious yellow-orange light almost like
sunrise' filled the sky.[5] Many thousands of East Enders gathered
at Liverpool Street station and demanded to be allowed down
onto the platforms. According to one of them, 'the authorities
wouldn't agree to it and they called out the soldiers to bar the
way'. But 'the people would not give up and would not disperse,
would not take no for an answer. A great yell went up and the

gates were opened.'[6] The news streaked across the city, and in the end, with great reluctance from the authorities, some 79 tube stations were opened to the public as bomb shelters. At the height of the blitz there were about 177,000 people sleeping – some virtually living – in the Underground.[7]

Conditions in the tubes were always smelly and overcrowded, but at first they were appalling: there was no sanitation, the stench was unbearable, and fights broke out over possession of 'pitches'. Gradually, the local authorities and the voluntary bodies stepped in, if only to avert the danger of epidemic diseases: chemical toilets were installed, first aid posts established, bunk beds and canteens provided, and finally (grudgingly, for fear of attracting more people) some sort of educational and entertainment services: 'gramophones, concerts, play readings, discussions on current affairs, religious services, film shows, libraries, even play centres for the children ... provided by outside bodies or improvised by the shelterers themselves'.[8] Which is where Zippa came in.

Zippa's ultimate employer was the London County Council (L.C.C.), but she worked for the Council by way of a private body known as the City of Westminster Shelter Welfare Committee, based in Caxton Hall, Westminster. The chairman of this committee was William Edwin Sangster, a Methodist minister, well-known and much-loved at the time, whose preaching could pack the huge Methodist Central Hall in Westminster. On the evening following the terrible East End raid of 7 September, Dr Sangster (as he was known), having just conducted evening service there, found to his surprise that hundreds of people from all over London were crowding into the shelter beneath the hall: 'Some bombed out the previous night, most too frightened to stay in their homes and share the fate of all those who had died.'[9]

Dr Sangster decided immediately to take them in and cheer them up with hymn-singing and storytelling. An official told him he was contravening regulations, but he ignored him, and within a few days he and his wife and helpers from the Women's Volunteer Service, were serving soup and sandwiches. Soon there followed all the things that were to come to the tube shelterers in time: concert evenings with comedians and sing-songs; current affairs discussions; cookery classes; films and lantern lectures; and for the young, darts and ping-pong.[10]

The Westminster Shelter Welfare Committee had clearly been inspired by Dr Sangster, but he did not run it day to day. This was done by the 'organising secretary', Zippa's Mrs Eden, who regarded it as her personal fiefdom. Mrs Eden's particular focus was on young tube shelterers, arranging 'socials' for them – entertainments and dances – the idea being, in the manner of Dr Sangster, to cheer everyone up. Zippa sets the scene:

> *Last night we had a young people's Social in the concert room at St James's Park station – young people from the shelters. An extremely good, hearty hockey-playing woman gave a talk about what one can do to brighten shelter life – and was amusing and nice – and then we all played relay games and charades … There were about 60 boys and girls altogether – they seemed to love it! and we had buns and lemonade.*

The only problem, said Zippa, was Mrs Eden: 'When she stood up to talk, the atmosphere was immediately turned into a dreadful church charity treat.' Zippa asked some of the girls if they'd like keep-fit classes. The idea went down well, so she told Mrs Eden and said she'd give a demonstration the following Monday, when there would be another 'Social'. 'But she hummed and emmed and said it would be better if I could teach them folk dancing, which I dare say it would, but I can't and I told her and she didn't seem at all keen on my demonstration idea.'

The next morning, the L.C.C. Education Officer came to the Caxton Hall office, and Mrs Eden introduced Zippa to him as someone who could give keep fit classes! Zippa's suggestion had become Mrs Eden's idea. Never mind – the Education Officer 'jumped at it, and asked me if I'd go round the shelters at once with him making contacts for possible classes – but Mrs E begged him to do no such thing – she was doing everything etc. etc.'

It was frustrating and confusing for Zippa, not helped by the hybrid arrangement they worked out for her employment:

> *Apparently now I shall be employed [by the L.C.C.] as a shelter warden which allows me to work for Mrs Eden and get 5/– a class for anything I do in the shelters ... She was in a great state last night saying she thought their idea was to kick her out and get a paid organising secretary in her place – I expect it is – but of course it is unfair because she has built the whole thing up.*

The trouble was that Mrs Eden 'insists on having her finger in every pie', said Zippa. One of her other pies was something called Abbey Entertainments, which operated out of the same office in Caxton Hall and was, I think, formally or informally, an arm of the Shelter Welfare Committee. It was Abbey Entertainments that organised the 'shows' that Zippa had to 'take round' – variety acts consisting of, say, a piece of folk dancing, followed by a song, then a scene from Shakespeare, then a tap dance routine and so on. Zippa called these Mrs Eden's 'potty little entertainments'. But potty or not, they gave her an opening. For some weeks in the autumn of 1941, she tried in spare moments to choreograph a dance that she herself could perform in one of them.

The difficulty always was finding enough time and space in which to work anything out. She found it intensely frustrating, and one night she exploded in a letter to Tony:

> When am I going to find time to dance, rehearse and show something to Mrs Eden? If I had something ready, it would be very easy for me to get it on the stage … it must be small enough for a little platform and must be comedy. And now all my time goes in just living and the 1000 odd jobs that make it up.

Above all she wanted quiet in which to think:

> I can't restrain that revolutionary feeling that shrieks for solitude and unrestrained peace – there seems to be so much effort in living and so rare the moments of vital happiness – Don't take any notice Darling – it's very late – I'm tired and a distraught mass of feelings –

Just living, the effort in living – it was a refrain heard everywhere: the rationing, the prices, the shortages, the queuing – 'endless queuing' writes Juliet Gardiner in her history of wartime Britain, 'the symbol of wartime drudgery'.[11] Zippa doesn't mention it, but it must have been part of what she meant. Everyone was caught up in it. Word would fly round that something had appeared somewhere – fish, for example, which was so scarce at the time that the government was trying to persuade people to eat eel.[12] One diarist of the period describes her hunt for fish that winter of 1941, and splitting forces with her husband: 'I went to

Selfridges [in Oxford Street] where I managed to pick up some conger eel, all they had. Ralph got nothing in town, but in West Hampstead he managed to pick up a small tail of cod.'[13]

Rations were now down to one egg per person per week, one ounce of cheese, meat to the value of a shilling,[14] and there were shortages of fresh fruit and vegetables. There was always the black market if you had money, but otherwise people managed largely on a diet familiar, until now, only to the poor – bread and potatoes. Tony and Zippa often talked to each other about food and she couldn't help sometimes envying him. 'You lucky Devil to have all those eggs,' she once wrote when he told her about getting some from a local farmer: 'Last night I just couldn't sleep. I got colder and colder and coughed and coughed – so I went down about 1am and got a hot water bottle and some bread, and then slept like a top!'

It was hunger, clearly, as much as the cold and the coughing. She then got an infected finger, which was lanced and stitched, became reinfected and was lanced again. She also got a huge stye, 'the worst I've ever had', which burst and 'then gathered up again', and which also had to be lanced. It sounds as though she was badly run down, though she herself thought it was only exhaustion:

> *I'm sure it's just tiredness that gave me the stye. The thing is, that going out at night for an energetic evening after a day of whirl at the office, is really too much, especially as I can't rest between because I must prepare my games and dancing for the evening. Last night's class was difficult because I had children of all ages. The little ones, under twelve, wanted games and the girls and boys of sixteen upwards only wanted to dance. The room was small so it wasn't easy … My other class was fun in comparison. The hall there is big so we can*

play wild games and everyone joins in ... tomorrow night I
take another new one and dread it.

Now she was about to follow Mrs Eden's advice and bathe her
sore eye in seared milk. Did Tony know what searing was? It
means warming the milk up and sticking a red hot poker into it.

Tony didn't say anything about the poker, but he did urge
her to get a tonic from the doctor and to take it properly. The
doctor gave her one, and added halibut liver oil pills. It seemed
to work. She went to her next class feeling stronger. She even
added play-reading to the mix:

I divided them into groups and gave them balls, a skipping
rope and the gramophone,* and announced that I was going
to read a play for those who cared to listen. It worked very
well. The children played ball and skipped, some of the boys
and girls danced, and about six keen ones sat round me
while I read a comedy by Mabel Constanduros. They are
now very keen to act it, and one girl is going to type out some
copies. The little children though were very disappointed that
I didn't play with them, so next week I'll give them about
20 minutes first.

Managing so many different age groups at the same time, on
her own, was an ordeal. Just getting to the end of the evening
felt like a small victory. Whether they ever did perform the play,
she doesn't say. It was the dancing that was always most popular.
It's a surprising sidelight on shelter life. The wartime craze for

---

* This wind-up gramophone had been a wedding present. I remember it,
with its heavy, curving arm into which you screwed brass needles from a
little box.

dancing at the big dance halls, and in the smart West End clubs, is well-known. Not so much among the shelterers. Here, on New Year's Eve 1941, Zippa describes their party:

> *There were crowds of people – soldiers and ATS* and old people as well, and 2 soldiers played the piano and an accordion and everyone danced. I danced with the old men and wallflower girls and shy boys – There was really no need for me to be there except that my gramophone was useful when the band got tired, and that I made people dance who otherwise would have just looked on. There was a ping-pong table going as well and I gave balls and skipping ropes to the kids.*

Zippa sounds exuberant, but at the end of this letter she apologises for being 'such a bore … fretful and discontented and not eager about things'. Partly it was because of Mrs Eden, she says. That problem, thank goodness, was now over. Zippa had decided to leave the Westminster Welfare Committee and work directly for the London County Council. And Mrs Eden? She would be allowed to carry on with her shows if she liked, says Zippa, 'but there is already an organisation to do it in a big way!† I think Mrs E thought she was the only one in the field.'

Office politics, exhaustion and a bad diet answered for much. So did London itself, holed and cratered London. The Blitz was over by June 1941, when Hitler began his invasion of Russia – Operation Barbarossa. But by then much of the city was a wasteland – Westminster with its government buildings, nearby Pimlico, and Victoria where Zippa worked, particularly so.

---

* Auxiliary Territorial Service, the women's branch of the army.
† Presumably ENSA.

'I walked through a number of streets behind Victoria the other day' wrote a friend of a friend of Zippa's,

> and there it all was … street after street of damaged houses; boarded windows like closed eyes; doors swinging unfastened; inside the staircase in ruins … Some of the basements were inhabited … civilization ruined above them. I can't tell you the impression of sheer misery and foulness that those deserted streets made on me; it was like falling through hell.[15]*

Londoners got used to it, but it took its toll. And like everyone else with a lover or a husband or a brother in the forces, Zippa was anxious and lonely. Alured just then was at the end of a leave. She had cooked lunch for him. 'Then I had to go off to my physical jerks refresher course at Chelsea Polytechnic … I came back at 5 hoping he'd still be here, but just found a little note from him and I shan't see him again. I am so lonely I feel like crying', she told Tony.

The war was into its third year. Most of Europe was occupied – a looming presence, just there, a mere bomber's flight away. After Pearl Harbor on 7 December, neutral America was now no longer neutral – but neither had it yet arrived. England felt very small.

---

* All this would become true for Germany too: cities such as Lübeck and Rostow, Hamburg, Cologne, Berlin, and finally, in the last months of the war, Dresden.

Chapter 4

'Soldier, I wish you well'

Alured's regiment, the Royal Ulster Rifles, had returned from India early in 1941 and was now re-training to become a glider-borne unit, part of Churchill's new 1st Airborne Division. Like Tony, he was moving around from camp to camp with infrequent and uncertain leaves, and there was always an anxious moment when it looked as though their two leaves might coincide or overlap. Both of them were writing to Zippa about their ops and schemes and exercises, and both felt equally ill at ease as soldiers. But there the similarity ended. Alured was not training to be an officer. He was a private in every sense – inwardly disengaged from the world and its hierarchies and privileges. His letters entirely ignore the progress and direction of the war, spinning themselves instead out of odds and ends of comic or peculiar detail – the musical voice, for example, of the Welsh boy in the bed next to him describing a memory of something that had happened on a Tuesday, no a Wednesday, no, it must have been the Tuesday because on the Wednesday they murdered the Catholic. Or it might be the sleeping bodies of his mates, packed so tight in the back of a truck, that a movement of a foot in one place started a wave through the whole mass, drawing curses and groans in its wake.

Alured's letters were, in effect, small acts of refusal. Tony was equally at odds with the army, but he was curious about it all the same, interested in what people thought about the war and the politics of it, and above all interested in what the world would look like when it ended. However much he complained that it was all a waste of time which he could be spending with Zippa, he was in fact deeply engaged.

What astounded him was the apparent indifference of his fellow officers. One morning in April 1941, for example, 'when at breakfast we opened the papers and read that we had cap-tured Addis Ababa and the Germans had invaded Greece and Yugoslavia, there was not a flick of talk. Any other people would have bubbled with excitement.'

Tony was always an avid consumer of newspapers, particularly the foreign affairs sections.* As the son of a foreign correspondent, it was in his blood. But it put him a little to one side of many of his fellows. Insular Englishness depressed him: 'I hate hear-ing them talk of horses and their public schools', he once wrote from one of his camps. He even liked to think of himself as not entirely English. His father, after all, was an Irishman and his first memories were of Persia and India.

A little later that year, a certain Dr Baer gave a talk at his camp. He was originally from Austria and, 'he lectured on German concentration camps. It was, of course a hate talk of sorts, but he was very very good. He had himself been for over a year in a concentration camp. He spoke … with tremendous emphasis and power which obviously came from his bitter experience.'

---

* Much of my childhood was spent abroad, and I vividly remember him behind the great, rustling, tissue-like pages of the airmail *Times*, and the peculiar smell of the ink.

In principle, Tony didn't like hate talks. So absolute, so undiscriminating, so liable to lead to blind vengeance. It was another thing that set him apart. What he feared was that people would say to themselves: 'alright all Germans are swine, after the war we will cure them by giving them some of their own back'. Of course, that was exactly the intention of these talks, and there were many who would have cheered.*

As it happened, Alured had a friend in his battalion who was influenced in just this way. This friend, having met Alured and Zippa's sister Geraldine on leave once, started a correspondence with her in which nothing could be clearer. In one letter, written much later in the war from a field hospital in Normandy where he was wounded, he describes the mixture of patients in his tent – Poles, Canadians, a Belgian, 'our own boys' and a few Germans and Austrians. One of the Poles, he says, wanted to throw petrol over the German and Austrian patients and set fire to them. He doesn't demur. He himself had been put next to an Austrian who had shown him photographs of his family – 'pathetically trying to win my friendship'. This Austrian soldier had been lying out in the field for four days with terrible wounds, and he smelt. 'They all smell the same these Huns', says the letter-writer, and goes on to describe the nurse helping the Austrian with his food as 'a little maternal girl feeding a chimpanzee'.

Fortunately, Tony would never have seen this letter, but it goes to show how horribly right he was. And yet, at the same time, he could see the point of some sort of propaganda: 'If we

---

* Such views were known at the time as Vansittartism, after Lord Vansittart, chief diplomatic adviser to the government, who broadcast a BBC series of talks in 1940 and later, arguing that the German nation as a whole was and always had been 'predatory and bellicose'. See *The People's War*, pp. 489–90.

are fighting a war as we are', he wrote after Dr Baer's lecture, 'we must do everything we can to win and must realize what we face.'

It was a lonely business making fine distinctions, and Tony was always delighted when he found someone who felt the same. He met an education officer, a Welsh schoolmaster, with whom he had a long talk – 'very refreshing' – and they were agreed on the dangers: 'He was horrified too at the army Hates'. It turned out that this man's grandfather had been a collier, 40 years down the pits, whose wife had scrubbed his back in the kitchen each evening. They had belonged to 'the old puritanical Methodists' and had been 'reduced to begging sometimes when on strike in the fights against the coal owners'. It was another piece of Tony's education, like his conversation with George, the Durham miner at Winchester. This time there is no trace of his old patronising manner.

The men in Tony's platoon were another eye-opener. From Cranwich Camp in Norfolk, where he went after Salisbury Plain, he told Zippa about them. They seemed to him 'to be distressingly fed up and bored and discontented'. He decided to find out what the matter was. He said a few words to them about trying not to let things fester, and suggested that it might help to stand back a little: 'Stopping and looking at the war and comparing life in Poland or Greece etc., and that for themselves they must try to set their own standards and take no notice of other people's mistakes or unfairness or anything.' No doubt it was his own way of coping.

He then asked them what they thought:

Various grumbles were shot at me, not enough time and so on, and they were mucked around. Then one of my drivers, actually my own personal truck driver, whom I like very much, a lad named Purves, said that they felt they were not respected and valued enough, treated like so many

animals ... they did not like the Company Commander and
felt he is not interested.

It was true, Tony thought. The man had no 'soul', was really only 'interested in himself and what his superiors think', and was constantly 'trying to avoid a rocket from above'. The trouble was that this put him, Tony, in an awkward position:

One of them said the real thing is something we can't say to
an officer, sir. Of course he's right. I can't let them criticize
the company commander ... All a platoon officer can do is
to act as a sort of buffer between sometimes wrong decisions
from the company commander, and his men. Fortunately
really I'm so little interested in the army I don't mind getting
rockets from above.

To make matters worse, a new sergeant major had arrived at the camp, 'a most trying man', he said, 'a complete bundle of nerves, always shouting at everybody'.

Tony had a great respect for good sergeant majors. They held the army together, he told Zippa. His first one, at Winchester, had been 'first class', he said, 'astonishingly vital', a hard drinking, hard living man, with a fascinating vocabulary on the parade ground – 'not the usual vituperation but really original!' He was also very patient at 'explaining and gripping the attention of dim recruits'. He was 26 years old, had joined the army at sixteen, and knew the job backwards. One evening they went to the pub together and Tony asked him why he hadn't taken a commission. 'He says he's better off where he is. ... His opinion of some of the young 2nd loots [lieutenants] with what he calls 2/6 [two shillings and sixpence] accents is dirt. His tales of Malta and the regimentally organised brothels of Khartoum are illuminating.'

A clever man, good company and a far cry from this new nervy, shouty sergeant at Cranwich.

All the same, as he said, all Tony could do was to buffer as the chance arose. Just the day before, he had had the men on their own, 'doing little tactical schemes' in the rain. Luckily there was a village nearby with a café, so after a morning of 'filthy wet', he took them in and 'bought them tea and buns for lunch'.

Generally speaking, the army comes across in Tony's letters as a close-up version of England at its most insular and hide-bound. Not everywhere and always – and wherever he could, he would seize on people who thought more freely. But there weren't many of those, and almost none at his next camp near Swindon in Wiltshire. It was now June 1942, very hot and dry, and he was writing to Zippa from the billiard room, 'with balls gravely clicking around, prodded by gravely concentrating majors. Nobody even mentions more than a few low words about the war, and never except for a few young officers do they criticize the causes of it all. We are an extraordinary people!'

~

The only thing missing from Tony's social education was women. It was a man's world and the more he began to develop within it, the more Zippa came to occupy a dreamlike, magical place outside it. Not that he saw it like that. For him, she was the real-ity, the compass, the north star. It was army life that was 'mad and unreal', as he wrote after one of his leaves. He longed for beauty, sophistication, gaiety and, to him, Zippa was these things. Wherever he found them, in a book, or a piece of poetry or a film, his thoughts would fly to Zippa. Everything reminded him of Zippa. Soon after his move to Perham Down near Salisbury Plain, he read George Moore's *Héloïse and Abélard*, in which a line about Héloïse was nothing less than a description of Zippa:

'A courageous nature is thine without alloy speaking always out of itself.' With her 'piercing quality of truth that admits of no compromise', Zippa was Héloïse. Later, when he was in North Africa, he would read Shakespeare whenever he could, and again Zippa would appear to him between the lines. A verse from *A Winter's Tale* about Perdita, 'made me think of you', he wrote, and he quotes it: 'when you do dance I wish you a wave of the sea that you might ever do nothing but this'. And when he wrote next it was with a snatch from *Twelfth Night*: 'I remember so clearly you reading Viola so beautifully. Do you remember it – "We men may say more swear more ..." and the rest ... I can remember every inflexion of your voice as I read it again.'

Zippa could even throw a little stardust on Tony. From Cranwich he writes of a film show at the camp – Fred Astaire and Ginger Rogers in *Shall We Dance*. He was thrilled to see it. Fred Astaire was a lovely dancer, a true artist, and 'the men loved it ... it was like a breath of gaiety and civilization':

I would so love us to be able to dance something like that together, and you to have lovely clothes to look beautiful in!

For a moment, she was Ginger Rogers, and he was – who else? – the man himself.

Héloïse, Perdita, Viola, Ginger Rogers – Zippa brought grace and beauty to his unlovely days. It must have been strange for her to be loved so poetically, intoxicating perhaps, funny too, a little alarming given the realities of life. And yet, little by little, perhaps without either of them realising it, Tony was thinning her out. She was becoming a creature of his imagination, weightless and transparent.

~

In March 1942, Oakley Street in Chelsea, where the family had lived before moving to Stansted, became vacant again, and Zippa decided to take on the tenancy, with friends to share the rent. It had never been an easy house to live in – no electricity, no gas, no telephone, with open coal fires for heating and a coke-fired boiler for hot water. But she loved it: the sprung floor in the drawing-room where she could roll up the carpet, push the furniture back and dance; the garden; and the whole position of it, the river at the end of the road, Battersea Park just across the bridge, the towers of Westminster to the east, visible from the upstairs back windows.

Zippa got the house wired for electricity at the terrible cost of £40, and then she and friends, a handyman and a cleaning lady set to work, stripping off wallpaper, painting, cleaning, and putting up blackout curtains. The Stansted furniture had been in storage at a warehouse at Bishop's Stortford since the summer of 1941. So when the moment came, she made the train journey back once more – partly to make sure the movers took care, but also to visit the farm where she had left a few things. It was 'icy cold and snowing' as she walked to the farm, she told Tony, but,

> the sun came out in fits and starts between the bleak, cold clouds and the little birds sang as they do in spring … then I walked over the fields … and everything looked so beautiful and sad and rich and so much part of me that I hardly knew when I was passing Watermill House. If I go there when I'm 90 it will seem only yesterday that we were there. The feeling is all mixed up with you and some sort of dream.

Watermill House was beginning to rival Mitcham in her mind and, like Mitcham, leaving it was like leaving a part of herself. Still, she had Tony, and at long last her spirits were returning.

Snow was on the ground, but spring was in the air. Only the other day she had walked in Battersea Park and, 'the air was sweet, and they had already begun to dig the flowerbeds and the earth looked black and rich and made me ache to get on with Oakley Street'. Her stye, her infected finger, everything was healed. She was dancing again and feeling strong – and 'very very loving towards you'.

This gaiety of Zippa's, this delight in everything 'vital' (a favourite word) was an irrepressible impulse in her. It's what Tony had fallen in love with. And it was especially striking just then when there were a thousand things for her to be anxious about.

Zippa in mid-air

Her brothers were either in danger, or imminent danger. Denny had been in Singapore in February when the Japanese invaded.* He got out on one of the last boats, but no one knew that yet, and the press was full of atrocity stories. At the same time, Alured had written to Aunt Jane (who passed it on to Zippa) to say that he thought they would soon be going into action. He told Zippa that his regiment was 'training for an air-borne invasion' – where, he didn't know. 'They have to do intensive glider practice next month', she told Tony, and they were learning, 'navigation, motor cycling, enemy positions, and how to use German weapons, etc. etc. They all have to learn more or less how to glide so as to be able to take over. He seems cheerful but looks very haggard.' In fact, it wasn't until the end of the year that gliders were deployed, but there were always rumours. Would the Allies open a second front in Europe? It was very possible.

A second front was a constant question at the time. In July 1941, a month after the start of Hitler's Operation Barbarossa, Britain and the Soviet Union had signed the Anglo-Soviet Agreement, and had become military allies. Ever since, as German forces advanced deep into Russia, Stalin had been pressing for a second front. The Russian winter of 1941–42 and an unexpectedly strong counter-offensive by Stalin was now wearing the Germans down. Would this be the moment? Could the tide be turning? In February 1942, Tony wrote excitedly if prematurely: 'Oh darling wouldn't it be glorious if Stalin won the war this year?'†

Another possibility for Alured was North Africa, where the Allied forces (the Western Desert Force, so called) had been

---

* Singapore was an important British colony. Japan had entered the war on the German side in September 1940 and in February 1942 invaded Singapore, defeating the British and Allied forces and taking 130,000 prisoners.

† Stalin as an ally, of course, rather than as a Communist.

deployed since the end of 1940, initially against the Italians in Libya.* That campaign had been successful, but in early February 1941, Germany had come to the rescue of the Italians. From then on, under the formidable command of General Erwin Rommel, the German Afrika Korps had had the upper hand. During the spring and summer of 1941, Rommel had driven the Allies out of Libya into Egypt, bottling some of them up – mostly Australians – in the port city of Tobruk on the Libyan side of the border. There they had languished under siege from April until the end of November when, after much fierce fighting, the Allies (now officially the Eighth Army) finally liberated them.

Egypt and the Suez Canal – imperial Britain's route to India and the Far East – remained seriously at risk. So Alured's guess that the next push might be in North Africa was a likely one. In the autumn of 1941, he had even told Zippa that he was 'thinking of joining Field Security† and learning Arabic with the hope of being sent out in the spring'. In the event Alured was never deployed in North Africa, and a second front in Europe was still more than two years away. But in the early spring of 1942, it felt as though something big and dangerous was imminent one way or another.

And then, as if all that weren't enough, in February the government introduced soap rationing. Three ounces of toilet soap per person per month.[1] It was a cruel hit – more personal somehow than sugar or butter. As Vera Brittain wrote scornfully in her diary, it made more of a buzz among some women than Singapore itself.[2] And it didn't help when the government

---

* Italy invaded Libya in 1911 and, despite fierce resistance, that country had become an Italian colony.
† 'Field Security' meant the Intelligence Corps which was being developed at the time.

suggested taking a tip from the peasants of France who washed their clothes in wood ash and water.[3]

But Zippa was not to be defeated, even by soap. 'My darlingest love,' she wrote,

I am in bed, in a delightful mood – I have found a new trick – to put on the gramophone and leap into bed before the first note is played. Then I switch off the light and lie and listen in the dark while the whole haunting tune comes from summer and far away … I have been dancing and feel gay. I love you so much.

~

Some time in March, Zippa decided to stop her shelter work. It was ill-paid, badly organised and exhausting. For all her exuberance, she was beginning to dread those evenings. She had been learning shorthand and typing in any case, and now their letters talk about a possible secretarial job at the Red Cross at £2 10s a week. Other letters mention an assistant stage manager's job with a fledgling repertory company. She might even get small acting parts in it. It didn't work out. She decided to try for the Red Cross, though not with much enthusiasm. 'None of the clerk's jobs I am likely to get strike me as important. Felicity [a friend] talked of a lot of slowness and muddly voluntary women around the place …' The only really important paid jobs, Zippa felt, were on the farms and in the factories and she had decided – 'rightly or wrongly' – that she wasn't strong enough for those. Everything else – all the heroic work of people such as the air raid wardens so vividly described by Frances Faviell in her memoir – was voluntary. Zippa needed a wage.

In the end, whatever the job, what mattered most to her were her spare moments making Oakley Street, transforming it, working her old Stansted magic on it – really for Tony whenever he could get away. It was something she would always do, all her life, wherever she lived. Perhaps it arose from the neglect and chaos of her childhood. She needed to create order and beauty – especially now when there was so much destruction and ugliness. Of course, any kind of art has its back to the wall in times of war, and Zippa's rooms, her drawing-rooms in particular (almost an archaic word now), were a kind of art. They were about shape and harmony, light and colour, putting this with that – and doing it all on twopence halfpenny. She had a touch for it and it was her delight – not just for its own sake, but because she felt obscurely (she wouldn't have spelt it out) that it would rub off on people, draw them together and lift their spirits. (She often reminds me of the passage in Virginia Woolf's *To the Lighthouse* about Mrs Ramsay's dinner party, when the beautifully arranged bowl of fruit on the table has the momentary effect of drawing together Mrs Ramsay and one of her more resistant and uncharmable guests.) Luckily it was something that Tony loved in her and by the end of April, she had done it: 'You have made it enchanting', he wrote.

~

Tony and Zippa had just had a week's leave together and now, suddenly, things began to move fast. Almost immediately – 1 May – his unit was off to Scotland for a fortnight, followed by six weeks in Wales. He wrote to her from the train as it neared Carlisle, excited to see Scotland, but, 'what a mess a lot of England is, all the country round Crewe, chimneys and slag heaps and raw dirty patches and odd corn fields here and there pushing into squalid houses.' In the event, those eight weeks were cut short, and he was back by the beginning of June.

By then, the regiment knew. They were being sent abroad. No one could yet say where or when. 'Rumour seems strongest for the Middle East, after all', Tony wrote. He thought there might be some weekends left, but she would probably have to come to him. Tucked into the same envelope is a farewell note from one of his old Cambridge friends – Wilfrid Noyce, a mountaineer who would go on to join the Everest expedition in 1953. His friend apologises for not being able to visit and say goodbye in person, but he was on fire-watching duty:

> And in some ways I'm not sorry. 'Parting is such sweet sorrow' … but it is sorrow and I hate saying goodbye … But at any rate you are now in it, and have the satisfaction of seeing this maddening thing through. Will I be able to see Zippa occasionally and cheer her up when you have left?

After a few more parting thoughts, he signs off with lines from Housman's *A Shropshire Lad* 'So goodbye Tony' he writes, 'wherever you are',

> Dead or living, drunk or dry,
> Soldier, I wish you well.*

---

* 'A Shropshire Lad', XXII:

> What thoughts at heart have you and I
> We cannot stop to tell;
> But dead or living, drunk or dry,
> Soldier, I wish you well.

Tony and Zippa

Chapter 5

'If I were killed'

There followed a period of stopping and starting – a sudden dawn move from Cranwich to Chiseldon near Swindon, followed by that peculiarly English limbo, full of talk of horses and public schools, which Tony found so exasperating: 'Chiseldon [camp] is full of peace-time minded people … None of them seem to have any sense of urgency and it is all deadening.'

For himself, he was trying – as Alured had tried in the spring – to guess whether the next move in the war really would be in North Africa, as the rumour was, or in Europe. At the end of May 1942, Anthony Eden and Vyacheslav Molotov, the two foreign ministers of Britain and the Soviet Union, signed another, more comprehensive, treaty of alliance – the Anglo-Soviet Treaty – and the government issued a communiqué which referred to 'the urgent task of creating a second front in Europe in 1942'. So perhaps it would be Europe after all.*

---

* Though it was noticed that within a few weeks of the signing, government spokesmen were already downplaying the idea. See Philip Jordan, *Jordan's Tunis Diary* (Collins, 1943), p. 8. Philip Jordan was a war correspondent for *The News Chronicle*, and covered the North Africa campaign for the same period that Tony was there.

And North Africa? 'Any further news from Egypt I am afraid is inevitably bad', wrote Tony, 'and I would not be surprised at anything.' He was writing at the end of June, a week after the Allies were defeated at the Battle of Gazala, 60 kilometres west of Tobruk, with Tobruk itself falling to Rommel again. Thirty-five-thousand Allied troops were taken prisoner and their comrades were now being driven steadily east over the border into Egypt itself.* Tony spoke almost as though the Suez Canal were already a lost cause. The general feeling, he wrote, was that: 'We are likely to go on July 17th, but privately I would not be all that surprised if we never went at all. After all there may be nowhere to send us and also they may just decide to put everything into a European invasion to take the Germans off.'

～

No letters from Zippa survive for these last weeks of June and July, but one of Tony's suggests a difficult moment between them on one of his leaves. Tony's quick irritability was something Zippa and her family had come to know. It was never more than a sudden burst and always quickly over, but it left people shaken. As a child, I vividly remember those moments – a chair suddenly scraped back; a newspaper clashed shut. Zippa must have talked to him about it, for he apologises and hopes she will forgive him:

> *I think perhaps the chief reason of my being snappy is that being an only child has made me selfish, and not used to fitting in with lots of people, while you have always had lots*

---

* The Axis forces were within about 100 kilometres of Alexandria, but were stopped by the Allies at the First Battle of Alamein in July 1942.

of people and it does not seem strange to you to have them
always around.

It sounds as though they had been at Oakley Street with a crowd of friends and family, when he had hoped they would be alone together. Perhaps she had been rushed and busy with cooking and getting things ready, and he had told her that it wasn't right, the others should help, and why should she, and so on. It was the sort of thing he was always saying to her – don't let people impose on you. At any rate, his letter afterwards admits that she was right to say 'that if I did not fuss but did the things with you, then it would be nice'. And he goes on to make a distinction between himself and Zippa that became habitual with him:

> *I must give up trying to apply logic, which is truly a cold use-*
> *less thing to apply to life which is really an affair of people*
> *and feelings … I don't suppose I shall be able to change with*
> *a bang because I am so impatient, but I will try and you*
> *must help me …*

No doubt they were both a little on edge. Tony was about to go into action. And not only that. Zippa, in her own way, was too.

It was over a year now since they had married and they had never properly talked about having a baby. Zippa had raised the subject first, and Tony's immediate reaction had been – 'Impossible!' Of course, he knew nothing about babies. He had never even met one – not to talk to, that is. It's easy to imagine him shying at the very thought of a baby. They had discussed it some more, but he had seemed to her immovably convinced that it was out of the question: 'If I were killed,' he had said, 'you would be very tied with a baby and less able to live your life, and dance and do things and I would hate you to be a slave to material drudgery, which does come with children however hard you try; I would like you always to be free and gay and not be housebound.'

This was kind. But from this distance, it's impossible not to see the real problem. He simply couldn't imagine it. Couldn't see her differently. Viola, pushing a pram? Ginger Rogers, doing the nappies? No – Zippa was eternal spring. Even if he were killed, she must always be as she was now. Zippa let the matter drop and he took care not to pick it up again: 'So when you never mentioned it,' he explained later, 'I thought to myself "Well, perhaps really it is just as well" and left it at that.'

In fact, she had decided. Since they had known that the regiment would soon be going, the war had worn a different face. It was no longer officer training. Tony was going somewhere to kill or be killed. 'If I were killed', he had said. If this, then that. He had spoken as if death were merely a stage in a logical sequence. Actually, it was a gaping reality. Besides, she had her own 'ifs'. If not now, when? How long would the war last? She was 28. A friend had written from America to say that 'the general opinion in New York' was that the war would carry on for another five years. 'My God!' she had thought. She would be 33. But she wouldn't argue with Tony. It wasn't a matter for argument, and anyway there wasn't time to win one. She would take it upon herself. During these last weeks, she would silently leave off precautions, and see what happened.

Zippa would never have counted herself a feminist. She was wary of -ists and -isms. But, in this, she was moved by an impulse any feminist would recognise. A baby, if there were to be one, would be her sole responsibility. Tony would be its father, but beyond that, she was on her own. She would carry and bear it alone, and for its first, second, third years of life – who knew how long? – she would care for it alone. If Tony were killed, then all the more so. But even if he lived, for the moment, the choice and its consequences were her own business.

By early July the regiment was on standby, and its destination was Egypt. The Mediterranean was full of U-boats and mines, so their route would be round the Cape of Good Hope. It was a glorious summer, and as the day approached, Tony and Zippa met whenever there was a chance. They found somewhere to swim, they paid goodbye visits to friends and family, she gave a dinner party for him at Oakley Street – 'lovely', he said, and she was such a clever hostess in knowing how to 'make everybody feel wanted and a success'. Now was the moment to tell him. He had booked a hotel for them in Marlborough for their final weekend, and before they met for the last time, she did.

It was a bolt from the blue. He was staggered – and hurt. It wasn't so much that she might be pregnant, but that she had felt she couldn't talk to him:

> Please please don't think I am so unsympathetic and snappy that I won't talk properly about something so important; and Darling, just because I point out strongly, seeming even to argue, the opposite side, it does not mean necessarily that I agree with that.

'I felt,' he said, 'that it was a thing open to discussion both ways.' And he goes on to recap the points for and against: the timing of it, how long he'd be likely to be away, their uncertain prospects – even postwar – and so on. This time, however, he tactfully concludes that 'taken all round you are probably right and it would be best now'. Tony was nothing if not rational and fair-minded. The only thing he seemed not to have any inkling of – and how could he, given his background and experience? – was Zippa's overriding desire to create a life. A life not only for its own sake, but now in particular, now in the face of death.

Talk of life and death was not their way. At least not in letters. Who knows what they said to each other in the small hours. But Zippa's decision had shifted the scenery. There was a starkness now about the lights and shadows, a touch of thunder in the possibilities either way. And yet, for all the unknown terrors ahead, somehow, on that last weekend, they found a kind of stillness together:

> *It all seemed so quiet and happy in Marlborough … I love you completely my Zippa and you make me so happy and contented. I feel so safe in thinking of you and completely and terribly trusting.*

~

Tony was writing from camp with everything packed and ready to go: 'parade in 15 minutes'. There'd been a bad moment – he couldn't find his revolver, searched everywhere, thought he'd lost it, it turned out his batman had packed it.* He couldn't believe he wasn't going to see her in a week or ten days. 'We have said goodbye so many times', and she had been so sad as they stood at the Chiseldon bus stop. But 'it won't be terribly long before I am back', he assured her. 'You must not be too unhappy', and 'I do hope you have a baby'. It was still 'you' and not 'we'.

The train left Swindon at midnight for Glasgow where they were to embark. It had been a stirring departure, 'just as it is in the films', wrote Tony:

---

* A 'batman' was an officer's personal servant.

A mass parade of everyone, the colonel saying goodbye to us, march to the station, then chaos, but finally all packed on. For the most part the men were very cheery, a lot of them a bit tight! Looking at them all as they marched by, they seemed a good lot … there were not many deserters, only 2 out of our 108 or so.

At 8.30 the next morning, Tony was writing again, the Yorkshire moors, bare and bleak, rolling past the carriage windows. He couldn't help an edge of excitement as he wrote. At last they were moving. If they were going at all, better just to go. And they were doing it in style, no hanging about. They arrived that day, went straight to the docks and embarked: 'for the most part' he wrote, the men 'singing away, though some must be very miserable'. How lucky we are, he said, to be parting as we do and not with some quarrel hanging over us. That same afternoon, they 'put off from the dockside and went gently down the river':

Really it was rather impressive. We passed ship after ship under construction, all surrounded with a forest of scaffolding and echoing with a hammering of drills. The troops all lined the decks and everyone on shore waved and the men broke into a discordant mixture of 'Tipperary' and 'There'll always be an England' at different ends of the ship.

For two days they waited offshore during which Tony wrote a final valedictory letter. With an eye on the censor, he says he can't say much about anything, and there are indeed neatly razored out windows from his pages wherever he had written anything about their whereabouts, or the date. For the rest, the censor spared him his descriptions, his reflections on his unreal and dreamlike state of mind, and his disbelief that he wouldn't be able to hold her close for another year. On board and later in North Africa, Tony himself would censor the letters of his men and would tell her how touched he was by them – 'through them all, a note of cheerfulness and no grumbling', and many of them 'extraordinarily like my own. All thinking of their sweethearts, wives and children, and all longing for letters from home.'

But as he wrote now, he wanted to convey something more. It was three years since the late summer of 1939 when they had first met, and he wanted to look back and sum up. He wanted her to know,

that you have done me an awful lot of good, and you've given me so many kinds of happiness in little simple ways that I always longed for but somehow never enjoyed because of my way of life, the attitude to everything. Your instinct as you call it is the wisest thing I know.

It is curious how like his early letters this is, letters where he had spoken of the help and strength she had given him. There's even a hint of his mother and his childhood in these lines. Those simple kinds of happiness he had longed for and that had been missing from his way of life. Zippa was still, as she always had been, the source of all comfort, strength and wisdom. 'So happy and contented', he had said after their last weekend in Marlborough, 'so safe … and trusting.' And now he was being carried thousands of miles away from her. Wherever he was, he said, whatever he was doing, his thoughts would always come back to her – to Stansted, to Dorset, to Oakley Street 'where everything now breathes of you. I feel so full of you and always shall, so safe and utterly certain of you as the best and purest gold. I have so much to be grateful for.'

And he does hope she'll have a baby.

~

On the evening of 18 July, the ship 'slipped away in pale sunlight, the shore looking all washed and green, the hills standing dark and near behind', and early the next morning, Tony went up on deck. It was an extraordinary sight. There, in a great company, was their convoy, picked up during the night, now sailing in formation around them: 'The sea was choppy and spray was blowing over the deck, a brisk wind and bursts of sun. The ships looked really fine, rising and falling steadily always in the same relation to each other.'

As he had said, it was like a film. Outside and in, it was all spectacle. The ship had been a luxury liner before the war, and his cabin – shared with seven other officers – had once been one of the grand state rooms. As for the mess, where the officers dined – it was tremendous. Four courses for breakfast, six courses for lunch and dinner. Grapefruit, oranges, meat, fish, French wines, cheese, coffee, whiskey – and waiters at one's elbow. It was a different world. Tony was now a 2nd lieutenant, the most junior of commissioned officers, but an officer nonetheless.

Seven weeks at sea lay ahead – a strange interlude in which he stood balanced between sea and sky, between Zippa steadily diminishing behind him, and ahead the vague and violent desert. They had no news of the outside world, no papers, no letters, no radio – even receiving signals would give away their position. From time to time, wild rumours would sweep the ship: that Japan had declared war on Russia; that Russia had bombed Tokyo for seven hours; that Vichy France had declared war on Britain. Otherwise everything was in abeyance. For much of the time, the sea was flat calm, glossy even. He had known the round pond in Kensington Gardens rougher. A few things happened. Once, the ship's guns were fired off for practice, and the whole vessel shuddered; once a neutral ship passed by, lights blazing in every direction; once there was an air-raid alarm, but it was only an English plane patrolling over the Atlantic; and for 24 hours there was a blessed fog – protection from enemy planes.

Time passed. Tony read – *Cold Comfort Farm*, Balzac in French, a book about the Russian educational system, anything he could get hold of. He watched people – the quick, slight Chinese crew and the waiters, also Chinese, with their fine hands: 'I wonder what they think of us, great guzzling hogs'. He discovered that they usually earned £4 a week, but now £16 – 'considerably more than I do'. He got into conversation with one of the military policemen on board who told him that they played cards in their quarters – fast, mysterious games for huge stakes, as much as £25 a hand. Tony worried about the men, who also gambled – like mad, he says – 'and of course some of them get fleeced, and then they start to sell their kit to get money'.

There were hours when he leant over the bulwarks and studied the water: 'deep ice green before it breaks and then creamy froth', while 'close to the side of the ship it looks pitch black'. He looks out to the horizon, where the sky was clear, and sees a line of vivid blue. Sometimes, porpoises rolled by, and birds, he didn't know the name, flying just inches above the surface, scarcely moving huge wings. Sometimes he played chess, badly, with an Oxford undergraduate he had made friends with – only two years at the university before being called up.

Tony's ship-board letters were written like diaries, over several days, and they are full of leisurely descriptions of the people he meets: the ship's doctor, for instance, a charming Quaker who used to run the Charing Cross Hospital, but whose career had been impeded, he suspected, by his homosexuality – 'a high degree of panseyness', was Tony's phrase. He liked the army doctors, he said, because they were less military than other officers.

There was an actor he wanted particularly to tell Zippa about, Peter d'Aubeny,* who had had some success and who told him about an interesting experiment in America – the Theatre Guild, to which people subscribed whatever they could, and which promoted plays that the commercial theatre would never touch. Once, someone took him up onto the bridge to meet the Admiral himself, 'a sweet old boy', Tony said, surrounded by people darting about with 'Nelsonian spyglasses'. The Admiral invited them down to his cabin for drinks. Apparently, he had been brought back from retirement, 'and was master of some fox hounds and talks constantly of hunting, his entire geography of England is divided into hunts, speaks of everybody as living in the Beaufort or Heythrop country etc. etc.' And then there was someone who had worked in Malaya who told him about the rubber planters there, and the local people they exploited.

Politics always interested Tony. One of the officers in his cabin was a man of fascist views who adored pistols and shiny leather belts and boots: 'just the kind Hitler attracted in hundreds'. The man believed that Germans should be exterminated, but that Hitler was right in his treatment of the Jews. 'Yesterday we had a tremendous argument in the cabin.' But Tony felt encouraged because 'nobody would agree with him, even about hating Germans, and everybody shouted him down and ridiculed him'.

There were more politics at a Brains Trust meeting the ship organised, inspired by a popular radio series of that name, first broadcast to the Forces the year before. The format was simple – a panel of experts discussing topical questions from the audience. 'I was inveigled into passing as a brain', wrote Tony, and he goes

---

* Or Daubeny. He lost an arm in the war and gave up acting to become a theatre impresario. He organised the World Theatre Season, which brought foreign theatre companies to London between 1964 and 1975. He was knighted in 1973.

on to describe his fellow panellists. On the whole, he said, the questions were political: 'Why suppress the worker?' and 'What part will Russia be given (yes, given!) in Europe after the war?' One of the panellists was a guards officer, a Mr Blow, described as 'a coming politician, journalist, future Prime Minister [sic]':

Mr Blow was called on with a flourish to pronounce on the political questions. Really I thought he was completely incompetent. He could not speak well. He had a blah accent and scrupulously avoided anything to do with Russia whenever he could. I was glad to see that on the whole they did not like him. I took him up with socialist arguments and did my best to discomfort him.

Afterwards, he came up to Tony and was 'most matey'. Tony asked him what he had done and wanted to do in the future and he spoke warmly of the idea of a 'Young Tory Party': 'He seems to think it can all be settled by progressive young men getting round a good dinner table. Really the most dangerous type, and just how every crusty old Tory starts.'

The next Brains Trust meeting was packed, 3–400 people. They're very popular, Tony says. He himself, 'seems to have acquired a reputation apparently as a violent socialist!' and he delivered 'an oration', he says, on the question: 'Should armaments be manufactured by private enterprise?' In fact the whole temper of the ship was highly political. The next gathering was for a debate on the motion 'that the house would deplore the spread of communism after the war'. Tony considered the motion too vague and refused to speak on it. As he had suspected, the debate degenerated into an attack on one side, and a defence on the other, of Russia, about which too few people knew anything. Still, he said, 'the men were very interested and for the most part very pro Russian. They do feel that Russia stands for the common people.'*

~

As the ship moved south, the days became hotter and damper. They stopped at their first port of call to take on fresh water – his first sight of Africa. A bit like Scotland, he says, hills behind hills, but green and forested to the top, and at evening 'bathed in a violet mist'. They were forbidden to go ashore for fear of malaria and their cabin reeked of the anti-mosquito ointment they had been given. He hadn't really expected any, but there were no letters from home. He was thinking of Zippa in Oakley Street, pining for her and 'most of all I am wondering if you are going to have a baby'.

Soon they crossed the Equator and at last it began to get cooler. He'd heard depressing news – that the Germans had 'got a hold on the Caucasus',† and that we've 'put Gandhi in jug'‡ – 'so muddled and topsy-turvy'. But they were approaching the Cape where they would go ashore and he would be able to find out more. He couldn't allow himself even to hope that there'd be letters from her there.

And there were none. Once on shore, the first thing Tony did was to rush to the shops and buy things for Zippa: food parcels (butter, marmalade), clothes (silk stockings, a leather bag, a pretty

---

* The 'average soldier in the British ranks … was at this point a long way ahead of his officers in his appreciation of the Russian question'. Alan Moorehead, *Desert War*, pp. 196–7.

† The Red Army was in retreat as the Germans advanced towards Stalingrad.

‡ Gandhi opposed India's participation in the war and on 8 August 1942 gave a speech which launched the Quit India Movement. He and others were imprisoned. Tony's father, Arthur Moore, who supported the Movement, was sacked from the *Statesman*.

French blouse with lace – too expensive but he couldn't resist it), face cream, powder and lipstick. What joy, for Zippa, in drab and rationed London. How like him. How like his father too. That dinner at the Berkeley; the case of wedding champagne. But it was also Tony's dream about Zippa, the Zippa he longed for when all this was over – when she would put on her silk stockings and her beautiful French blouse, powder her nose, paint her lips, take her little bag and off they'd go to a restaurant and eat butter and marmalade to their heart's content. And he never stopped to think that by the time the French blouse reached her in London, the buttons might not meet all the way down.

Tony seems to have been operating on two entirely different levels. In some ways, he was becoming a sophisticated observer of life, perceptive and curious about people, interested in everything they could tell him about the world. He was by nature an impatient man, easily bored, but so far, from the Admiral on the bridge to the waiter in the mess, everything had held his attention. And the same with everything else – the creatures over the side, porpoises, flying fish, phosphorescence, above all 'the immense solitude' of the sea: 'It is extraordinary that this vast emptiness is always here when we are leading our ordinary lives. I can understand people getting bitten by a love of the sea.' Literally and figuratively, Tony's horizons had been widening.

But about Zippa he remained as he had always been – oddly unsophisticated, childish even. Nothing had moved since that first love-struck autumn of 1939. Perhaps it was inevitable. They had never had much ordinary, continuous time together. Waiting at bus stops and on station platforms, blowing kisses from carriage windows, had been as much a part of their love as having breakfast together. Now she wasn't there at all. As he lay on deck looking at the stars, he tried to conjure her. Without her letters, her voice, her thoughts, she became her image merely:

*I think of all the details of you in Oakley Street, and what it
looks like, and all your clothes, and what you are wearing ...
I can remember you in a hundred thousand attitudes and
all of them graceful ... I have been thinking of you so very
closely this evening, till I could almost imagine you beside
me. I thought of you dressed up in each and all of your jewels
and wearing your Cinderella frock and can see you dancing
in that show.* *

Tony had always been inclined to fold her away in a compartment
of his mind quite separate from anything to do with army life.
Now everything was army, everything was khaki, and he needed
more than ever to keep her separate and unblemished.

The trouble was that this Zippa wasn't the real one. That
Cinderella, for example. She had been working on it in the
autumn of 1939, and she had written about it to Alured at
the time:

*I've got my entrance, and a play with birds and flowers
which everybody is charmed with ... The whole thing is such
a charade though, that I'll burlesque the part quite a lot – I
mean exaggerate the wide-eyed innocence touch, only not to
the extent of spoiling the dance bits.*

Zippa minded as much as Tony about how she looked and
moved. But she was funny too, with a turn for nonsense. Had
Tony forgotten? or had he simply been charmed by the birds and
flowers and never noticed the burlesque? Now, he simply erased
it. Cinderella was just part of Zippa being graceful. They had a
film show on board, featuring a Norwegian ice-skating champion

---

* This was a Cinderella she had danced in early 1940.

Zippa (left) as Cinderella

of the day, Sonja Henie, who was also a Hollywood star. 'I could watch her for hours', he told Zippa, she 'reminds me of you dancing': 'wouldn't it be fun to learn to skate so that we could dance on skates a little?' When she wasn't Cinderella, or Ginger Rogers or Shakespeare's heroines, she was Sonja Henie, and all of them together would take him by the hand and dance him away from war and stupidity and ugliness.

Chapter 6

'Millions and millions of flies'

Early in September 1942, the ship ended its long sea journey and everyone was loaded onto a train bound for the Infantry Base Depot. A frantic scene awaited them. As soon as the train drew in, wrote Tony, it was 'hung round by people screaming for baksheesh and offering "filthy pictures"'. The military police drove them off, but they 'flowed back again'. As soon as he could extricate himself, he saw it all, there it was: 'a vast camp, tents in miles and miles of omnipresent sand'. His heart sank.

But it wasn't quite as blank as that. The camp was inter-sected by little irrigation ditches, one of which ran by his tent. 'Everything depends on water,' he wrote. 'The desert blooms like Kew where it can be irrigated by my little runnel from a canal, and it has only to be scratched by a wooden ox-drawn plough.'

He found himself observing the locals, long-robed men, some squatting for hours on their heels, others riding little donkeys 'set right back on the rump', trotting along 'at a tremendous twinkling pace'. The sea was only half a mile away, and he had bathed already. Glorious, 'warm as warm'. How she would love it. But there were no letters from her.

A few days later, Tony and a group of others received orders to proceed to Alexandria. He doesn't give the name but, in a sort of code, he refers to an old Cambridge friend that Zippa knew named Aleck, by which she would have understood.* From there – shockingly soon, it seemed – they were 'whirled away' into the desert:

> *A fantastic and unbelievable drive by lorry over miles of open sand, everywhere looking exactly the same, trying to find a certain place to report; it took us 7 hours, only 50 miles, and now it is just getting dark, and the whole situation seems completely extraordinary and unreal.*

The next morning they reported to their battalion HQ – First Battalion, King's Royal Rifle Corps (sometimes referred to as the 60th), Seventh Armoured Division. This was Tony's home now, his bit of the Eighth Army, the famous 'desert rats' so-called, under the command of General Bernard Montgomery ('Monty'). He looked about him. The emptiness and desolation were overwhelming, 'and none the less so for being full of army'. The certain place they had been aiming for was a hill called Himeimat, which marked the southernmost point of the Alamein Line.† To the west of this line lay the German-Italian army, lit up by the morning sun in the east – Tony's first sight of the enemy, actual men, guns and tanks. At noon, they became invisible in the heat haze, but in the evenings, there they were again, silhouetted now with the setting sun behind them.

To the south of these armies lay a dried up salt lake known as the Qattara Depression, a huge and almost impassable sinkhole, 145 metres below sea-level, capable of swallowing tanks and

---

* This was Aleck Crichton, who remained a close friend of both my parents all their lives, and at whose farm in Co. Sligo, Ireland, I remember many happy holidays.

† This and the following details come from a letter written a year later when the information was no longer sensitive.

men. It was an 'eerie' place, Tony wrote, dominated by a 'strange-shaped hill of sand rather like a miniature Matterhorn'. Together, Himeimat and the Qattara Depression shut the armies in, cutting them off from the wide flanking movements they had been used to so far in the campaign. This was close-in confrontation across a no man's land which doubled as a graveyard.

And there were no letters from Zippa. It was now almost two months since he had heard from her.

~

During Tony's time in North Africa, he often begged Zippa not to worry about him. He had always been lucky, he said, and he wasn't going to stop being lucky now. It irritated him to hear BBC reporters describing the desert troops as heroes, 'sweating and steaming in the heat' and 'tormented by flies'. Not at all, he assured her: 'the weather and conditions are not nearly as bad as all that'. As for the dangers, he hardly mentions them. Once or twice, when friends were killed or wounded, he told her – for example, when an American soldier he knew was wounded by 'machine gun bullets from the air through his knees'. But this was written later, after the German surrender in 1943 when there was no further cause for alarm. Only then could he admit to having been '20 yards away and rather frightened!'. 'I remember it well', he adds – but he said nothing at the time.

Sometimes his attempts to make light of things sound a little absurd. When he was given command of a platoon, for example, he explained the fact to Zippa by saying that it was only because so many officers had been off 'with small wounds caused by their vehicles blowing up on a mine'. Rommel's minefields were notorious, nicknamed 'the devil's gardens', probably the world's biggest and most deadly and sown with about half a million mines. The mines themselves were intended for vehicles, but they were often surrounded by anti-personnel booby traps, consisting of explosive canisters full of ball-bearings which a man's weight could detonate.[1]

I don't know if Zippa was convinced by Tony's bland assurances. But one of his other comforting lines was to say that, of all the places to be in this war, the desert was the best. The North African campaign was in fact as bloody as anywhere else. But in one way he was right. Much of it was away from towns and villages and civilians. On the whole, the armies confronted and manoeuvred around each other across vast empty spaces. In his trilogy, *The Desert War*, Alan Moorehead famously compared desert warfare to war at sea, with tanks for ships. But he offered another equally striking analogy taken from a Cairo G.H.Q. statement issued in June 1940: 'One of the few advantages that soldiers experience in having a desert for their theatre of war is that the auditorium is empty.'[2]

Not completely empty. There were the Bedouin, and Tony mentions them from time to time. In one letter, they had just passed a small encampment with 'women at the doors and children wild with excitement and a flock of sheep and goats with baby lambs nuzzling at their mothers'. As they left them behind, 'five absurd camels trotted along with great raking strides beside our truck, doing a good fifteen miles an hour for a long way.'

It was extraordinary, he wrote, how the Bedu managed to live and wander about, 'unperturbed in the middle of battles', putting up their 'low black tents near wells', their camels subsisting on nothing but 'tufts of harsh green scrub'. The worst of it, he said, was that their black encampments were sometimes mistaken at a distance for tanks, and shelled.

But on the whole, there was less collateral damage in the desert, and when in the spring of 1943, the Eighth Army entered

farmland on its way to the endgame at Tunis, Tony was immediately struck by the difference: 'War seems somehow worse in
cultivated land. It seems so wicked to drive crashing through
standing crops.' The farms too were a sad sight: silent, empty, the
houses burnt black, 'their farmyards still full of McCormick har-
rows'. Tony wrote those words after eight months of living in the
desert. He had by then begun to know its seasons and beauties,
its rosy dawns and grand sunsets. Yet for all that, nothing in the
desert quite matched the eloquence of an abandoned McCormick
harrow in a Tunisian farmyard.

~

For a couple of weeks after he arrived, Tony's letters stop completely. All he said when he wrote next was that he'd been
moving about a lot and that 'things have been a bit difficult'. It
was the start of a new rhythm and language in his letters that
Zippa would come to know. 'A bit difficult' or 'rather trying' were
his habitual euphemisms – possibly worse than plain-speaking
would have been. Worse still were the sudden silences, like this
one, or the disjointed letters that began arriving later – paragraphs
abruptly broken off, half sentences left hanging, small neat hand-
writing ambushed from one word to the next by wild scrawl.
And then there were the letters that failed to explain what happened next.

What had happened this time was the aftermath of a battle
at a place called Alam el Halfa, south of el Alamein. Montgomery
had only recently been appointed Commander of the Eighth
Army, and this was his first engagement with Rommel – the
prelude, as it turned out, to his victory at el Alamein itself in
November, two months later. At Alam el Halfa, Tony had come
in at the end, 'in the middle of the battlefield', and had crossed
into no man's land and behind the enemy lines:

*Miles and miles of waste and gravel and stone and every-
where flies, millions and millions of flies. Everywhere you
see pathetic scraps of waste. Chianti bottles … German cigarette packets, letters and snapshots, German, Italian and
English. Odd graves here and there with tin hats, German
and English. Another thing everywhere – white snail shells,
the Germans make crosses with them on their graves.*

He had met a German prisoner of war as he was being
brought in and had talked to him. The man had been at Leningrad
three months before 'where he said things were very rotten'.*
He had a mass of photographs of his family, 'strong fine faces'
says Tony, 'prosperous middle class people, they looked, and
now he was a pathetic sight, a week's beard, suffering from diar-
rhoea, dashing off with a spade to dig a little hole'. And then,
almost surprised, he adds 'He came from Dusseldorf.' Prosperous,
middle-class Dusseldorf – as ordinary as a McCormick harrow.
So odd to be fighting a man from Dusseldorf.

Tony's description of the battlefield and lines captured from
the retreating Germans understandably leaves out three things
– tins of half-eaten rotting food, excrement and corpses. These
were the causes of the flies, and the cause of the affliction suffered by the man from Dusseldorf – as well as by thousands of
his countrymen. A report published later, on the sanitary situation
in the El Alamein area spoke of the 'indescribably filthy condition' of the German and Italian lines, 'revolting in the masses of
human faeces and camp debris lying everywhere', and it quoted
an Eighth Army hygiene officer who called it 'one huge fly farm'.
A special unit was assembled to clear 'refuse, debris and bodies',

---

* The Germans laid siege to Leningrad from 8 September 1941 until
27 January 1944 – 872 days later.

especially in no man's land where 'corpses and other organic matter made one of the worst fly-breeding sources'.[3] Rommel was a
brilliant military tactician, but he was surprisingly neglectful of
the hygiene of his army – to such an extent that during the period
from October 1941 to December 1942, 'for every German
absent from duty because of battle injury, three were lost because
of disease. Through sickness, Rommel lost temporarily or permanently a force equal to twice his average strength.'[4]

No doubt Tony had some sympathy for his German POW, for
he himself was writing his letter from hospital. Dysentery, he said
– 'a very mild attack of a mild form of dysentery'. The sanitary
arrangements of the Eighth Army meant that the problem was
not as acute for them as it was for the Germans and Italians. Still,
Tony was one of 1,793 dysentery/diarrhoea admissions to Field
Medical Units in September 1942.[5] It was all nonsense, he told
Zippa. He had 'never been really ill', he was now 'almost better'
and the whole thing had been 'all rather ludicrous'.

Tony's next letters were written not from the field, nor from
Alexandria or Cairo, but from a hospital in Palestine, as it was
then known. All that summer, according to the diarist Hermione
Ranfurly, then working at the High Commission in Jerusalem,
wounded soldiers had been 'pouring into Palestine because the
hospitals in Egypt are overflowing'.[6] Tony had been transferred
there as a 'lying patient' by hospital ship. The doctor had just seen
him and had said he would have to remain there for another three
weeks: 'there is a definite though mild germ' Tony admits, before
moving swiftly on to talk about something else – the Italian and
German prisoners of war working at the hospital, with whom he
has had interesting conversations. The truth – as he told his son
decades later – was that there had been nothing 'mild' about his
dysentery. He had been very ill indeed, and had become so thin
as to be practically skeletal.

Once he was on the mend, his main worry was Zippa's letters. He had received nothing from her since leaving England. Everyone else was getting letters. Where were they? He wondered whether they would catch up with him in Palestine, or arrive after he had left and be sent chasing him round the Middle East for weeks. Day after day he fretted until at last, on the 5 October, nearly three months since he had left England, while he was still convalescent, several arrived at once. 'I was so excited, I could hardly open them', he wrote. Inside, sure enough, there was her news:

I am terribly pleased you are going to have a baby. I would have been very disappointed if nothing had happened.

But he could hardly grasp it – such a 'funny thought, an entirely separate person'. More letters from her began arriving, out of order, early and late. Soon he was reading terrible things: 'I can't bear to think of you feeling so terribly ill with nausea and hunger, and I wish more than ever that I could be with you all the time and look after you.' He was amazed: 'I had not known that the early time of pregnancy was so very horrid. I thought it was just morning sickness.'

But maybe, after all, he could help. He could tell her what to do: 'find out all the things you should and should not do, should and should not eat'. Gradually he began to fit it all together. But even though he soon knew she was feeling better, he couldn't get over how horrible it had been for her, and how little he had realised.

~

None of Zippa's letters for these months have survived, but Tony comments so closely on them that it's as though they had. It seems she had taken a little holiday at a cottage somewhere with a friend, and had lain in the orchard and dreamed about the future. Now he was lying in his hospital bed and doing the same thing, both of them romanticising about peacetime: a cottage, a garden, children and lots of friends.

For Zippa, it was the old temptation that she had felt when she had first met Tony – to live in the country 'and be happy ever after'. 'I could too', she had said to Alured at that time. 'But', she had added – and that 'but' had thrown a shadow over her thoughts of life after marriage. Now, it wasn't life after marriage that she was thinking of. It was life after war. In the face of war, and with a baby coming, simply not-war was enough. Peace in a cottage was enough. Tony too was beguiled: 'I think I feel the same as you were feeling in your orchard when you wanted to live in a cottage and never to go back at all.'

Even if they had to live in London, he said, they would somehow get a cottage too,* 'and you will make it lovely and enchanting as you make everything ... and will turn things to sunniness, and I will get a job and work furiously ... I can't for the life of me really think what I shall do and don't honestly care tremendously so long as it is something worth doing.'

As time passed, the cottage grew in his mind and turned into 'a large house, with lots of people in it' – rather like Stansted or Oakley Street – 'the sort of place people come to, and that is the best way always to keep fresh and alive'. This house of theirs would have children in it too, but 'not necessarily our own!!', he wrote. In fact, children were a bit of a sticking point:

The one thing we must never forget ... is that the most important thing is to be happy together ... We must never

---

* The housing market was different then. You didn't have to be very rich to buy, and renting was cheap too.

*have no time left to be together, we must always have time
to go away ... we neither of us must get so taken up with
children that the children are more [to us] than each other,
as Mummy has done.*

Was Tony already jealous? I don't know whether he was right
to connect his parents' estrangement with Eileen's devotion to
him. But he clearly saw himself in competition with their coming baby. The answer was to get a nanny, 'preferably French', able
to 'do everything': 'She will love you, and she must love babies
because then we will be safe to leave her with baby and be able
to do things together without being too tied.'

He was excited. He began to think about names. He didn't
think he minded whether it was a girl or a boy, but somehow it
was always girls' names that came to him. Little versions of Zippa,
perhaps. What did she think of Tania? Too foreign sounding? Or
Sheila, or Madeleine? Rosalind sounded nice, so long as it wasn't
shortened. Only later came Lawrence, or Bryan, definitely not
Daniel. Meanwhile, she had mentioned a dress she had bought
and white shoes – 'tell me about them' he says. That at least was
simple. The baby was ungraspable, but there was nothing difficult
about a dress and white shoes.

Tony was now out of hospital and recuperating, spending his
sick leave visiting places of interest in Palestine. He went for a day
to Tel Aviv, where he bought himself a complete Shakespeare in
three small Everyman volumes – concentrated essence of Zippa,
as it were. The city impressed him but left him cold. It was 'about
the size of Oxford', he explained, had sprung up since the 1920s
from almost nothing, and was now all shining new buildings, 'bal-
conies and sweeping curves', wide boulevards, trees, and expensive
shops: 'All very nice and lots of the buildings very good, but somehow it seems to lack any form and has no character of its own.'

He then spent a week in Jerusalem, and paradoxically it was there that he felt a real sense of new beginnings. At first he was a bit lost, but the 'Jewish Agency' there soon introduced him to the secretaries of everything: 'the marvellous new hospital, the university, the Art school and museum, and the agricultural settlements'. He was invited to their homes for tea and dinner, where he 'talked furiously' and was delighted 'to see everyone interested and educated and with ideas, people looking alive and attractive': 'The war has not yet affected the life of the place yet, and everybody really thinks about the ordinary things. There seems to be so much doing, a general atmosphere of growth and creation.'

Tony doesn't mention meeting the diarist Hermione Ranfurly, still at that time in Jerusalem, but he would have been surprised to read her description of the place – tense, unhappy, with an 'unspoken mental undertow of suspicion' everywhere, no one asking but everyone wanting to find out 'which side you are on – Arab or Jew.'[7] Much later in his life Tony was posted to Israel and would have understood, but now, with only a few more days of leave to go, his mind was in a kind of dream – or, as he put it, under a 'magic spell of peace and happiness'. He had been given an introduction to a charming Polish family who lived on a co-operative farm – not a communal farm where everyone lived in common – but one where people lived as families, worked their land, and only sold in common. It was, he said, 'like a dream of paradise', as far from human strife as it was possible to imagine: 'To live here makes me ache and long to have you here beside me and for us to stop and love in this spot and forget the war.' Like so much else, it was an impossible dream. The next day, he left the country, and began his journey back to that very war.

The last of his leave he spent in Cairo, also beguiling but in a different way – very French, full of luxury shops, cafés, smart patisseries with delicious cakes and rows and rows of bonbons. Someone took him to a rooftop restaurant under a full moon. The orchestra played the Gold and Silver Waltz, and he was so sad because Zippa wasn't there, dancing and looking lovely. He tells her he has sent her some blue silk to make herself pretty underwear.

These letters of Tony's sometimes took six weeks and more to arrive, and Zippa's reply to this one – the first of hers to survive – was written in the middle of December. She envied him his patisseries, his moon and restaurant, but could offer him nothing in return but rabbit and pigeon. Food prices in England were fantastic, she says. She was spending more than she should, but she couldn't get by as she used to on vegetable stew alone. Zippa would have had her precious green ration book with extra milk for expectant mothers, concentrated orange juice and one or two other things. But still, she was often hungry: 'If I can't get a good fish or meat meal a day, I feel down and sick, so when there is nothing to be had, I am forced to go out – that happens at least twice and sometimes three times a week.' It was one of the oddities of rationing. Food at restaurants and cafés could be bought without coupons – but it was expensive.

She prayed for him and thought about him – more than she thought about the baby, she writes. But she doesn't mention his blue silk. She does say, however, that she has 'bought woolly knickers now – huge!' It was winter. She was by then six months pregnant. Was she reminding him? She says goodbye. Beyond anything she missed him: 'Darling, darling Tony, I want you so much I am going to cry.'

~

Tony was back with his unit at the end of October, and was immediately plunged into 'great excitement', as he says – 'tremendous cautious optimism … We will know by the time this arrives'. He had missed most of it but wasn't too late for the excruciating moment of hope and fear mixed. 'If only this battle works', he wrote, 'it is the beginning of the end. If not, it means we must start again. I so hope and do believe it will work alright.'

This battle was none other than the Second Battle of Alamein,* one of the most significant engagements of the war, and it did indeed work alright. It was Rommel's first major defeat. Almost within sight of Cairo he had been stopped at the last, and Churchill allowed himself to declare – more cautiously than Tony – that it was 'the end of the beginning'.[†] It was 'a new experience', he said, 'we have victory – a remarkable and definite victory', and he marked it by ordering church bells – silent since the invasion scare of 1940, when it was decided they should be rung only in alarm[8] – to be rung out the following Sunday, 15 November, from Land's End to John o' Groats. Zippa would have heard them near and far in Chelsea and all over London. Tony would have heard them in a special broadcast by the BBC Overseas Service from Coventry Cathedral. Maybe they raised a glass to each other.

A few days after his first letter of cautious optimism, Tony found a moment to write again, partly to say how pleased he was because they had given him a new job – 'understudying the Battalion Intelligence Officer':

> *In practice it means that I am the Colonel's odd job man, but it means I hear a lot and get sent off to places to find out things. The battle from the little I can …*

---

* The First Battle of Alamein having been fought in July 1942. That battle halted Rommel's advance towards Alexandria and Cairo and this one turned him back.

[†] In his speech to the Mansion House on 11 November.

And there he breaks off. Five days later, on 8 November, he picks up the same letter again, and in a wild scrawl says he can't now finish his sentence and 'Heaven knows when I shall write again … have been travelling a lot'. All he wants her to know is that there are 'great hopes that everything is terrific' and that 'there is no need at all to worry about me'. She mustn't worry either if she doesn't hear from him 'for long intervals'. That letter got posted, and nine days later, he managed to post off a few more words: 'One second, absolutely well, no need for any worry, everything fine'. Not until the end of November could he say 'at last we have a day or two of rest', before settling down to write at leisure.

Unfortunately – but inevitably, given the eyes of the censor – Tony says not a word about what had been happening. Zippa might have guessed something from his words about travelling a lot. That was exactly the point. During the weeks and months following El Alamein, the Eighth Army chased Rommel westwards, out of Egypt into Cyrenaica (eastern Libya); out of Cyrenaica and into Tripolitania (western Libya) and beyond. It wasn't, of course, a joy ride. There were minefields to pass through, and dummy minefields full of buried scrap metal. There were rearguard actions, and Rommel's engineers cratered the main coastal road behind them. At the beginning, Montgomery thought he could catch up with the enemy straightaway and entrap it at a place called Fuka, just 60 miles west of El Alamein. He hoped that that would be that. But between Tony's dropping his pen halfway through his letter of 3 November and picking it up again on 8 November, they were held up by a dummy minefield, then they ran into a defended position and somehow Rommel got away.[9]

Rommel was known as the Desert Fox, and in his determination to save as much as possible of his defeated army, he managed again and again to slip past Montgomery's efforts to outflank and entrap him. All the same, the gap was closing, and it wouldn't be until the spring of 1943, when he had been driven over the Libyan border into southern Tunisia, that Rommel was able to make a stand and go on the offensive again. Meanwhile, battle by battle, the Eighth Army re-took the places he had pushed them out of in the other direction during the years before. On the day Tony finished his letter, 8 November, Mersa Matruh fell; in the gap between that and his next letter on the 17th, the Halfaya Pass was taken – then Tobruk, then Derma. After that came Benghazi on the 20th, and in December El Agheila. Finally, on 18 December, hostilities came to a temporary stop 100 miles further west, with a short, fierce fight at Nofilia – where Tony lost his watch:

Did I ever tell you that I lost my watch? … washing one morning during the battle for Nofilia which is just beyond Agheila. All my things were on my jeep and suddenly orders came out and I had to drive off and left the watch on the jeep.

I remember my mother telling me this story. The 'orders' Tony mentions so vaguely in this letter were nothing of the kind. They were bombs. An enemy plane came over and dropped one a few yards from where he was shaving.

∼

Churchill's speech about the end of the beginning was broadcast to the troops, and Tony was impressed. But something he heard on the evening of 29 November impressed him more. It was the announcement of William Beveridge's Security Insurance Scheme, the report which was the basis for what would become the National Health Service and the Welfare State – in fact, the whole post-war social settlement. It was the culmination of work Beveridge had started almost 40 years before at Toynbee Hall, where Tony's father had lived and worked – 'an all-in insurance', Tony told Zippa, 'covering unemployment, old age, sickness, maternity, funeral, everything for one level of contributions paid by all, and one standard of receipt for all, regardless of means. If it is accepted it is a tremendously good and important thing.'

The war had shone a stark light on British society. As one observer put it, it had brought 'the great unwashed right into the bosoms of the great washed'.[10] In his report, Beveridge identified what he called five giants – Want, Disease, Ignorance, Squalor and Idleness – and in a very direct way the victims of these ogres were emerging for all to see: bombed-out families from the slums; undernourished, pasty, lice-ridden children on the evacuation trains. Frances Faviell in her memoir about the Blitz describes working for the Red Cross and having to wash and de-louse women from the East End who had never seen a bath.[11] It was becoming obvious to many – to the men on board Tony's ship to Egypt, for example – that something was wrong with the whole system. In Beveridge, Tony recognised a practical plan to match the scale of the problem.

There was one thing, however, that he hadn't reckoned on – the mutters of the men gathered round the wireless listening to the announcement. 'When did they ever give yer anything, they'll take it off yer somehow', he quotes them saying. It 'horrified' him, he said: 'People are terribly irresponsible.' He shook his head. But in the event, the men turned out to be more politically savvy than he was. There were powerful interests against Beveridge, not least the insurance companies. On 2 December 1942, almost at the same time as Tony was writing to Zippa, the member of parliament for West Leicester, Harold Nicolson, wrote in his diary: 'The Tory line seems to be to welcome the Report in principle, and then to whittle it away by detailed criticism.'[12] It was a tactic that, at one point, led Beveridge himself to believe that his 'principles of security and freedom from want have been abandoned'.[13]

Nevertheless, the old edifice was beginning to crack. Beveridge would soon be followed by white papers, debates in parliament, articles in the press, all acknowledging the need for a new order. It was a breath of fresh air. As the months passed, the outlines would begin to emerge of a society in which Tony could at least imagine 'something worth doing' – even if he couldn't, for the life of him, think what it was.

All that was to come. For the moment, he was stuck where he was, in the army, rooted as it was in the old order – 'a little behind the times' as Alan Moorehead gently put it. Moorehead had been sending dispatches to the *Daily Express* from North Africa since 1940, and had been struck by how class-bound the army still was, how wedded to the whole 'ritual of the salute and the hierarchy of the commissioned officer'. Having Russia as an ally was an embarrassment to it. The officer class hardly knew where to look. Tony had observed on board ship how carefully the Guards officer on his Brains Trust panel had avoided speaking of Russia. Likewise, Alan Moorehead noted that:

> The entrance of Russia on our side caught the serving officer off balance … It was not easy for men reared in the public-school-university-city-regular-army atmosphere to adjust themselves suddenly to the idea that they were fighting side by side with Communists … Some made no attempt. Others avoided the whole issue.[14]

These, on the whole, were Tony's fellow officers. He might be inwardly excited by the sniff of change, but for the moment there was nothing for it but to keep his head down under his perfectly plausible public-school-university camouflage.

So, Tony got on with it and made himself useful. The colonel had chosen him as the battalion's intelligence officer – or at least the understudy. Now, he was given command of a platoon, and promoted to lieutenant. As he got to know the men he began to tell Zippa about them. It turned out that his sergeant kept a tobacco and sweet shop in civilian life. Tony liked him, found him very reliable, a bit slow but 'quite imperturbable'. He came from Southall, knew the nearby borough of Heston, and even the church where he and Zippa had got married. Then there was his lance corporal, a big cockney coal-heaver from Fulham, which neighbours Chelsea, who knew Oakley Street well. Another was a boy who could neither read nor write – 'an extraordinary discovery', says Tony.* Almost as amazing was one of his corporals, an Edwardian figure with a bushy moustache, straight out of the 1914–18 war, he said, who turned out to have been valet to Sir Anthony Eden, the foreign secretary, and was now on a retainer of six guineas a week.†

This man, Tony says, was an absolute 'rock of reliability', but he couldn't say the same for everyone. Another corporal was a 'loud-mouthed, shoddy man who cannot manage his men or look after his food etc., but is good with his gun, a constant nuisance'. The whole question of morale interested him:

Men's temperaments are awfully important in the desert and things like efficient management of food avoids a lot of trouble. I have only just come to this lot and it is impossible

---

* In fact there was a lot of illiteracy in the ranks. See Chapter 4 of Anthony Burgess's autobiography, *Little Wilson and Big God* (Penguin, 1988).
† About as much per year as Tony had wanted, ideally, to marry on.

to re-organise it in the middle, but later on it will be quite
interesting to get them together and make them live better ...
it is the only part of it I could be at all interested in.

As for their politics – he talked to the men and, again, like
the ones on board ship, he discovered that most of them, 'have
strong Socialist views, and I found I agreed in everything nearly!
They are determined to change things.'

And yet, like the men listening to the Beveridge announcement, or like George the ex-miner at Winchester, they were
habitually and deeply suspicious. They talk, said Tony, of a 'mysterious power "they", who are out to do them down'. On the
face of it, Tony himself should have been one of 'them'. But it
sounds as though they liked him well enough. He found them
well-disposed – 'good-hearted', he said – and 'they call me the
guvnor which always tickles me'.

~

Now there was a new excitement. In the early part of December,
as they were moving westwards towards El Agheila, the battalion made a significant rendezvous. This was with some of the
American forces that had landed in Morocco and Algiers the
month before, and which, together with a new British contingent,
the First Army, had been working its way east in a joint operation
known as Operation Torch. For the last three days, Tony's men
had been picking stones off a piece of desert to make a landing
strip for the American planes – grumbling rather, he said, at such
an impossible task. But they kept at it, and in the end he hurried
them off only just in time:

It was a most impressive sight, plane after plane circled and
came in, the slipstream raising a feather of dust, then a cloud

as it landed. The sun was just setting and the whole ground
was a cloud of red and golden dust, with planes taxi-ing
about in ordered confusion.

The arrival of the Americans was a dramatic turn in this long
desert saga. As they got out of their planes, Tony looked at them
with interest. The mixture of races struck him and the fact that
they were mostly pretty big men. He couldn't help noticing,
though, that they didn't look particularly healthy. Still, they were
welcome – 'it is most encouraging to see them here'.

The Battle of El Agheila started on the night of 11 December
and, unusually for him, Tony mentions it – 'the battle coming',
he says. On the day it ended, with Rommel once more in retreat,
he allowed himself a little more: 'the war here continues to succeed', and he thinks it is 'the end out here and the prelude to
the end in Europe'. But he sounds a little flat. There is none of
the excitement there had been at El Alamein when he had said
something similar. It's as though, with Rommel so clearly on the
run and the tide so obviously turning, there was nothing ahead
but grinding slog and the always-present chance of a shell or a
bullet at the finishing line.

In their book, *Alamein: War Without Hate*, John Bierman
and Colin Smith remark on a sort of burn-out in the days after
Alamein. The men were physically exhausted, of course, but
they were also nervous about their luck. In the words of Michael
Carver (later Field Marshal Lord Carver), having 'miraculously'
survived so far, there was a feeling that 'it would be folly to fling
away one's life too recklessly when victory was at hand'.[15] Six
and seven weeks after Alamein, Tony noticed a general discon-
tent among the men. They were fed up, he said, especially the
ones who had been out there a long time – 'browned off and
full of grouses'. They wanted to go home, they were worried

about their families. His sergeant from Southall, for example, who told him about his mother. She was apparently 'a wonder' who 'worked herself to death'. She had died in May, while he was in Egypt, and his sister was unhappily married: 'he is much worried', wrote Tony.

It was also very cold now in the desert, at least after dark, and they were all still in shorts. The supplies of trousers hadn't arrived yet. It was warm enough in the day, so long as it didn't rain. But when it did, things were 'utterly miserable' – though it did bring out an extraordinary growth of grass and flowers, even in the sand: 'purple snapdragons, and vivid orange miniature marigolds, a lovely yellow flower like an anemone, and most lovely of all a flower like a double Christmas rose, only it grows low to the ground and pressed in like a button on a sofa.' Night fell earlier too, about 5:30pm, and living in the open, with no blackout, meant there could be no light for anything but a brew of tea and bed. They had been living for a long time on half a gallon of water a day each, for all purposes – 'washing in a mugful', he said – but to the men 'the Brew-up' was sacred. They did it on cut-down tins over petrol fires in the sand, and 'if anyone stops this Brew at night', wrote Tony, 'they are almost mutinous'.

Now Christmas was approaching, and for some of them it would be their second Christmas away – even their third, if they'd been in the campaign against the Italians before Rommel's arrival. It was tough on them. Tony himself was struggling after a mere five months (including the journey time): 'Chelsea and you seem so very very far and remote'. It was a low point for everyone, not helped by a dreary carol service where no one could remember the words – 'though they did Good King Wenceslas and the First Noel bravely enough'.

But there was one stroke of luck. Tony sometimes describes the quite nice flour and water, bully beef and onion cakes that his sergeant would cook for them both. Now, at Christmas, he feared that there would be nothing else, nothing special for the platoon. Then this happened:

> *I was travelling independently with my 30 men and man-aged to find a bulk canteen store and bullied them into selling me three legs of pork, two turkeys and 35 pounds of Christmas pudding. We cooked it over petrol fires on dixie lids! And it was jolly good. The Christmas pudding was excellent, full of good stuff.*

Better than tea and buns on a rainy afternoon in Norfolk.

Chapter 7

'Blood and pain'

Tony once used the well-known dictum about war being marked by 'long periods of inactivity and intense bursts of excitement'. The bursts of excitement speak for themselves – those broken off sentences, wild scrawls and abrupt, week-long silences. But the days of idleness were almost worse. For a restless man like Tony, they were sometimes unbearable. There were duties: 'checking men's equipment, clothing etc. etc., training them, watching their action reserves … check[ing] to see they do what they ought'. But he found it hard 'to work up any interest or enthusiasm' for these things. Rules and regulations sent him to sleep, though the pamphlets setting them out did occasionally contain the odd gem. This, for example, which he thought might brighten Zippa's day: 'the numbers of brassieres and pantees washable per week per A.T.S. member at the public expense'.

At least now, January 1943, they had two gallons of water per person per day and they had managed to get hold of tarpaulins to make a kind of blackout. They had dug themselves a mess in the sand, ten foot by five, and had covered it over so as to have a light to write by and not be obliged to go to bed at sunset. One way or another, Tony filled the hours as best he could – getting to know the men, writing letters, wondering about the future, worrying about Zippa and above all cursing the army postal system which seemed to pile up letters for infrequent deliveries and never seemed to have anything recent.

Everything depended on letters. Sometimes there was a gap of a month, two months even. From early December 1942 to early February 1943, he heard nothing, and the last letter from Zippa had itself been two months old. In other words, all he knew in February was how she had been in October. By the end of January, it felt as though she were slipping away. 'It hardly seems true,' he wrote,

> *that you really are there, alive and real, that you are now this minute perhaps sitting by the fire in Oakley Street in your long red dress … I can't help worrying about you now my darling, especially as I cannot hear from you. I can't tell you how much I hate that and how utterly out of touch from you it makes me feel.*

He was writing just then from Palestine again, where he had been sent on a course for intelligence officers. On the face of it, he was having an interesting time. He re-visited his old Polish friends at their farm co-operative, and he made a trip to Jerusalem. He had stopped off at Cairo on the way and would do so again on the way back. His letters from all these places are full of stories, descriptions and conversations. Perhaps it was something about him, or his uniform, or the fact of war, but wherever he went, particularly on the buses in Palestine, people fell into conversation with him: Arabs and Jews from all over the Middle East and Europe – Iraq, Bulgaria, Poland, Russia, some newly arrived, and some established there for generations. Everyone was interested, talkative, friendly.

There was one man, however, who boarded a bus Tony was on, and spoke to no one. Tony was fascinated by him, as was a little girl sitting in front of him, aged about nine, who had been examining everyone on the bus, 'with a candid appraising air, somehow so different from a grown-up. There were as yet no prejudices, bitterness or unhappiness to spoil her.' The man they were both watching was a soldier, 'tall, fair and goodlooking', with a face that was 'somehow shocking':

> *Tremendous lines under his eyes, his mouth loose and sagging. He smoked incessantly and vulgarly, puffing out of his mouth and nose. He seemed oblivious of everyone else. He looked as though he had been through a great deal of suffering, and this had made him somehow elemental and physical. Probably once he was cultivated and sensitive, but it was all gone. Rather frightening. It was odd to see the little girl looking at him with a puzzled face.*

It's a powerful moment, emblematic even: the Lucifer figure of the soldier; the innocence of the child; and the whole thing framed – double framed – by the watchers.

And yet, for all his interest in everything and everyone around him, Tony could sometimes strike an entirely different note – vacant, lost, above all, lonely:

> *I have got nothing to say but I am missing you so much and longing for you, so I can only write … I so want to be back with you living a real and live life … sometimes it sweeps over me. I find it awfully hard to concentrate on anything even if I do find something intelligent either to think of or read. And then too I find myself becoming terribly lazy about people, even quite nice people.*

He tells her of a dream he has had: of coming into the drawing room at Oakley Street and finding her sweeping the floor in a blue overall – 'and there was sad little music going on. Then, oddly, you had a cigarette hanging from your lips'. He watches her a moment, and the dream ends with her rushing into his arms: 'your head was buried in my shoulder and I kissed your hair, and then I woke up so sad!' But the broom and the overalls and the cigarette linger. Zippa was not only slipping away, she was changing into someone else.

Tony always worried that Zippa did too much and that people imposed on her. He meant the work that went into Oakley Street, and the many friends who came and stayed for meals and nights, or who just lived there as tenants. He felt the charm of the place, and the sunniness which drew people to her: 'I was thrilled to hear of your party', wrote Tony at about this time: 'It sounded such tremendous fun … you make such a good party atmosphere. People always love them. I should so so much like to have been in the Oakley Street drawing-room with it all full of flowers and candles and you there, my sweet.'

But these things had never happened by themselves. There had always been mops and brooms in the background, coals to be carried, fireplaces to be swept and laid. Oakley Street – like all those tall Victorian London houses with their basement kitchens, coal holes, open fires, and flight upon flight of stairs – was a monster. Veronica had cursed it in her diaries when the family had lived there before the war. She and Zippa had tackled it together, without full-time servants or mod cons, and had looked the other way – like swans riding above their ugly black paddling feet. Tony called it drudgery, and it was. Perhaps he was haunted by a common sight at the time – which I remember still in the 50s – of working women looking old before their time, broken down, legs rickety and feet deformed by bunions.* It wasn't as bad as that,

---

* Beveridge's NHS made a great difference to the lives of their daughters.

but the family had very little money. If people didn't help – and Zippa wasn't good at asking – he feared for her, for her health, for her looks, and ultimately, for himself. What he wanted was to preserve her as he imagined her in his waking dreams. In his sleeping nightmares, she became Mrs Mop.

So, in letter after letter – especially now with her advancing pregnancy – he begged her to rest, to sleep, to make everyone help. Of course, the real change in Zippa was her pregnancy. But on that subject he was at a loss. He had no way of thinking about it. He tried, he strained to imagine her, but could only think that she was ill, tired and unable to dance – 'you can't do it now, poor sweet'. He tried to think of her body: 'my poor Darling, are you hating terribly getting tubby', becoming 'swollen and uncomfy'. Zippa was always careful of her weight, he knew that. But he was foggy about pregnancy, couldn't make the distinction or hit the right note, and blundered into baby language. His whole sense of her was of fragility and discomfort and he wanted desperately to be helpful and sympathetic. He meant well, but – poor man – he was flying blind.

As for the baby itself, it was a blank: 'I can't think of the baby at all, I don't know it at all, and have not been near any of the preparations for it, and I can only think of you.' He could think about the responsibility of it (a book on parenthood, read mostly in his truck, left him horrified). He could plan its education (definitely not boarding school). He could imagine it spoiling their fun. But as a being in itself, separate and real, it was beyond him.

So, when at last her letters came, one dated as recently as 31 January, he was both thrilled and astonished by what she had to tell him:

> I feel so excited to hear you writing of the baby as a separate person. I never realized it was as individual as that before

*it was born, for instance that it went to sleep independently
of you.*

Zippa's letters still have to be guessed at. Apart from the one
in which she tells him about her huge woolly knickers, there are
none extant until after the baby is born. But reading between
his lines, it is possible to hear her voice. 'Indeed, indeed, darling,
I agree with you,' Tony says at one point, 'it is to be our baby.'
She sounds nervous. Had he forgotten that the baby was his as
much as hers? She had reason enough. In one letter he marvelled
that a baby was to be born, 'created by you' – as though it had
nothing to do with him. And he was forever looking forward to
the time when together they would travel, entertain, dance the
night away, with someone else to look after it.

If nothing else, Tony's parcels alone might have given her
pause. From Cairo, on his way back from Palestine, he sent more
silks, blue and dusty pink, more silk stockings, sadly no jewellery
because it was so expensive, but honey at least, and sultanas: 'I
do so adore buying things for you my darling darling one. It is the
only thing I like spending money on.' In reply, she told him she
was wearing an old moleskin she had found and he laughed, he
said, to think of it. 'Still, nice and warm.' She said she had varicose
veins, and he commiserated: 'My poor sweet … but surely they
will go down'.

I can imagine Zippa clowning a little about these things,
burlesquing herself for his amusement. But she may have been
dropping a hint too. If the war in North Africa was nearly over,
as he had said it was, there was a chance he could be back soon.
He had often told her that he missed her most when he was
in the places where she might, theoretically, be – not in the
desert among the military, but in Cairo or Palestine where civilian life was largely unchanged. Here lights blazed and no one

bothered about the blackout. Here there were restaurants and orchestras and pretty clothes. He couldn't really picture her in Chelsea any more, but he could almost feel her beside him in the orange groves of Palestine, or under the moon in Cairo. All the more vividly, perhaps, for the silks he dressed her in. But all this might have made uneasy reading for Zippa. After all, she might have thought, silk and sultanas are another world. I live in wartime London. These are my varicose veins and that's my old moleskin jacket.

~

From Tony's own account of himself, anyone might have thought he was having a 'cushy' war, as the expression was. But of course the censor skewed the balance of his letters. He couldn't tell Zippa about his intelligence course for example, or anything specific about military matters, and in any case he always wanted her to believe he was safe. In fact, just as Zippa was entering the ninth month of her pregnancy, so Tony was about to enter the most gruelling phase of the campaign that he had known so far – the final push through the mountains and ravines of Tunisia to Tunis itself.

By mid-February, he was back with his battalion, now as an intelligence officer on the Colonel's staff, no longer understudying, and in charge of a small intelligence section. Everyone felt that the Allies were on a winning streak and the news from Russia earlier in the month had only seemed to confirm it. On 2 February 1943, after more than five months of bloody fighting at Stalingrad, and terrible bombing from the Luftwaffe, the Germans had surrendered the city. 'The war is terrific now', Tony had written. 'The Russians are being tremendous, today concrete news of the Stalingrad army and the German Field Marshall's surrender.'

The view ahead seemed suddenly lighter: 'If only nothing goes wrong, it really might be over this year', he had said. All the same, he was cautious. Zippa must have written in great excitement, for he writes back with a drop or two of cold water: 'Don't be too optimistic over the war,' he says, 'I am sure it is really won now, but for all that it will take some time to finish, unless the Russians do it all. Tunis I am afraid must be a slow affair, and then there are the Japs, but for all that it will get better and better from now on.'

Sitting one morning before breakfast in the mess – 'a lean-to against the side of a 3-ton lorry' – he describes his fellow officers for Zippa, from the colonel ('no fool') to the padre ('a considerable wit') – 'a very pleasant lot, all friendly, nobody whom one could dislike, but again nobody with whom I could become great friends'. Tony found it easy to get on with people, but he rarely found a great friend. He often mentions meeting people he has found refreshing, whom he could imagine getting to know, like the education officer at Winchester who agreed with him about the army hate talks. But too often these were fleeting encounters. Unless a man served with you in the same unit, the shifts of war would move him on. Even bumping into old friends could be a sad business: 'George and Malcolm go off tomorrow', he had written from Palestine: 'I feel sad to say goodbye. I feel very fond of them both and heaven knows when I shall see them again.'

Luckily, there were two people in his battalion Tony could talk to. One was Michael Fyfe, the chess-playing Oxford undergraduate he had met on board ship, and the other was Jack Brister, one of several American officers who had joined the battalion on their own account before America entered the war. These two friendships apart, Tony was essentially lonely, always slightly out of tune, unable quite to surrender himself to the expected sentiments of wartime. There was, for example, a Hollywood film of the day, enormously popular, called *Mrs Miniver*. He saw it in Cairo on his way to his intelligence course. It was about an ordinary English family from a quiet English village and their stoicism in the face of war. He enjoyed it very much. It reminded him of England and Zippa. It brought tears to his eyes. All except the last scene which takes place in the bombed-out village church where the vicar delivers a stirring patriotic sermon and the villagers strike up with 'Onward Christian Soldiers'. It left him cold, he said, 'because I always think of other families as nice and charming in Germany who are suffering the same from our bombs.'

Mrs Miniver was a huge propaganda success on both sides of the Atlantic. But in small ways, its assumptions were everywhere, little rubs and snags to be silently borne. Now at battalion headquarters, they had General Wilson, Commander-in-Chief Middle East, coming to tea – an enormous man, Tony said, nicknamed Jumbo Wilson. He was 'in military circles a very big noise', and he gave 'a great impression of solidity and confidence, which is, I suppose, rather the main point of a C in C's job'. As it happened, Tony found himself liking him – 'kind and friendly'. But he was amazed at the deferential fuss and scurry around him:

> It seems to me a pity that in the army one is always supposed to be overawed by great authority. In peace time one could have sat next to him at dinner and chattered away, but here it was all rather stilted.

~

In the event, the great man was probably visiting the battalion for more than a cup of tea. Tony apologises for a dull letter, and adds enigmatically, 'some of the things I could write about I cannot'. Something was in the wind just then, and this may have been what he meant. No doubt the General had come to fill

129

them in. Intelligence had been emerging from the codebreakers at Bletchley Park about plans for an attack by the Axis forces at a place in Tunisia called Medenine. Medenine was just south-east of the first of three bottlenecks between the mountains and the sea that the Allies needed to break through on their way north towards Tunis. Montgomery was therefore preparing – moving Allied ground forces, air forces, and supplies into position.

A week after Tony's letter, on 6 March, early in the morning, the attack took place. Montgomery was ready with overwhelming firepower and by late afternoon, all was over, with significant German losses in tanks and men. Tony himself was still in Libya at the time. In fact, on the very afternoon of Medenine, he was near a town called Agedabia where a group of them had gone to erect a cross over the roadside grave of a young officer of the regiment who had been killed there three months before. Tony and Zippa had known him in England, and in one of the rare moments when Tony so much as mentions death, he described the whole incident: dusk, setting up a roadblock, a shell-burst from the supposedly departed enemy, the young officer's shattered leg, loss of consciousness, bleeding, death. So sad, said Tony, 'such a silly thing, just one odd German gun left behind … I liked him awfully'. As for Medenine, Tony mentions it with a sense of surprise and relief: 'they really did lose 52 tanks against our guns' – which just goes to show that after all 'they are not really any more clever than we are'. Altogether it reinforced his hope that 'Tunis will be ours in about 2 months'.

Tony was in high spirits. His pen races along like the jeep he'd been in all day. He tells her about a broadcast he had heard the day before, about the Eighth Army advances – 'much talk of the green jackets as the rifle regiments are called, and description of many of the things we did'. Now as he wrote, he could hear the men in 'my little intelligence section' cracking jokes and telling each other stories. At the same time Joyce Grenfell was on the wireless doing a sketch on a knitting party: 'she *is* good, even if she always does the same thing'. He mentions another comedy sketch, a piece of German propaganda about Poles and Americans in England sleeping with the wives and sisters of the desert soldiers: 'Fortunately, I think we all laugh'. But did Zippa know that much of 'the best wireless comes from Germany, often in programmes of propaganda to us'? 'We listen nearly every night to a wonderful sentimental German song we call Lili Marlene. It closes their programme at 10pm. This is one for their own army and is a sort of home sweet home to them.' And he tells her about the swallows gathering on the telegraph lines along his route that day, 'ready to fly north to you'.

In the event, Medenine was the last German-Italian offensive in the North Africa campaign and it marked the end of Rommel's command. Tired, ill and convinced that the whole thing was now a lost cause, Rommel had left the planning and execution of Medenine to the Italian General Giuseppe Messe. On 8 March, he bowed out altogether – though it was kept secret from the Allies until the end of the campaign – and the next day he left Tunisia and North Africa for good. The command passed to General Messe.

On the day after Medenine fell, Tony received a month-old letter from Zippa in which she told him that the baby – which had been riding high under her ribs – had now dropped. It sounded odd to him, but no more. There was no knowing what was going to happen. He wasn't sure when the baby was due even. He guessed the end of March. Two timetables jostled in his head. The baby in under a month, Tunis in two. 'To people in England it may seem slow,' he says, 'but it takes a long time to bring an army and all its supplies up. What will be decisive I think is the air strength we can bring to bear.'

On 13 March, he wrote apologising for his silence. He had had to 'dash off with the Colonel and Company Commander of the Battalion to a conference', driving for two days in the staff car ('very comfortable') to somewhere, he doesn't say, though on the way they stopped at Tripoli – taken by the Eighth Army on 23 January while Tony was on his intelligence course in Palestine. It sounds as though his conference was over the border into Tunisia, for on the 15th, he was sitting in a distinctly Tunisian landscape – 'in a most charming little position' among 'smallish brown hills' with green gullies full of palm trees and grass and flowers: 'From the hill top we can see right away over the plain to the distant sparkling sea, and the other way over to a high chain of dark striking hills with sharp gullies and ravines.'

It was probably somewhere north of Medenine on the way to what is known as the Mareth Line. This was the first bottleneck – a series of fortifications which had been built by the French in the 30s against Italian-occupied Libya, and which ran from the brown, green-gullied Matmata Hills in the west, to the Mediterranean coast in the east. It was where the next great battle would begin a few days later. For the moment all was quiet, the country like a picture postcard, except for the distant churning of military traffic: 'just like a toy war' he wrote, 'everything so tiny and clearcut'.*

As the days passed, the picture postcard became more menacing. In the next letter night has fallen, and in the background his wireless is playing the 'Chattanooga Choo Choo' in Portuguese. At the same time, he can hear planes roaring in the distance, 'and Ack-ack just like a London raid'. It wouldn't be long now before

---

* Tony was reading *War and Peace* at the time. Elsewhere in these letters from Tunisia, he describes the distant trails of smoke from shells – like Tolstoy's Pierre Bezukhov at the Battle of Borodino, gazing at the scene spread out below with its little puffs of gunsmoke.

the ground battle. At least Zippa's letters were arriving more frequently, via Tripoli now rather than Cairo. She was waiting too, telling him about it, apologising, as he had done, for being boring. He might not want to hear the details, she thought, her worries about stretch marks and not being slim afterwards. He tried to reassure her. Of course she didn't bore him, he said – 'I am more interested in it than anything else in this world, and I love you far far too much to mind whatever scars you might collect', or anything else.

As he wrote, he realised she might not read his words until after the birth. He tried to think of her as she might be then, lying in bed 'with a funny little pink thing'. But what filled his imagination more vividly than anything was the pain she was about to suffer:

> *Oh Zippa, I am so worried, I know it is stupid and that having a baby is natural and not a sickness, but Zippa I can't bear to think of you suffering. Birth is such an unbelievable mystery, it is even more mysterious than death ... But why in Heaven's name birth should come with blood and pain is impossible to understand. It is the one thing I cannot share and help you with.*

It was a conundrum. He had by now seen enough of death to rob it of its mystery. Birth, on the other hand, still seemed holy to him – 'the experience which of all things on earth is nearest to God, or whatever is', he wrote. And yet what of the suffering, the blood and pain that birth shared with death? He could not experience her holy mystery – but of all perverse things, he could vividly imagine her unholy suffering.

It was rare for Tony to invoke God in any situation, and his little hesitation – 'or whatever is' – is characteristic. The military were less shy. Just before the battle, Montgomery visited the troops, made a speech, and issued an Order of the Day with a pious flourish: 'With faith in God', Tony quotes him saying, 'and the Justice of our cause, we will go forward to Victory.' 'It seemed so forced', he thought, 'to bring the Almighty into it'. Still, he trusted Montgomery: 'a very competent man [who] certainly gets everything set before he embarks on anything'. The attack on the Mareth Line was due at any moment now, and Tony believed that by the time his letter arrived, not only would there be a 'little pink thing', but also 'considerable news of the 8th Army, I hope and think good news'.

Tony's letter was written on 20 March. That night, the attack began, named Operation Pugilist. Also that night, Zippa went into labour. On 21 March, the fighting on the Mareth Line continued. At the Fulmer Chase Maternity Hospital, Gerrards Cross, there was victory. A baby girl was born. They named her Rosalind.

~

Nothing reached Tony about the birth of his daughter for another ten days. Meanwhile Operation Pugilist was proving tougher than Montgomery had expected, and he decided to turn everyone back and round to the west to join a flanking movement that the New Zealand Division had already begun some days before. This had been intended as a diversionary tactic, but it now became the main attack route towards the second bottleneck, north of Mareth, at a place called Wadi Akarit. It was a huge movement of men and guns and vehicles, mostly by night, through rocky, desert hills, under constant shelling from the enemy occupying the high points. Crucial to its success was the use of fighter planes as bombers by the Desert Air Force, as well as the support of American air power. Tony's letters tell of planes no longer in the distance but 'rushing about overhead and Ack-ack shells bursting'. He writes of 'fairly exhausting night-driving', of 'a wind, hot like a furnace from the south, everywhere gusts of sand and dust', and of dreams about ice-cream sodas. He mentions being 'awake at night on the wireless set' in his truck, 'collecting and reporting information'. The wireless connection had to be kept open 24 hours a day, he said, so he had very little sleep. He came to admire the riflemen signallers working in the field – very intelligent men, he said, necessarily so, for they had 'a most extraordinarily difficult and responsible job'.

It was a new kind of engagement and a new kind of terrain for these desert soldiers – close mountain warfare, hand-to-hand fighting for every hilltop, and vehicles and artillery hemmed in by narrow ravines and passes. The reports that appeared later in the regimental yearbook for 1943 describe hours of slow grind, long stoppages, sudden high-speed bursts, units arriving twelve hours late, and altogether 150 miles of slog for a westward gain of 30 miles. In the words of one company commander: 'really bloody going'.[1]

By 31 March, they had arrived at a place from which the Wadi Akarit was visible two or three miles away. Here the battalion halted in the lee of a ridge, out of sight, with its headquarters tucked into a fold of the hill. Tony described himself sitting in a gully, as he had done before Mareth, in 'foothills which surround a wide rather arid basin. The bare little hills here with sharp gullies look like a backcloth in one dimension, especially in the early morning light.' He doesn't say, as his company commander Major John Hogg does, that these bare little hills were full of German and Italian gunners – 'the wily Hun and Eytie' was his phrase. Luckily, their guns never found the battalion's gully – or wadi, as it was called – a 'wadi of good omen', Major Hogg wrote: 'Shells fell short of it, over it, to the left of it and to the right of it, but they never managed to get one inside.'[2]

In among the explosions, Tony sat at his wireless controls, headphones clamped to his ears: 'I hear all the information that is passed back by the units, plot it on a map, tell the colonel anything I think matters, and pass back our own stuff. It only becomes trying when stuff pours in and the colonel is not here and I have to start issuing instructions!!' His truck, he said, was 'so constructed that one can really see nothing of the actual ground itself', while at the same time, he could hear everything – the signallers on the ground, sometimes 'Italians talking furiously on the air and sometimes American pilots calling for signals'. It wasn't difficult, he said, but it made him nervous, 'afraid of suddenly … not having codes, or maps or something.' And there was a special kind of tension whenever things went quiet. This was when he quoted the dictum about war consisting of long stretches of inaction punctuated by bursts of excitement. As he sat in his truck at 4am, his thoughts would drift to Zippa with a sharpened sense of the madness of it all – he in the cold grey dawn with his headphones on, and she, gracious in her 'lovely clothes, full of gaiety and sweet sanity'.

Tony's visions of Zippa were always unreal, but she might have laughed at this one. Sleepless and red-eyed with a ten-day-old baby, she knew those 4am watches well. The 2am and 6am ones as well. Were it not for the time difference, they might have been sitting up awake in the dark at the same time. But in the circumstances, she probably forgave him. For his part, he was frantic for news. He had been reading *War and Peace* and *Anna Karenina* and was badly frightened by the birth scenes in both books: 'In *War and Peace* Andrei's wife dies, and in the other, Kitty, Levin's wife, has a fearful time!' But even if Zippa was alright, he was still fundamentally stumped. It was extraordinary, he said, to think of her 'with a baby occupying all her time and thoughts'. He tried 'to picture what it looked like', he said, but had to admit that he could arrive at 'no conception of it'.

That evening of 31 March, a telegram arrived from his mother: the baby was born, it was a girl, and they were 'both doing perfectly'. The word 'both' gave him a jump: 'It is so strange to think of her now as a person to be included in the word both'. He was unutterably relieved, tumbling with questions. How was she, what did she feel, how had it been, 'Zippa Darling, was it really all as normal and alright as could be? ... Is the pain too agonising and unearthly Zippa, I cannot grasp it.' Were people being helpful, he wanted to know? Was she being 'ruthless in thinking of herself and the baby now'? As he writes he tries to think about the baby itself. What does she look like? Is she fair? He thinks she might be ugly – ugly at the moment, that is, because you never know what a baby will turn into. Soon he

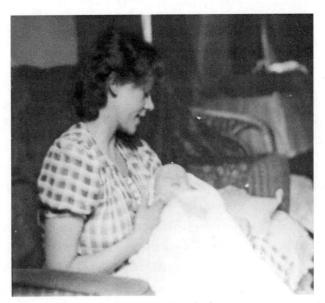

Zippa with Rosalind

was imagining her development and how best to bring her up. He doesn't know, but he thinks that 'a tremendous amount of influence over a person's character is exerted by its life as a tiny baby'. He couldn't imagine a better person than Zippa for creating the right atmosphere for a child to grow up in. He agrees that it's best to avoid 'elaborate systems', but still Rosalind must learn early on not to expect everything to be done for her. But in the end, 'all I ask Darling one, is that she is as charming and as good and true as you'.

Now letters from her were arriving from the middle of March, and to crown everything, they tell him that his parcels have arrived – best of all the French blouse: 'I am so terribly pleased'. The French blouse at last, the blouse of blouses, so real, so graspable, so unlike the baby, in fact almost like his vision of Zippa herself: 'I fell in love with it so much and it was rather extravagant'. Now he must go. The post corporal was coming round and there wouldn't be another chance for days.

The Battle of Akarit began before dawn on 6 April and continued all day and into the next night. He hadn't yet heard about the birth from Zippa herself, but this battle at any rate was a fierce and bloody 24 hours. Montgomery wrote in his campaign diary: 'We had on this day the heaviest and most savage fighting we have had since I have commanded the Eighth Army. Certain localities and points changed hands several times.'[3] Tony managed a scrawl that day: 'No time for a letter. Hot day, much excitement on, and I am very busy on the wireless, the news I think is good and the battle going well.'

The next day his letter starts as though he had more time, and he even begins to tell her about the book he's reading, Siegfried Sassoon's *Memoirs of an Infantry Officer*: 'I like his simplicity and his admission of doubt, and inconsistencies, even his pacifism he admits not to have been a reasoned logical thing, and he felt at once pacifist and yet proud of having been in France.' Tony understood such doubts and inconsistencies. They chimed with his own. He could have gone on. But suddenly his writing lurches:

Zippa Zippa your letter March 23rd just after Rosalind was born has just come in. Oh Darling I can't bear the thought of you having had such an awful time. Oh Zippa Zippa ... thank heavens it is over, but I shan't forget.

Oh and one of 25th came too. I have no time to read before answering. You have done something colossal ... I'm so glad you are delighted, it is wonderful ... A battle is going on and I can't write, am on the wireless. A million million thoughts and wishes ...

The main battle at Akarit was over, the enemy had withdrawn, but they were now chasing them and there were rearguard actions. It is extraordinary that the battle for Rosalind coincided, not just once but a second time, in Tony's mind, with major conflicts in the Tunis campaign: first with the Mareth Line, and now with Wadi Akarit. He wrote again two days later, reliving Zippa's 'wild nightmare', horrified at the picture of her 'gulping joyfully at gas and chloroform'. He hadn't realised that it could all take so long. 'It is such a bloody life sometimes' he says – as indeed he might have said of the scenes around him. The casualties on all sides were great, thousands dead and wounded.

Now all was calm. They had driven that day through 'lovely country', he wrote, 'a great range of hills on our left, blue shadows over the slopes, a salt lake in the distance, patches of breast high wheat, bearded kind, and the wind chasing silken ripples over barley, with little crimson poppies in it.' He had spent the previous night with Jack Brister trying to locate 'a certain party' six miles away in the pitch dark, had got lost and had driven into a disused well, twenty-feet deep. The jeep had overturned, but luckily had lodged itself across the top of it, so hadn't crushed them. They had climbed out and spent the rest of the night trying to find their way back without being mistaken for the enemy. His eyes were dropping as he wrote. He was utterly happy, he said, and no, of course he didn't think of Rosalind as just a nuisance. It's an arresting moment. Zippa must have said something. 'I am delighted with Rosalind', he assured her, 'tell me all about her'. But for now he must sleep: 'how I long to be close to you and hold you in my arms again'.

Chapter 8

'A considerable achievement'

After Akarit, the exhausted battalion halted for six days at a place called Bou Thadi, about 160 miles south of Tunis. To get there, they drove through a country of almond and olive groves, of corn and banks of flowers, and when they finally stopped, they found themselves, said Tony, in an 'enchanted valley'. The letter is torn, with a hole in the middle, but around the edges it's possible to make out yellow daisies, convolvulus and poppies. As he sat writing, the air felt like June, he said, and somewhere in the torn part there must have been water, a stream perhaps, for he had managed to wash himself all over, including his hair for the first time in weeks. He had just been watching a praying mantis with its 'spindle delicate legs' and its 'pin shape very human head': 'when he stops he lifts up his front legs and clasps them in an attitude of prayer'.

Altogether he was feeling optimistic:

This campaign is very nearly over now. All seems well, though there may be a close in struggle if he [Rommel]*

---

* No one yet knew that Rommel had left. The Germans kept his departure a secret from the Allies.

tries to make Tunis a Tobruk. I hope he does not insist on fighting to the last!

The next day, in a second letter, they had just had supper, the light was fading, and he was in a mood for poking a little fun at the grandiloquence of the war:

Considering we are fighting a war, fighting a great campaign, and are, as Monty says, perhaps the best fighting machine the British Empire has ever produced, I have just had an extraordinarily good dinner!

The menu had included the local wine, 'like Soho vin ordinaire', also tinned cream and a cigar, and he was now feeling 'as much at peace with the world as is possible away from you my darling'. It was a fleeting moment, he knew, and he warned her that she 'may learn of us again in the news soon'. But she mustn't worry:

Have no fears for me my darling, I assure you that so far, anyway, we have not had nearly so bad a time as you will have imagined. This war here is not nearly such non-stop horror as you must think. Of course there are nasty moments …

and he reminds her how lucky he is.

~

During these March and April weeks, as the baby became a reality, so did Tony's old anxiety about a job when the war was over. He was shocked at himself for not having a firm plan. He couldn't go on dithering. A few days after the Battle of Mareth, towards the end of March, he wrote to Zippa about a broadcast speech he had heard – Churchill setting out his vision for post-war Europe.[1] He was writing from his 'little cell': 'About 6ft square, 5ft high walls of piled up stones and a tarpaulin like an umbrella over the top. Through the opening I see my huge olive tree and blue sky and silver planes miles up.'

The prime minister, Tony said, had been full of warnings against exaggerated optimism. He hadn't wanted even to guess when the end would come – not this year anyway, maybe not even next. He hadn't wanted to make fairy-tale promises either. That was for a future government, Churchill had said, and it would be wrong to bind it. In any case he didn't think this was the moment to be planning for anything other than military victory.

But in among the caveats had come passages of hope: there was a section on Beveridge, on social change, on educational reform. 'The one best thing in Winston's speech,' wrote Tony, 'was his talk of equality of education.' But then he hesitated: 'I wonder how much he really means it, or how much it is the old aristocratic tradition of giving way gently in time, just before it becomes inevitable.' Tony was beginning to sound like the suspicious men round the wireless when the Beveridge Report was first announced. So far, they had been right. That mysterious and invisible 'they' that Tony heard them grumbling about so often – in this case, the MPs debating the Report in parliament – had already, in February 1943, voted to postpone a decision on legislating for any of Beveridge until after the war.* It had been at Churchill's insistence, and his March broadcast was in line with that. In fact, when Tony heard it, he wondered whether the whole thing was really 'an attempt to sidetrack Beveridge' altogether.

---

* Though there was a sizeable backbench revolt. See *The People's War*, pp. 531–32.

Still, it revived in him an old interest in education. He reviewed the various jobs he might do. The Civil Service? There might be 'good interesting jobs' there, he thought – 'after all, there will be all sorts of extensions of government control of things'. Business? He couldn't get interested in it. Journalism? A 'cut-throat' profession, and he was 'frightened' of being a fail-ure – unlike his father, though he didn't say that. What he came back to was teaching – 'because it is the only thing I see that I ought to be capable of doing, which does mean something really worth doing'.

He sounds a little diffident. But if Zippa imagined a man in front of a blackboard, she was in for a surprise. He wouldn't teach in England, he thought, or only for a year or so. After that, he would try

to get a job in Russia for at least a year, and then, either directly or after coming back to England, spend a year teach-ing in America. … Then, after some years teaching, having been abroad and seen different systems, I might try for edu-cation administration or organising a place for the training of teachers, for that is really what is wanted, a far far higher standard of teachers. Perhaps I could go into politics.

Zippa knew he wanted to travel, but this! Russia, America – was it really teaching he was after? Her letter is missing, but Tony's answer suggests she had put her finger on something. 'Yes, Zippa', he admitted, 'I <u>am</u> more attracted by politics than by teaching, but …' He hardly knew what he thought.

Tony's desire to travel came partly from a curiosity about the world, but also, I suspect, from a hesitation about England. If England was to be shaped by 'the old aristocratic tradition' of Churchill and the officer class, he would rather look further afield. Whenever England showed signs of changing – equality of education, for example – he was excited. But he didn't yet trust it. Russia and America, on the other hand, seemed more interesting. He didn't really know about Russia, but he had seen what it meant to the men on board ship, what hopes it stood for. Besides, Russia's resistance to the Germans had been extraordinary – and life-saving for Britain. 'Terrific', he had said, 'tremendous'. He was not alone. By 1943, even the die-hard officers that Alan Moorehead spoke of had begun 'to take pride in the Red soldier'.[2] Churchill's speech itself had paid elaborate tribute to them – 'our Russian allies ... fighting for dear life and dearer honour in the dire, deadly, daily struggle against all the might of the German military machine'.

As for America, Tony didn't know much about that either. He had had his first glimpse of Americans in December – those big men he had described for Zippa, whose planes had landed in the desert in a whirl of golden dust. He had heard their pilots on his headphones before Akarit, calling for signals. They were over here. North Africa was their first campaign and the Supreme Command of the Allied forces had passed to General Eisenhower.

The war had brought both Russia and America into greater focus. They were the major powers. Churchill in his speech had tried to claim parity with them: 'the three great victorious Powers', he had said, 'the British Commonwealth of Nations, the United States, and Soviet Russia'. But Tony was under no illusions. 'He has done wonders', he said later, towards the end of 1944, but 'poor Winston has a tough job. After all, we are only a 2nd class power, and he has no cards to play against Joe and Roosevelt except prestige.'

What was really beginning to interest Tony – though he may not have known it yet – was essentially that game of cards: how the nations of the world, particularly Russia and America, might play their hands. But in 1943, he didn't yet see how that could be a job. Teaching was a job; educational administration was a job. The best he could do was to give those things a Russian and American twist. He would take his schoolroom to each in turn.

It must have been dizzying for Zippa, and for a moment, he seems to have realised it: 'The greatest doubts of all I have is what it would be like for you … whether you would like living for a year or so first in Russia and then in America … I really don't know, Darling, whether it is a mad idea.'

It was. In the event, he didn't pursue it. Perhaps she said something. But his sense remained that, in the post-war world, those would be the countries to watch.

~

Tunisia in the spring of 1943 was scarcely the place or time for making career decisions. Tony's valley at Bou Thadi was a haven, but war crashed all round it. Only the other day an enemy plane had burst in, hurtling down a few hundred yards away 'with billows of black smoke and leaping flame'. It had been a gruesome sight, but everyone, he said,

> *almost literally jumped up and down and began clapping as at a show. Our signals officer, a boy of 20 or so, was thrilled and later kept saying how wonderful it was and that it had made his day. I only felt rather still and horrified at the thought of the German inside. He could not possibly have got out.*

A few days later, they were on the move again. Tony tried to describe the scene for Zippa. The Eighth Army were generally an eccentric lot, old sweats who'd been in North Africa longer than anyone else, and who didn't give a damn what they looked like.

146

Tony's battalion was no different. Over the years, the men had picked up dogs, mainly in the desert, and these had multiplied: 'The regimental Sjt Major's had puppies the other day and the whole family now travels in the truck!' But it wasn't just dogs. Now that they were in farming country, the men had diversified: 'clucking chickens flap from every truck', he wrote, 'and an occasional sheep or goat maa's plaintively beneath a canopy'. The whole caravan set off, he said, looking like 'a moving farm'.

As it happened, they were about to join up with another more conventional part of the Allied forces. With Tunis itself within their sights, the Allies were now re-arranging themselves to make the final approach. Part of the Eighth Army had gone east, up the coast towards the third of the bottlenecks at a town southeast of Tunis called Enfidaville (now Enfidha). Tony's division meanwhile was deployed west, then north to join up with a division of the First Army, newly arrived from England and still relatively smart. The rendezvous came as something of a shock to both sides. Here's Tony's commanding officer, Major Hogg, writing in the Regiment's yearbook about a platoon from the battalion taking over from a newly arrived company of Welsh Guards:

> [Captain] Sandy [Goschen] drove up to find these immaculate and tin-hatted figures awaiting us, and vastly surprised them by the order of de-bussing: first of all the Section hens (the providers of the breakfast egg) fluttered to the ground; then the platoon dog jumped off, then some rather scruffy, unshaven, and sleepless Riflemen.[3]

With and without livestock, with and without tin hats, all the armies – British and Commonwealth, US and Free French – were now converging on Tunis from every direction, hemming the enemy in against the sea. It seemed the end would come by the end of April.[4] In fact, it came just a little later than that. The Axis had decided, just as Tony had feared, to fight to the last. 'On the very day that the line at Wadi Akarit broke', writes one historian, 'Hitler and Mussolini met at Salzburg and agreed that Tunisia must be held, whatever the cost, to keep Allied forces engaged in North Africa rather than allow them to invade Europe.'[5]

And the cost was high for both sides. The mountains through which the Allies fought were heavily defended. Enemy guns occupied the vantage points and covered every pass and gap. Their shelling was relentless and the accounts in the regimental chronicle record many miserable days exposed to it, and many moonless nights of silent, creeping patrols and reconnaissance.

It was a strange few weeks. The beauty of the country was breathtaking. Tony was not alone in speaking of it. Major Hogg, a dry, humorous, hard-bitten man, couldn't help including the flowers and almond blossom in his report for the regimental chronicle – 'most attractive', he said. He even went so far as 'enchanting'[6] for the next place they stopped at, further north. The diaries of Philip Jordan, a journalist travelling with the First Army, are likewise full of the flowers of Tunisia. He writes of fields of gentians, and roads of poppies, of 'wild snapdragons, lilies, violets, vetch, marigolds, plump yellow daisies'. He describes many things Tony would never have mentioned to Zippa: 'smashed and burnt cars and tanks', and the air thick with the smell of death: 'The Germans, during the time they occupied this area, buried no dead, neither their own nor ours, so the air here is beastly with the sweet smell of decay.' But even in his descriptions of death and the engines of death, he couldn't escape the profusion of that spring. Spitfires, he said, took off with 'their wheels … tangled in flowers', and soldiers arrived at field hospitals 'with wild flowers embedded in their wounds'.[7]

The army was now among villages and towns. Ordinary people, civilians, begin to appear in Tony's letters: farmers, shop-keepers, women. The battalion could buy its own food and he encounters bakers, saltfish-sellers, egg-sellers – one of them a gnarled old man on horseback, with a high-backed, velvet-covered saddle stitched in silver thread. He found them friendly, hospit-able and more honest than he had been warned. They invited him to drink tea, to smoke their long-stemmed pipes, and they drew him into the rituals of bargaining. He loved it. 'To do a deal is to form a friendship' he told Zippa – 'tremendous fun'. I can almost hear him. In later life, when work took him to the Middle East, bargaining was one of Tony's greatest pleasures. He had an eye for beautiful things – carpets, pots, pieces of embroidery – and I remember his leisurely haggles with glasses of sweet tea in the souks and bazaars. Now, as I write, my eye travels over the glow-ing colours of some of his prizes, and behind them, dimly, I see those Tunisian village men of 1943.

In fact, were it not for the war and the absence of Zippa, Tony in Tunisia might almost have been happy. Once, when he was writing to her in an olive grove, a small boy came near with his goats. He 'makes strange throaty noises to them from time to time', he said, while 'an adorable little black kid is butting ecstati-cally at its mother with a furiously wagging tale'. It was a Biblical scene. His boy differed 'not a scrap', he thought, from 'a little boy, who did the same thing in the same place 2,000 years ago.'

It seems fantastic to have aeroplanes and all the parapher-nalia of war rumbling around while the little Arab boy watches his goats.

But he also desperately wanted to tell Zippa more about that war – those planes, the battles, the plan, what next: 'I do wish I could write to you more, it is so cramping not being able to say just where I am and what we are doing'. All he could offer were the usual bursts and rushes that she knew well, here strung along from letter to letter:

> *No time to write ... things are somewhat rushed ... am sitting on the wireless set having had a short night of one hour's sleep ... had a fearful job ... had to find a route across country and lead the battalion to a place it was rather important for it to get to on time ... almost black, no moon ... more than a little relieved it worked O.K. Oh I shall never be able to finish this letter ... Charlie Zebra Charlie ZEBRA (that's me), information, or have you any request etc. etc.*

These last phrases were written on 1 May – just short of the second anniversary of their wedding day. But Tony forgets it in his sorrow at the death of his great friend, Jack Brister – caught by 'an unhappy shell', wrote Major Hogg.[8] 'He was one of the few people I felt I could really know permanently' Tony wrote; it seems 'fantastic that all his rich personality should suddenly not exist'. It was, no doubt, one of the things he meant when he said to Zippa at about this time: 'If it were not for you to think of, life would be very dark.'

Two days later, hot and fly-ridden, Tony wrote to say that the battle was 'more difficult than I expected ... great deep ravines and some salt lakes make it difficult to go anywhere except up certain narrow valleys'. They were still 30 miles or so away from Tunis, and over the next days – according to Major Hogg – 'the Hun gunners shot off everything they had with them ... in one final orgy'.[9]

~

The game was up. The final orgy was its last throw. On 7 May Tunis fell to the British, and nearby Bizerta to the Americans. As soon as the news reached him, Tony snatched a wet, smudged and crumpled airmail letter:

Please forgive awful scrawl. It is all I have and only hope it will hold together. Yesterday Tunis and Bizerta fell, it has come very quickly at the end, though there will still be some resistance on the peninsula. I have no time to write much, but just so that you know I am well! ... It is exciting here now about Tunis. Really it has been a considerable achievement. What now? is the question we all ask. ... I am clamped to the wireless and must go back to directing the battle.

'Considerable achievement', was like him. 'Considerable news', was what he had hoped for at the Battle of Mareth. It was the nearest Tony would ever get to waving the flag or sing-ing 'Onward Christian Soldiers'. He doesn't say anything about the people of Tunis climbing all over the army trucks and tanks, throwing flowers and shaking hands with everyone. 'We were literally mobbed', says one officer in the regimental chronicle.[10] True, Tony was still up in the mountains during those first few days, but he would have heard about it. All the same, his 'con-siderable achievement' only barely conceals a sense of pride, the kind that Sassoon had felt in having fought in France. He may have resisted it at some level, but he felt it – just as Tony felt, couldn't help feeling, the *esprit de corps* of the Eighth Army when finally it came together and met up with the First Army in Tunis:

There is a great feeling by now between the 8th Army people, particularly people who have been out here a long time. To look at they are not particularly orderly but have learned how to get along and look after themselves. One of our trucks looks like a scrap heap. There are always heaps of things piled on it, things the men have picked up, and blackened fire tins hanging on the side … In the desert it used to be a question of long journeys and short halts, and the rifleman prided himself on the ability to produce a cup of tea on a petrol fire in about 2½ minutes. As a result we look rather a ragamuffin lot. The 1st Army on the other hand have very much the stamp of England on them, for instance they always wear tin hats and we never do. They are full of road discipline which we are bad at being used to the desert. They camouflage their trucks with great care but crowd them together. We don't camouflage at all but try hard to disperse them so that they are not a target for aeroplanes. … The 1st Army feel they have been out here a long time if they left before Christmas! … Still the 8th army has a good deal to learn about fighting in close country.

Alan Moorehead, at that time with the First Army, put it with more of a flourish. 'After months in the muddy Tunisian hills, we were pale and wearing thick battle dress', he wrote,

These others, from the Nile, 1,500 miles away, were dressed in shorts and open-necked shirts and were burnt by the sun to a walnut brown. They were covered in dust, and their blackened tea canteens and cooking pots rattled about on the back of their armoured cars. Our equipment was clean and new, theirs was battered and dirty. They were a colonial army, dishevelled and exultant, coming up from an expedition in Africa; we were of Europe and relatively new to the war. The serjeant in the leading 8th Army car was not a tactful man.

'Who are you?' he called out.

'The First Army.'

He considered it a moment. 'You can go home' he said.[11]

~

Though Tunis fell on 7 May, it wasn't until 12 May – Zippa's birthday as it happened – that Tony was able to say that 'the last of the fighting in North Africa is over':

All yesterday afternoon and all today thousands of Germans have been surrendering. They have been driving themselves, crammed in lorries past the road where I am sitting. It is strange to see Germans as prisoners in such numbers. Apparently well over 100,000 prisoners so far.* I really don't think he [Rommel] has been able to get any at all away ... The Germans seem to have had no organised plan for evacuations, or attempting to hold on on the peninsula.

A few days later he 'drove past a long trail' and got a closer look:

It was strange to watch them all file past, thousands of them carrying blankets, packs and all they could. Among those thousands there must have been charming men, clever men, kind men and bad men ... really what a tremendous potentiality there is in Germany, if only it were wisely directed. A waste was what it all seemed.

---

* In the end, more than 230,000 prisoners of war were taken.

Tony was curiously downbeat. Admittedly he had caught a stomach bug just then and felt too ill to join in the celebrations. But all he says about the general atmosphere was that 'all our people are full of excitement and high spirits'. Everyone was scrambling to get their hands on the cars of the German officers:

The technique is to go down to the prisoners' camp and wait till some Brigadier drives in in a smart car to give himself up, and then drive off in his car. In a few days they will all be called in to a dump, but meanwhile, everyone has a car!

A few days later he was better enough to go for a bathe in the sea – 'wonderful to twirl and float free in the water' – and to look about him. It was a pleasure to be among French people, he said, 'so nice to see and talk to them'. They were 'delighted to see us', and when he stopped at a farmhouse, he was 'pressed with wine and liqueurs'. The daughter of the family 'was going to have a baby in a month', they said, 'and now she will be able to have it in peace'. The only discordant note in all this was 'the bad behaviour of some of our troops, smashing up houses and pinching things. If there is a single person in a house, they would not take a thing, but when they come to deserted houses … they just break things up. This of course is by no means the rule, but it does happen … and it makes me furious.'

As for the city, Tunis itself, it was doing its best, with 'a struggling gay French air, trying to be a little Paris'. This, in spite of food shortages and no electricity. Shops were beginning to open, but there wasn't much in them. Everything had been taken by the departing Germans, people said, and there were queues at all the banks trying to get rid of their German currency. Tony always loved the French, read as much French literature as he could find, and seized every chance to practise speaking the language. He wished he could stay and get to know people. But the battalion HQ was somewhere in the surrounding country, he doesn't or can't say where.

In the end, for all the high spirits, for all the smashing and rejoicing, the capture of Tunis fell oddly flat. 'Well, that was that', wrote Major Hogg, 'though it did leave me, and even more so some of the older "sweats" and "Desert Rats", feeling relaxed and at a loose end'.[12] Tony wrote of a sense of 'anti-climax, nobody knows what is going to happen'. One thing he did know. Churchill, in his speech back in March at the time of the battle of Mareth, had talked of bringing some of the men back soon, of demobbing and re-deploying. But there was no plan for Tony to come home. He doesn't explain, but he sounds definite. Churchill had also spoken of war continuing in the Far East even after the defeat of Germany. 'The only thing I hope for,' wrote Tony, 'is that I don't get sent to Japan!!'

It was now a year, he noted bleakly, since he first heard he was to go abroad. He had said then that he would be home in a year. And now? 'If only I could be sure that in another year I would be home'. He had been dreaming of England for so long. It was spring there too, of course, and a letter from Zippa about walking in the bursting beech woods had been almost unbearable. His own equally beautiful walks only made it worse: 'A winding path led up the side of a narrow valley … bordered with lovely flowers. Masses of snap dragons, foxgloves, brilliant large vetches and little yellow irises … the air was full of birds singing, particularly thrushes! It seemed so like England!'

Tony often tried to see England in the landscapes of Africa – England or Ireland. The Tunisian hills could be in Ireland; the rolling fields of corn were like Surrey; a rocky bay in Algeria reminded him of Cornwall. Or he would turn it around, and imagine Zippa there. He wanted to see Algeria with her, maybe

Palestine again, and Syria. What fun they would have. And then he would check himself. Of course – Rosalind!

Rosalind, the fact of her, changed everything. Zippa was right. Whatever he said about being delighted with the baby, he couldn't remember to include her. She was extra, extraneous even. 'I think of you,' he wrote, 'and try to imagine what you're doing. I can't picture you with Rosalind at all!'. Poor Zippa. It was true – she was no longer simply Zippa, his Zippa. She was Zippa-and-Rosalind. She had tried to make him feel a little of what she felt for the baby. But what could she do? What could either of them do? He could not grasp, let alone love, something he had never seen. He could be pleased for her – 'that you do feel positively happy with Rosalind and that you do love her'. But he blundered badly too: 'otherwise' he went on, 'the load of work she must be would be nothing but a drag'. He didn't really know what to say: 'Tell me, when do they cut teeth, start to walk, start to talk etc. … when does she start to recognise people?'

And yet intuitively, Tony had grasped something. The other night, he says, he had a dream. He dreamt he had come home, and that he had been greeted by Rosalind. The child – a child now – had looked at him for a long time, then 'burst into a fury and had said "Don't like you!"' It was 'funny and horrid', he said. 'I hope it does not work out like that.' He doesn't say what, in his dream, he felt about her.

Chapter 9

A turning point

All this time, Zippa's voice has been muffled. None of her letters between Christmas 1942 and the summer of 1943 have survived, though they can be guessed at from Tony's. Now suddenly, in early June, she bursts out in person. She has been celebrating. Tunis maybe, but also Rosalind's christening and, in his absence, Tony's birthday. She's bought him a present – some old glass, his favourite thing, one a tiny liqueur glass (and she draws it for him), which, 'would do for Rosalind to have a sip out of when we're leaning back and imbibing some rich and rare liqueur!!'

Also, she thinks she's about to move. There had been some worries about the Oakley Street house in Tony's letters – the lease, the landlady, a hike in the rent. What was she going to do? Would she move? Must she? Yes, she thinks she will. She can't afford Oakley Street any more. She can't afford anywhere else nearby either. She doesn't mention it, but the arrival in England of the Americans had pushed up rents all round.[1] The only place she can afford now, is Wapping – miles away to the east, down in the docklands. She doesn't mind though: 'I shall like it I think, though it is rather cut off with Rosalind to look after.'

Tony was appalled. Wapping of all places! It's 'a very dangerous area if bombing starts again as is quite possible'. He wished she wouldn't. He'd be prepared to pay a higher rent if necessary.

Anyway, she'll exhaust herself, packing up, cleaning at both ends, painting Wapping, unpacking, arranging furniture, making blackout curtains: 'Rosalind is all you can manage,' he says. 'Do realize it, and please, for my sake, don't try anything else. I do want a well and lovely darling.'

Tony often spoke like that – 'If you aren't careful you will stop looking so lovely, and I couldn't bear that', he once said – and it always leaves a suspicion that he was concerned as much for his own sake as for hers. And yet, it's too simple. What he really wanted, in his romantic, chivalrous way, was the chance to make Zippa happy. It sounds old-fashioned now, but I think he saw it as his responsibility as her husband. The trouble was that his idea of happiness was always entangled with the idea of youth and beauty:

> *We must have a lovely gay time these next few years. I don't want the wild extravagance of the '20s but I do want us to have fun and gaiety and travel and for you to be beautiful … if only I can give you a happy life I shall be content.*

At the back of everything was his sense of time passing. Youth was temporary, beauty fragile. The war was using up their moment now, but if they were careful they could still come into their own.

Zippa never paid much attention to people who told her she was doing too much. As for the dangerousness of Wapping ('the number of imploring letters not to go is amazing', she laughed), her answer to that was simple. She had no choice – and 'I definitely do not want to live for the duration at Derby or the vicarage'. 'Derby' meant a house in the country, near Derby, called Hilton Lodge, where her cousin Betty lived, the daughter of Aunt Jane. Betty was very close to Zippa and her siblings, more like a fourth sister than a cousin. She had married into a Midlands

Hilton Lodge, near Derby

brewing family and during the war her big, comfortable house, with its vegetable garden, chickens and fresh eggs, was an escape from the bombings and grimness of London.* But however much Zippa loved Betty and Hilton Lodge, she didn't want to live there.

So, Wapping it was, 8 Pier Head, a charming Georgian house on the river, and cheap – leased from the London Port Authority. When Tony told his father about it, Arthur wrote back full of enthusiasm. He knew Wapping well from his Toynbee Hall days in neighbouring Whitechapel – an interesting neighbourhood, he told Tony, 'a sort of East End Chelsea, with a less precious and more wildly romantic flavour'. He knew Pier Head too – had nearly taken a place there himself once, the Harbour Master's house. Tony began to come round to it, though it would mean he could no longer picture her so clearly.

---

* Though Derby itself, with its Rolls-Royce factory, was a major target and there was always the danger of a stray bomb.

And of course he was right. Zippa did exhaust herself – though what he always forgot was that she didn't much mind exhausting herself. Besides, she had good friends to help, two in particular, Dorothea and Franz Dessauer, brother and sister, Jewish refugees from Nazi Vienna, whom the family had known since before the war.* I remember them – a striking pair, both of them tall and gentle with softly accented voices, Franz a little stooping, with his viola, and his piercing blue eyes; and magnificent, green-eyed Dolly (as she was known), with her raven hair and cigarettes. Dolly had been one of the Oakley Street lodgers, and was moving to the Wapping house, where Zippa's sister Geraldine and her children would also live.

The move was a mighty work, but Zippa was undaunted – exuberant even:

I dashed down this morning to see how the man Judith [another friend] got us is doing. Rather a fool, I thought. I got some white paint, which is almost impossible now, and am doing the drawing-room woodwork with it – or rather he is, and I've had to stop him because he is sloshing it about so badly … I've told him to get on with something else and I'll spend the day there tomorrow and do it myself. I am far the best painter!

Franz was distempering the walls a very pale duck egg green, while she had made a list of things that didn't work and had gone to the engineering department of the Port Authority to see about repairs. There she had found '2 delightful men in the office doing nothing, stewing by the fire. We talked of all sorts of things and they disclosed their hobby to me which was drawing pictures of

---

* Franz later changed his name to Davenport.

the views out of the windows and printing in old English characters. I think they really have nothing else to do.'

Zippa was fascinated by the whole Wapping area, had walked
along Monument Street as far as the Tower and had found the
fish market where the men wore 'extraordinary hats like ribbed
toffee, made for balancing sacks on'. Then – rather like Tony himself – she would sometimes break off abruptly and apologise the
next day: 'I really am working without a minute between, except
eating and feeding Rosalind, and then I can't write and when I
get back usually by 10:30pm, I have supper and flop off to sleep.'

But he mustn't worry, she says: 'I'm quite well and have lots
of milk, and Rosalind is doing well and loves being carted back
and forth on the tube!'

> *This sort of thing amuses me when I get down to it and I am*
> *well and excited ... Everything always takes three times as*
> *long as I think it will, but I'll never learn!*

No doubt Tony shook his head, but he was tactful on the whole,
and only gave a rather routine warning about making sure the
others shared expenses with her.

By the end of June, they were in. It had been, she agreed, 'a
colossal job' – 'too much kitchen stuff, too many blankets, pictures, gas fires, tools etc. etc.', and the grand piano wouldn't go
up the stairs. Annoying. It would need lifting tackle to get it in
through the drawing-room window, so for now it was in the hall
'on its side with its legs off'. She was so tired she couldn't sleep
the first night, but last night she did – and 'the darling Rosalind
didn't wake me till seven!'

There was a reckless side to Zippa, a kind of raw, spontaneous
energy which got her through. It was part of her attraction. And
of course she made the place glow. Tony wanted to know every

detail of the house, so he could imagine her. She told him about the Persian hanging here; the red velvet Oakley Street curtains there; the steps down in the hall, and the arch, and if you turn left you see the river and boats; the other way, you see 'a wave of green from the plane trees'. She also told him about the people round about.

Zippa could make friends on the spot – the men in the engineering department; the publican next door; the policemen on the beat whom she had charmed by the end of the first week: 'The policemen on duty on the Pier are sweet and have invited us to take our deck chairs out and sit on the edge of the river whenever we like!' She would leave the pram outside in the cul-de-sac and they would rock it as they passed whenever Rosalind cried. They had made a pet of her, she said, and rather spoilt her, but she didn't think it mattered. Now she was writing from the train on her way to Betty's at Hilton Lodge, where she would have a proper rest for a few weeks. She was taking his Cape Town marmalade – just arrived, 'such a joy':

I have just fed Rosalind, feeling very embarrassed – especially as she now makes loud sucking noises and gurgles, and shrieks with laughter and throws her legs in the air in her ecstasy over food! No regard whatsoever for my feelings!

Feeding, sucking, gurgling, shrieking, ecstasy – strange reading for Tony at any time, but now scarcely comprehensible. All Zippa's laughter died as it reached him, and he was left with nothing but a piece of military timetabling. 'Poor sweet,' he writes, 'how trying having to feed Rosalind in the train! I suppose she has to be fed exactly on time wherever you are, most trying.' The whole business of feeding amazed him. 'A frightful full-time

Zippa with Rosalind

job', he called it, 'I had not realized a baby had to be fed so often that you only get three clear hours between.' He was right in a way, but he could never quite grasp that frightfulness was never the whole story. Zippa knew it, not just with Rosalind, but with all the other things he grumbled about for her sake – the house, too many people, parties, clearing up.

For himself just then, life felt more frightful than not. The fighting had stopped, but the army was everywhere. It seemed to him 'crazy still to be in the army' at all. He felt swallowed up by it, particularly in Tunis where there seemed to be more uniforms than civilians:

> *I do hate feeling in a city that I am not just me, Tony Moore, but part of the mass of British soldiers, just another British officer.*

And then there were the inspections, the parades, the spit and polish. By early June, they had moved somewhere close to Tripoli where there was to be an inspection of the troops: 'We are all dressed up in our best ironed shirts, creased trousers, belts scrubbed white', wrote Tony on the morning of the inspection: 'It will entail standing for about two hours, and unless the general tells us to stand easy, we will have to keep completely still and the flies will drive me mad.'

There are photographs of the occasion in the regimental chronicle – and of the next one as well, on the 25th, when the King came to Tripoli, and the battalion provided the guard of honour. There is Major Hogg, says a caption, and Sandy Goschen, last seen in his truck full of chickens and dogs and scruffy riflemen. And there in the list of officers present, is Tony's name. But among the stiff lines of ironed shirts and creased trousers, it is impossible to distinguish him. As the King drove away, says the chronicle, they gave him three cheers. A good show, it seems.

Tony doesn't mention the King, nor any of the pomp and ceremony of those days. Just a few weeks before, on 23 May, he had listened to the news about a bombing raid on Dortmund, the coal and steel centre in the Ruhr valley, in which 2,000 tonnes of explosives were dropped in half an hour – a third of the total dropped on London during the 90-day Blitz.[2] He hated the thought, but conceded that it would have 'a tremendous effect on Germany' and that 'the war might end before I dare hope'. Personally, all he could feel was 'rather tired and stupid'.

~

1943 marked a turning point in the war, and so it did in different ways for Zippa and Tony. For Zippa it was a year of birth and death – the birth of Rosalind in March, and in May, the death of her mother, Hortense. Her father and grandmother had both died in the mid-1930s, and Hortense was almost the last link to the older generations of the family. Now, only Aunt Jane was left (not counting their step-grandfather, Uncle Tony), and she was seriously ill with cancer. In fact she was dying. That summer at Hilton Lodge where she was living with her daughter, Betty, would be her last. When Zippa travelled up to Derby, she knew she would be saying goodbye.

It had always been the plan that the Derby holiday would be continued in North Wales, in a cottage by the sea. They were a crowd. Zippa and Rosalind were joined by Geraldine and her two children, and Betty and her two little boys came on after Aunt Jane's funeral. Then friends came and went for a few days here and there – Dolly and others, some with children too. It was all big meals, picnics, wet bathing costumes and nappies drying everywhere, toddler tantrums, and different bed times. It was the kind of thing Zippa took in her stride, but which put Tony into a fuss. No doubt guessing just that, she assured him that she was 'strong and well again':

I carry Rosalind with me everywhere – jumping about on rocks and up steep cliffs – some people would be horrified, but she seems to love it, and coos over my shoulder, pulling my hair and laughing. She has practically cut her first tooth!

No one had a car, of course, but they made friends with a local man who had a pony and trap, and one day he took them up the mountain to a ruined spot where his family had once lived, and there they all had a picnic while the man leaned over a wall and wept to see the places of his childhood.

It was on this holiday that Zippa noticed a subtle change in herself:

Do you know, I suddenly feel much older. Uncle Tony is the only one of that generation left to us ... and since the baby arrived and Mother died, I have had to make my own decisions, and be much more definite in every way – and then there is this holiday and Geraldine and I running the house for a pack of children, with the inevitable responsibilities that go with it. ... I find I have a lot of authority with the children and servants.* I imagine the same thing happening to you in the army – you get a very firm idea of what you want, or anyway what you don't want in this war ...

Tony agreed that she was good at running things and that people loved her for it. But he found it hard to grasp this new tough Zippa. It was easier to commiserate. 'Zippa,' he wrote again not long after, 'you have had a hard life to lead since I've been away':

You have had Rosalind. Hortense and Aunt Jane have died, and you have had to move Oakley Street. All in just over a year. Poor Darling, and all the time when I should most of all have been there to help you and could not. I regret it so much ... No wonder you feel you have a lot on your shoulders.

Zippa had gone through a great deal, it's true – but so had everyone else, including the other women on that holiday. Worse. Dolly's story was unimaginably worse: arriving in England at the age of fifteen, home and parents left behind in Nazi Vienna, she

---

* There were servants at Hilton Lodge, though it was hard for Betty to keep them when the Rolls-Royce factory in Derby paid so well.

and her brother unable to learn their fate.* As for Betty, she had spent three years nursing her dying mother, during which time her husband had had home leave and she had had a second child, now a toddler of two. She was, said Zippa, 'white with exhaustion'. Geraldine, meanwhile, had made a disastrous marriage and had nearly died in childbirth. But in spite of everything – at least in Zippa's telling – there was always an edge of hilarity in their doings. That summer, they found a local babysitter, and after the children were in bed, they'd go riding together, breathing 'a long sigh of relief', she wrote, as the door shut behind them. One evening, 'after our ride. … we walked about a mile and a half to a little pub at the cross roads, below a mountain … we all felt very tight and laughed a lot … and Betty turned a cartwheel in the road on the way home in the moonlight.'

Tony would have smiled at that – though, in one of his next letters, he somehow manages to transform all Zippa's horse-riding (she had been riding at Hilton too) into a sequence from the film he always carried in his mind about her: 'I should love to see you on your grey horse with flowing mane and tail, and you beautifully dressed looking wonderful. Oh darling I want you always to look wonderful and be beautifully dressed because you … are so lovely.'

What Zippa thought of Tony's make-believe she never says. But even he would have been hard pressed to find any glamour in her next description – the whole caravan of them on the return journey from Wales by train: children sticky, screaming and pretending to be sick so as to deter anyone from sitting in their carriage; Rosalind's feeds; passengers tut-tutting. And then the

---

* After the war, Franz returned to Austria to find out what he could. He discovered that they had been taken to Auschwitz and murdered.

discovery – horrors! – that they had left all their luggage behind on the platform at Bangor. They had to laugh.

~

Two months after the fall of Tunis, on 10 July, American forces under General George Patton and Eighth Army troops under General Montgomery, invaded Sicily. Tony wrote immediately to Zippa. He had been expecting it for some time, he says, though he feared 'it would not be an easy job. If it succeeds … it should open the way to a general assault on Italy and S. Europe. We shall then be able to cover Italy from the air and use the Mediterranean entirely without hindrance.'

It did succeed. The massive air and sea assault on Sicily took the Germans by surprise,* and led to the fall of the Italian government with the arrest of Mussolini on 25 July. Then came the landings in Italy itself, in early September. Tony was at a conference in Tripoli at the time, discussing 'tactical problems', and he was amused by the Italian interpreter there who, when told that 'we have invaded Italy', replied 'oh have <u>we</u>?' Zippa, still in Wales, heard about Italy from the local baker – 'you'll go there, I suppose', she wrote. He wished he could. But no. There were no plans for that.

Tony's battalion was not, at that stage, part of the campaign to liberate Italy – something which might well have saved his life (casualties in that campaign were very high on all sides). Still, restless as he was by nature, not being part of the action was intensely frustrating. Tony had never been far from black periods,

---

* Hitler had been taken in by an elaborate hoax. It involved a corpse washed up on a Spanish beach, disguised as a British officer and carrying plans for an Allied invasion of Greece. The author of this deception, Ewen Montagu, wrote a book about it in 1953, *The Man Who Never Was*. A film based on the book followed in 1956.

and for him, the months after Tunis were an arid wasteland. There wasn't enough to do. It was inherent in the army system: 'In an ordinary fighting Bn [Battalion] except when there is a battle going on one does not really do much regular work.' There were various routine duties of course, and there were his men – checking their equipment and supervising their training. He was also roped in to sit on a court martial panel deciding cases against alleged deserters. He hated it, especially when the soldier was very young:

Of course stiff sentences must be given or you will get others doing it, but I find it awfully hard not to think of it from the personal side of the wretched gulping nervous lad in front of me, and imagining him in prison and thinking of the effect it will have on him.

Otherwise, there was his work as an intelligence officer, though he could never say anything about that.

Searching Tony's letters for clues is fairly thankless. Every now and then there's a hint of something. A conversation, for example, with a stranger he picked up on the road, a man in European dress whom at first he took to be French. Then he noticed the star and crescent on his ring. The man said he had been a prisoner of war in France, and told him about the German anti-British propaganda in Tunisia which most Arabs believed. Knowing the anti-British feeling among Arabs, Tony was inclined to believe him. They end up having coffee with the man's father, a local sheikh, where there were also two Frenchmen who turned out 'to be directors of all the local arts and crafts, pottery, weaving etc. in two big districts'. It's a rambling tale, without any clear object, but by the end of it there is a sense that Tony has made some contacts, friends even, among both Arabs and French, and that he has tapped into a local network. It might be nothing. Or it might be Tony keeping his ear to the ground.

Another time that summer, he visited the British political administrator of a mountainous district south of Tripoli. It was an extraordinary journey across the desert towards 'a wall of sand and rocks rising to about 1000 feet', up which his road twirled, hairpin after hairpin, to the top. There he stopped and looked back, 'over miles of yellow sand, and shadowed dark purple where it undulated. On top … it was like a different country, everywhere olive trees, and not scruffy little ones, but gnarled old giants, some of them at least 800–1000 years old.'

He drove on to the town and stayed for two days, observing the administrator's work with both Arabs and Italians. In the evening they were joined by a French officer in the British Army, 'an unobtrusive, shrewd little man', who had 'clearly knocked around all over the world and who may well have spent some time in the Foreign Legion'. Again, it's intriguing, but frustrating. Tony doesn't expand. All he adds is that it was a charming place, his hotel very simple, with a garden – and there was 'a constant tiny clattering of donkey's hooves outside'.

Tony travelled a good deal during these months – which must have been some relief from the routine of the battalion. Sometimes he would be sent on intelligence courses to the cities – Tunis, Tripoli, Cairo and Algiers. And sometimes he'd be in the mountains, conducting and umpiring training exercises with the men in preparation for Italy. Landscapes were a safe subject and the letters are full of them. Full too of the people he met along the way, and of the books that somehow or other he managed to read in quiet moments – just as he had between battles in Tunisia. From the summer, autumn and winter of 1943, through to early 1944, here he is, glimpsed from letter to letter, in tents, under mosquito nets, moving around, sometimes by day, sometimes by night, going about his various tasks, reading, eating, making chance acquaintances, practising his French, and observing anything that came along:

It is a full moon and it throws the shadows of the olive leaves on my net and everything is silver and cool … partridges walk about on the stubble just like England … a blast furnace howling all day, temperature 127 in the shade … ploughing through Montaigne … wise and shrewd … can't write … sand whirling about the tent … compass march … full moon … hilly country past sleeping prosperous farm houses … two men working furiously at 10 o'clock by moonlight … back from leave … got onto a Flying Fortress … travelled literally 6 feet above the water, skimming along like a great bird … travelled with a couple of American dough boys, escaped from prison in Italy … had walked for a month … lying in an orange orchard reading George Sand … mountains hazy gold … air full of birdsong … a reconnaissance to see if a route were possible … camping up in the mountains … conditions impossible … stopped at a little village hotel … delicious omelette… all gossiped and eat round the enormous kitchen stove … French officers billetted at the hotel and we had long and amicable talks … sleet, snow, thunder and lightening … this morning was breathtaking … deep in crisp frozen snow … everything dazzling, the air like Switzerland …

~

In one of his letters that winter Tony describes sitting in his farmhouse billet, in front of a 'gently bubbling wood fire with my feet on the mantelpiece!', reading Plato. He had also just read a letter from Zippa, posted from Wapping six days before. She had written it, she said, sitting at her desk at the window looking out over the river. 'It does make you so vivid and near to get a letter so quickly', he replied. It made him long for her. She was not only his beloved, but his home. In fact his love for her often sounds like a kind of home sickness. She was his haven, from the world outside and from himself. Plato, Montaigne, orange groves, mountains, nothing could reconcile him to her absence. 'Away from you,' he wrote, 'I relapse into rather twisted melancholy, the influence of Mummy, and you make me so much nicer and better.'

However busy he tried to be, time hung heavy. It became an obsession. Not only the waste of it, but the mist it laid over his memories of Zippa. It frightened him. Every now and then, he would be overcome by a vivid, almost hallucinatory sense of her presence, her body, her smell. Then he would lose her again in a general blur.

And so, for both of them, the war itself came to be about time – about anniversaries, memories, forecasts, and calculations as to how close the end was. After Tunis, Tony had imagined it would come quite quickly. That had soon faded, to be replaced by a leap of hope in July and August with Russian victories at Kursk and Karkhov. That too had waned. Then in September, with the invasion of Italy, his spirits soared again.

Oh, the news is so exciting, I feel so thrilled and delighted. It opens up endless possibilities, and I feel with a rush and a jump, that anything might happen. All the Italians and Balkans will pack in and the Russians are advancing at a remarkable speed and there must be nothing but despair in Germany today.

But nothing, after Tunis, happened with a rush and a jump. September was thrilling, but it also marked a dismal anniversary.

Four years since 1939. Tony and Zippa each wrote with the same thought – four years! It was the period of the whole of the First World War. 'I'm becoming so pessimistic' wrote Zippa, 'every step seems to take such ages.' One evening towards the end of that month, Tony found himself both fascinated and horrified by a small performance on his verandah. He was sitting out under the stars when he noticed a lizard crawling along the wall towards a butterfly as it fluttered against a light. The lizard 'kept its beady eye glued on it', he wrote, 'working closer step by step; then he dashed in and seized it. The poor lovely butterfly was fast in its vice-like jaws and fluttered furiously till it got slowly weaker and the lizard carried it off, still and drooping. Somehow it seemed so savage.' A parable for their savage times.

And so the war ploughed on into its fifth year. Even with the fall of Taranto and Naples, peace seemed no nearer: 'Oh, if only a miracle would happen,' Tony wrote, 'and it would all end'. When on 12 October Italy declared war on Germany, he allowed himself a cautious hope:

> *It should have a considerable effect on the Balkans at once.*
> *Also it must be very depressing to the Germans. Oh, how I*
> *hope and hope nothing goes wrong from now on ... it should*
> *be over next autumn.*

October was their month, the month of their first meeting at the Chelsea Town Hall. It sent him back to 'that long golden autumn' at Stansted, to their walks together, to the scent of her hair, and he declares himself again with John Donne's poem, 'The Anniversary':

> *All other things to their destruction draw,*
> *Only our love hath no decay.*

> *This, no tomorrow hath nor yesterday,*
> *Running, it never runs from us away,*
> *But truly keeps his first, last, everlasting day.*

'I like Donne', he says, 'Goodbye my darling, darling Zippa'.

It was a weary time all round. Everyone was thinking of home. Tony's instinct, as always, was to send a parcel. Oranges, grapefruit, lemons, mandarins, and a lovely fruit he'd discovered called a clementine – it was the season. 'I heard of someone going home by ship' he wrote,

> *and had only two hours to organise it! … I told our carpen-*
> *ter to nail down the packing case and paint the address on,*
> *and when I came to collect it I found quite a crowd gath-*
> *ered round and one rifleman highly excited because he lived*
> *300 yds from our house. So I promised to collect his address*
> *and ask you to take his wife a few oranges.*

For one rifleman, at least, Tony's oranges had lighted everything up: a street in Wapping, a wife, children perhaps. For Tony too. It was why he did it.

Of course there were other bright moments here and there. At the end of September, an enormous party was arranged for all the officers in the Division, with entertainment provided by musicians and performers from an Italian prisoner-of-war camp nearby – 'absolutely wonderful', Tony said, particularly the band, led by a brilliant flautist. But the tour de force of the whole evening

> *was a female impersonator. He sang in an absolutely pure*
> *and strong soprano. I have never heard anything like it. …*
> *Also he danced as a girl, Spanish tangoes and Oriental*

dances. I almost burst with laughter to see him tango up to some colonel and blink languishingly at him over his shoulder. Obviously he adored it and had the whole thing taped ... patting his hair, feeling to see if his earrings were in, patting his breasts into shape. It was better than any Cambridge equivalent, and all in Italian.

And then there was Christmas. Christmas set everyone counting again – how many since the war started, how many away from home, how many more. In London, Zippa heard rumours about the men coming home. Someone had said something in the pub. Tony gave a hollow laugh:

I assure you darling, you can ignore all rumours passed you by engineers in pubs!! All the riflemen get letters from their wives saying 'we hear you are coming home!!'. But lots of our men have been here 3 and 4 years and have no prospect.

To cheer everyone up, regimental dances were organised, and Tony describes meeting 'a charming French girl' at one of these, 'who danced extremely well and loved it'. It was fun – 4am before he got back to his farmhouse, 'Arabs leading out horses and putting them to their carts, and a noisy cock beginning to crow'.

As for Christmas day itself, it was a magnificent affair laid on for the men and served by the officers: white table linen, candles in lanterns, even a piece of mistletoe which Tony had got hold of, and 'plates piled high with turkey, pork, beef, peas, cabbage, carrots, roast potatoes, and some had at least four helpings, then Christmas pudding, mince pies, stewed apricot and custard, wine and tea to drink.' Later on, the officers sat down to their own feast. Quite fun, said Tony – considering: 'all the time my darling Zippa, I was thinking of you and wanting you terribly'.

Nothing could ever really console or distract him. In the New Year they had an evening of big band music with Nat Gonella ('even I have heard of him') on the trumpet. It made his feet itch to be 'whirling and gliding about with you'. Oh, how he wanted to dance with her again. 'Is there a Wapping Palais de Danse?' he asked. And he closes his letter with a sudden fearful thought: 'Don't forget me darling. It is over 18 months since I kissed you last.'

Chapter 10

'A lovely ambassadress, darling'

In June 1943 Tony picked up a six-month-old copy of the weekly edition of *The Times*, and read in it an article about a government white paper on reforms to the Diplomatic Service. In all his reflections about a future job, Tony had never thought of the Diplomatic Service – presumably because candidates for it had always been expected to have private means. Now, in true Beveridge fashion, all that would change. The reform that chiefly caught his eye was that the service should be open to everyone on the grounds of merit (not women, though – not until 1946) and that they should be paid properly. As the government spokesman said in the House of Commons: 'No young man of ability, personality and character will be prevented from going into the Foreign Service through any lack of means.'[1]

'I am distinctly attracted by the idea', he told Zippa. In fact, it took scarcely a sentence or two before he was imagining her as 'a lovely ambassadress, darling!' At a stroke, the new proposals – already approved in parliament by the time Tony read his article – had turned all his curiosity about the world beyond England into a job. He was more excited by it than he had been by anything else, teaching included. He thought he could do it. What did Zippa think? Would she mind 'living a lot abroad?' Would she, 'hate the idea of being the wife of an official and as such often having to entertain and know people you would not normally be interested in?' He worried she might not want to lose sight of England: 'The service also includes the Foreign Office at home ... one could be abroad, then part of the time get a job in the Foreign Office.' Zippa wrote back gaily to say 'I love the idea of the Foreign Service.' Tony decided to write off to them for information about 'possibilities of joining'.

~

Tony may not have known it yet, but he had found what he wanted to do. He had always been interested in foreign affairs, and had always been amazed when others weren't. It wasn't just a matter of politics either. He genuinely wanted to know and understand other people and countries. Not all. Europe, America, and Russia mainly, and now that he was in North Africa, the Arabs of the French and Italian colonies. Those Arabs working in the fields at night, for example. Why were they doing it? Was it that they were on piece rates, he wondered, and needed the money?

Tony noticed those particular Arabs when he was on exercises in Algeria – but in general the condition of the Algerian Arabs shocked him. Their situation in the countryside was, he thought, better than in the city. Their houses were only bamboo huts or whitewashed mud, but they had little plots of 'carefully earthed up vegetables and small patches of corn'. The old men had 'fine lined faces', and there were 'quite cheerful bright looking boys'. The city, on the other hand, was a hellish place, especially in winter: 'An enormous number of them are filthy, literally dressed in a patchwork of dirty rags, barefoot and shivering. How they manage in the cold I can't imagine. They are diseased, largely syphilitic and the children look miserable.' Just a fortnight before, he had dealt with one of these children, hit in a car accident, 'and I had to take it to hospital, where it died, poor little scrap'. There were thousands of them, he said, 'ragged, pale, mostly soulless looking urchins. Their filth and poverty is unbelievable.'*

Children figure quite often in Tony's letters: the wildly excited Bedu children in the desert soon after he arrived; the little girl fascinated by the soldier on the bus in Palestine; the Biblical goat boy in a Tunisian olive grove. Once, in Tripoli, Tony came across a Jewish boy, about twelve years old, whose father had died and who was about to walk 150 miles to a town where his uncle lived. Tony got involved, tried to help, took him to a kindly Jewish bookseller he knew. He was moved by the whole situation, by the boy's plight and his determination. He seemed to be a sign of something, of survival and hope. Hermione Ranfurly's diary mentions the importance in wartime of flowers and trees, birds and animals – 'silent allies', she calls them, 'very precious'.[2] Tony would have agreed, and he would have added children. But the children of Algiers were in a class of their own – hopeless, 'soulless' as he put it. It was almost the blackest thing he could say about the place. If they were signs of anything, it was of death.

Tunis, on the other hand, he thought relatively benign. There, it was not so much the poverty as the corruption – so transparent as to be almost a joke:

We go to arrange about getting eggs or meat or something and they explain that if they sell them to us they are robbing the civilian population, but that that would be O.K. if we help the civilian population in return. This can apparently best be done by supplying the 'controlleur' with essence

---

* He doesn't say it, but it would have been hard not to see something brewing. Not long after, just as the war was ending in May 1945, there was an uprising, brutally put down. It was a foretaste of what was to come, in 1954, with the Algerian War of Independence.

*[petrol], the souscontrolleur with chocolat and his office boy
with cigarettes!!*

Still, from what he could see, he thought them basically decent:
'they do not set themselves on a superior pedestal above the
people of the country. One frequently sees ordinary French
people talking friendlily to Arabs. I bet we would not see that
in India.'

Tony loved people-watching – in the streets, in cafés, on buses
and trains. But more than anything he wanted to meet them
and get into conversation. One of Zippa's jobs was to send him
French novels if she could find them – Balzac, Flaubert, Stendhal
– and also French and Italian dictionaries. He wanted to learn
the languages properly. He worked at it whenever he could and
found that it opened doors. When his jeep got stuck in the mud
somewhere in the Algerian mountains, a forester – a 'Brigadier
des Forêts' – with '50 Arabs at his heels', dug him out and he was
able to strike up some sort of conversation. The man invited him
back to his house, and there, over a delicious lunch cooked by
his wife, Tony found out about him, his background, his job, and
learned more about the workings of the French forestry service
than he could ever have guessed.

Another time, he was in a café in the old Arab quarter of
Algiers, where there was a group of Spaniards 'singing Spanish
songs, lovely voices, lovely songs'. He sat over his coffee, watched
and listened. Then one of them came across and invited him to
join them. Tony had no Spanish, so what followed was probably
in French, the lingua franca. It turned out they were naval officers,
all refugees from Franco's Spain, and were celebrating the anniversary of el Alamein. 'There was much kissing on both cheeks,
me included, every five minutes', he wrote, and he didn't get to
bed until two in the morning.

These were brief encounters, but there were more lasting friendships too. Tony's intelligence courses were usually followed by a week's leave and he would take these leaves in whichever city he found himself. Usually he had introductions to various people, and in Tunis there was a French Jewish family that he was especially fond of. They were charming, he said, very bourgeois, rather narrow, but they were kind to him and invited him to join them in the evenings – evenings which would end in everyone singing old French songs and arias from the Italian operas. Their Sunday gatherings, involving the whole extended family, were hard work, he said, everyone speaking simultaneously in both French and Italian. But he persevered. Gradually, the family confided its secrets to him, especially the young women, so that his letters about them often sound like episodes in a family drama: the daughter deserted by a caddish British officer; an American officer caught kissing an aunt; the beautiful friend married off to an uncle in the family. It turned out that arranged marriages were normal. 'Life here is absolute death for a girl,' he said: 'There is no prospect and no future except to become a producer of children for a husband you do not love.' Sometimes in the evenings, he would take the daughter, the aunt, and the friend to a restaurant, where the other customers would mutter darkly: 'What does he want with so many? Leave us a few.'

Something similar happened in Cairo, where again all his contacts were with foreigners. Cairo was a different proposition altogether, a big cosmopolitan city, 'fantastically rich and the majority fantastically poor', he wrote. Tony was sent there on an intelligence course in the spring of 1944, finishing with a week's leave for which he was 'laden with introductions to the most upstage people': one to a Baroness Bentinck, from the Dutch legation; another to Princess Irène of Greece ('which I think I will present, for fun'); and another to an Egyptian business family, very rich, where the son was engaged to a beautiful Jewish woman whose family were refugees from Nazi Austria. This was the Cairo of swimming pools, fast cars, expensive restaurants and parties every evening. He loved it, in spite of himself, and had a wonderful time being driven around by the beautiful Austrian, and spending more than he should on parcels for Zippa. Silk stockings again, blue shoes, bits of haberdashery impossible to find in England – ribbon, elastic, hair grips – and still more and more:

> *Blue and white wool for things for Rosalind … A pair of red slippers for you, and a tiny green pair for Rosalind … Also a parcel of food and another one of sweets, sugar and butter and peel and Turkish delight and things … Oh Darling, it would be such fun if you were here.*

On his last evening, his business friends took him to a Gala performance of the Russian film 'Stalingrad':

> *Tickets £1 each and all Cairo there, the King of Egypt incl. … It amused me to see all the Egyptian dignitaries … they must hate it as they are the most grasping anti-idealistic clique possible. The hall was full of Egyptian flags and only one small red flag.*

In the end, though dazzled, Tony was glad to get away. 'I really don't think one could live there for very long', he wrote from the plane back. It was, 'fantastic that these people here live like this all the time, not just for a week or two as I do when I happen to be here.' 'A thoroughly parasitic peacetime existence', he told himself severely.

There was something unreal about these city interludes. Tony felt it, and yet, indirectly and obscurely, they fed into a more serious intent. Tony always deprecated insularity, the Johnny Foreigner attitude, wherever he found it – and he probably found it in the army more than in most places, except, perhaps, at his public school. He would watch British officers at regimental dances trying to flirt with French girls with scarcely a word of French between them. The arrogance of it depressed him. I think he saw it, not only as a courtesy, but as a duty to make the effort, especially at that time. When the nations of the world were so disastrously embroiled, every foreign friendship, every exchange in another language carried a certain weight. An evening of French conversation with his Tunisian family was a step towards international understanding. A discussion in Italian with a conference interpreter was as hands across the sea. Even a week in Cairo (though it was pushing it a bit), hobnobbing with the international set, was a chance to sow the seed of amity.

In the autumn of 1943, Tony put himself forward for the job of unit education officer – despite the 'general disapproval of the necessity for educating the men now at all'. His idea was to start a course of French lessons – his small contribution to the international effort:

> 2 o'clock I gave my first French lesson. I had 9 pupils, all very keen and attentive … we went on for an hour and twenty minutes and I was pouring sweat and exhausted at the end. You know I quite enjoy teaching and I think I can teach if I know my subject. One gets results in exact proportion to the amount of energy and enthusiasm one puts in oneself. That is why it is so exhausting.

Within a few weeks, he had organised classes for 60 men (not all taught by himself) and in the New Year of 1944, was pleased to see the whole scheme given an official boost by a new

Education Bill.* Tony read it in January 1944 and was impressed, though it said nothing about better rates of pay. It raised the school-leaving age and required local authorities to offer education and training to adults, including soldiers. 'All so very right and proper,' Tony wrote, though 'by the time it has filtered down to the Battalion, and is received as a directive by a not very interested Colonel and a generally sceptical selection of officers, it is very hard to make much happen. People seem to feel that any suggestion of education will impair a man as a soldier.'

It was the old Beveridge story. High intentions and low whittling. Tony was writing just then from a 'vaguely depressing' three-day course run by the Head of Education in North Africa – a nice old boy but dull. 'Oh so pedestrian.' Interestingly, the letter is silent on the question of a post-war career in teaching.

～

From October 1943, Tony's battalion was stationed in Algeria, and while he was there he was sent on an intelligence course which he actually called 'fun'. It's a word he never used about any other of his courses. Fun, though hard work. Or fun *because* it was hard work. What's more, it meant living 'in a very pleasant little French town', all pink-and-white houses on the sea some fifteen miles southwest of Algiers. What made the course stimulating was that it was a joint British-American affair. The arrival of the Americans in North Africa at the end of 1942 had changed not just the command structure, but the whole atmosphere of the place. When Tony had been camped near Tunis, during the summer, he had gone into the city to see a film and had been 'amused by the commentary of applause and disapproval from the audience', with 'terrific enthusiasm at any mention of the Americans':

---

* Known now as the Butler Act, after R.A. Butler, who introduced it.

They do enjoy a reputation as being the new world which somehow we lack, as people are suspicious of England. Also of course they are such good publicity agents for themselves.

Now in Algeria, he could see for himself and, a little to his surprise, he found himself making friends with Americans easily. Some things about them seemed very foreign – having supper at 6:30pm, for example, and drinking French Benedictine before the meal: 'Drink to them is just drink', he said, 'any kind any time.' They were also embarrassingly sentimental. An American officer had come to give a lecture and stay to dinner:

He was very interesting and nice, but really very different ... saying all the things English people usually leave unsaid, and obviously puzzled by our jokey way of talking about the war and what we are fighting for e.g. 'The right to be inefficient', which I think is quite a good definition.

But the main thing for Tony – at least when he first encountered them – was that the Americans were so good-natured. Charming, he said, and generous, and he was interested to observe their effect on himself:

In the Battalion I am considered as really a bit odd but alright, but anyway not as a good fellow or good company. I find that with these Americans I behave quite differently and am almost regarded as a wit!!

It was liberating. The only drawback was their attitude to the French. 'They dislike the French', he wrote, 'and are desperately suspicious of being done for money. They feel very much that they have been had for suckers, that they are honest trusting

185

Americans and that the wily European does them down.' Perhaps they were right, but it was partly their own fault 'as they have too much money and fling it around'. No wonder they were cheated. It was almost a joke how much they had. Their pilots, he told Zippa, were issued with seven pairs of gloves.

For himself, he loved the French. There was a café run by a wizened old Parisian with whom Tony had long political conversations, delighted at being able now to speak the language easily. As for the city itself, Algiers, it was lovely to look at, 'climbing up a hill round the harbour', but he didn't really like it – too much army, and too big for him to find and get to know people like his Tunis family, 'which is what I always like to do'. Still, he liked the international atmosphere generally, and it reinforced his desire to try for the Foreign Service: 'I am sure I can get on with foreigners better than most English people.'

Early in November there was great excitement in the battalion. A special parade was ordered, and they were told it was for an inspection by the Colonel. No one believed it, and it turned out that the parade was for none other than the Foreign Secretary himself, Sir Anthony Eden. He was on his way from Moscow to London and would be stopping off briefly to inspect the troops.* Tony was detailed to go with the Colonel to meet him at the aerodrome. The minister landed mid-afternoon, after a nine-hour flight – did the inspection, made a speech, attended a political dinner and flew out at midnight. It was a fascinating few hours:

---

* Anthony Eden had been at the Moscow Conference, held on 30 October, in which the three Allied powers, plus China, agreed, among other things, on the establishment of the United Nations.

He took great trouble, spoke to every officer and sjt, walked round all the men, * he made a short speech congratulating the battalion on its splendid record (which, incidentally it has, having fought up and down the desert ever since war was declared), a few words most optimistically about Russia, and that was all.*

Tony watched him closely:

He possesses a most remarkable charm, and retains a capacity for seeming sincere and enthusiastic. I do actually think he is sincere. Anyway he was a great success with the men who cheered and clapped him spontaneously and that is not a thing riflemen do very much. They are on the whole suspicious, shrewd, rather Bolshie cockneys. Afterwards, when we were having drinks, I talked to him for several minutes, and got the same impression … very clever besides being charming, but I feel as I always felt that he lacks the drive and force required for the first rank in a statesman.

Tony was particularly interested in what he had to say about Russia. Eden said the Russian army was 'well fed and clothed' – as were the children – but that there was much suffering among ordinary people. 'There was a very definite official class,' he said, 'which does much better.' As for their relations with the Allies, they 'were very friendly', he said, 'more appreciative than he had dared to hope, and had definitely decided to co-operate with us, now and after … The Russians are longing to finish the war and get on and re-build.' Re-build Stalingrad, for example. Eden's

---

* Tony doesn't say whether he caught the eye of his old valet.

plane had flown over that city, and he told them that he had 'never anywhere seen such desolation'.

A few weeks later, the minister came again – telephoned the colonel to ask himself and two others to dinner. The two others were the permanent under secretary for foreign affairs, Sir Alexander Cadogan, and the American ambassador to London, George Winant. Again, Tony was fascinated and observed them closely, what they wore and how they carried themselves – Eden and Alexander distinguished and impeccable, Winant long-haired and shaggy, a gap between his waistcoat and trousers and a hat too small for his head. They sat down twelve to dinner, Tony next to Winant and opposite Eden. This time, the Foreign Secretary had come fresh from the Tehran conference attended by Churchill, Roosevelt and Stalin and the conversation naturally turned to that topic.* Then someone dropped a clanger:

> *One of our Company Commanders, a nice but rather stupid man, chimed in in the middle of a general pause – 'And did the Americans play better this time, sir?' Frantic grimaces by Anthony at Winant – a total silence, broken by me frantically groping for something to say with an enquiry about Mme Shang Kai Shek.† So you see darling, I have already embarked on my diplomatic career!!*

---

* The Tehran Conference was held between 28 November and 1 December, to decide the final strategy of the war and to set the date for opening the second front.

† There had recently been a conference in Cairo, attended by Churchill, Roosevelt, and the president of China, Chiang Kai-shek – recognised as such by the West until 1975. Madame Chiang Kai-shek had acted as her husband's adviser and interpreter.

Afterwards Eden spoke to the men again, 'as charmingly as last time', said Tony, followed by Winant who impressed him more. Not that he said much, or was particularly clear – in fact 'I have never', wrote Tony, 'seen a man more nervous':

> *He was obviously deeply moved at being among a crowd of British soldiers who have been out here some time ... he was so obviously desperately sincere that they all loved him.*

The battalion then put on a boxing match for the visitors – not especially expert, said Tony, but 'plucky': 'The crowd were very English, very good humoured, and I must say I don't think he [Winant] could have got a better picture of the English soldier anywhere.'

Later, over drinks, the talk resumed and went on until midnight. Tony was amazed by the frankness of their guests ('though of course they did not give any facts'):

> *Apparently everything is completely settled. It was odd to think I was talking to someone who knew exactly when and where all our countries are going to strike. I was very impressed by Winant and had a long talk with him ... [he] told me to come and see him in London and promised to make my 'itinerary' for me if ever I came to the U.S.A.!! Altogether, it really was a most interesting and pleasant evening. An odd place to meet famous people.*

Tony's appetite for the workings of international diplomacy is palpable, and equally his interest in the people doing it. As they whizzed across the world, chance had put them briefly in his way, and almost for the first time since coming to North Africa, he gives the impression of being confident and at ease.

Chapter 11

'Largely centred round Rosalind'

Tony's excitement at the idea of diplomacy, even his slightly jaundiced glimpses into the educational system, suggest that he was beginning to find his feet. The trouble was that it didn't feel like that to him at the time. Or not for long. Melancholy, as he called it, was always his bugbear. He never believed he was getting anywhere. While Zippa was gaining ground, enjoying Rosalind, becoming more confident, Tony felt as though he were only just hanging on.

Part of it was his homesickness for her. 'I am getting so very weary of being away from you', he wrote, 'and find I miss you and long for you more and more ... sometimes it seems a lifetime since I was last in England with you. I do really hope I shall see you before another year is out.'

But much of it was a chronic sense of waste and futility. The French lessons, the mountain training exercises, the intelligence courses, none of them amounted to anything. He felt himself slipping – 'tired and stupid', as he had said after Tunis, 'half alive', 'vaguely empty', 'more lazy and less intelligent', and so on. The phrases run through almost every letter at this time, increasingly as the year turns. He could sometimes manage a wry smile about it:

I went out and had dinner alone with Michael Fyfe at a restaurant in the city, very good soup, delicious prawns, lamb and oranges. We enjoyed our dinner and talked sadly of how dull life was, and apologised to each other for being so uninteresting and having nothing to talk about, which is quite true because we don't do anything.

It didn't help that the battalion was beginning to unravel. As the war moved north through Italy, attention turned towards France and a possible second front. Many of the officers that had been with him in the desert and Tunisian campaigns, were now leaving. New ones were coming out, and the old camaraderie was dissolving. When the colonel himself was replaced in early 1944, Tony summed up the situation gloomily:

I must say, looking back to the time when I joined we have not anything like such a pleasant lot of officers. I am almost becoming like an old desert rat who says things are not what they were … I sometimes think of trying for another job but can't face the thought of all the fuss and string-pulling to get one, and anyway I have not any strings and don't know how to set about it.

Ideally what he wanted was something that would fit with his Foreign Service hopes, but he couldn't think what. 'I shall probably just continue to drift. It is useless to try to influence one's fate in the army.'

~

Tony spoke at this time of feeling 'disjointed'. Nothing connected. Nothing fitted. Zippa was more fortunate. For all the danger and drabness of wartime London, her life was at least joined together.

She was at home, among familiar places, friends and family. Some of these people wrote letters to Tony about her, saying how well she was, how attractive, how good with Rosalind. He was pleased – but a little nervous: 'I hope you are not getting used to life without me,' he wrote when she moved to Wapping, 'arranging everything on your own and in your own way.' When she sent him a sad letter, he replied:

> *Oh darling, I was a little glad to think of you being a bit lonely for me among all your house full of people. I want so terribly to be back beside you to take care of you and look after you and help you with everything.*

Zippa loved him and missed him and wanted him to come home. But she didn't really need looking after. Help, yes – a decent water heater, for example, and modern kitchen equipment. He agreed: 'After the war we must indeed spend money on all possible kitchen gadgets to make life easier – especially a water heater.' She wrote about shopping with 'a filthy Rosalind and a pram full of washing'. Tony laughed and hoped it wasn't all too slummy. She told him she had bought a drying cupboard. He was beginning to get the picture. 'Your drying cupboard must be a joy if it works,' he wrote back, 'Poor Zippa, I hate to think of all the messy work and washing you must have to do.'*

Woven through everything, was Rosalind, shared and admired by everyone, a sort of household mascot. Again, the idea seemed to please him: 'I love to think of Rosalind already getting used

---

* I remember that drying cupboard – a large metal box with a hinged lid and rails inside for hanging clothes on. The heat came from gas flames at the bottom. Dangerous, I now realise, but it did work.

to people and learning from you to be charming.'* People would write to him about Rosalind too, Dolly for example, who told him that she adored Rosalind and thought Zippa was 'wonderful with her'. But it was all faintly disquieting: 'It is going to seem very strange,' he said, 'coming home to a house largely centred round Rosalind, who is my daughter.' She was his daughter, and yet she belonged to everyone except him. They had even given her a pet name – Dumbo, from Disney's cartoon elephant, because her ears stuck out. He didn't like it. They mustn't do it. 'You know how names stick.'

Tony tried to think about Rosalind. It had never been easy. Zippa had told him that she had red hair. It fascinated him. Where did it come from? Who in the family had red hair? Veronica, he remembered, had reddish hair. And hadn't he heard that their grandmother, Mimi, had too? It became Rosalind's sign, the thing he knew her by, something his mind could fasten onto – like Zippa and her clothes. Tell me about Rosalind's hair, he would say, what's happening to it now? What kind of red is it? Flaming? Gold? Carroty? Gold, said Zippa. He liked the sound of that:

> *Red gold hair can be lovely, and so can proper red if the girl is lovely. It's just that it looks more than ever awful on a plain girl. … I can't bear the idea of her having anything ugly!*

But apart from Rosalind's hair, there was something dutiful about Tony's interest:

---

* Being charming was always a great point with Tony (and Zippa), though it did fall heavily on the girls and women of the family.

*I would like to see and know her now. Other people's babies
are ugly and boring, but one's own is interesting because of
all the changes one can watch from day to day.*

To anyone else, in other words, Rosalind was probably just ugly
and boring. A few months later, the sister of someone he knew
had a baby – 'the first very tiny baby I have seen consciously':

*I examined him closely, really they are funny things, everyone
says he is a wonderful baby and is delighted, but he looked
ugly to me, a big head, and big tummy.*

When Rosalind was about six months and cutting her first
tooth, Zippa told him she would start weaning her. Oh good,
said Tony. She thought the whole process would take about six
months. Six months! He was aghast: 'What a long job babies are.
I don't see how we can ever have another.' She wrote again to say
she thought that at last she was slim again. He was pleased, but
again – 'such a fearful waste of time'. A little later, he wanted to
know how long before Rosalind was 'reasonably house-trained?!'
And when Zippa explained her routine, he threw up his hands: 'It
appears to be more or less one long pot!'. Everything took such
ages. 'I cannot quite picture how much she is going to alter our
lives,' he wrote, 'I hope there won't be too many things we can't
do because of her.' It was like the war. Rosalind was stealing their
youth, their moment, their chance of fun.

In fact, it wasn't just Rosalind he was up against. It was the
whole Wapping scene. Tony always begged Zippa to write to him
about everything she was doing, all the little daily things – 'anything or nothing', he said. And so she did. Besides water heaters
and drying cupboards, her letters are full of people – friends, and
friends of friends. Tony said it sounded like Oakley Street with

'crowds of people and enormous meals'. He said he loved it, but he grumbled, as he had then, about the work. He was also worried about the renewed bombing of London that autumn, which only confirmed his original doubts about Wapping: 'I hate to think of the air raids, are there ever any bombs dropped near you? Does it seem as though the raids have any objective?' Yes, bombs did drop on Wapping. But Zippa took it all easily. Her letters were written on the spur of the feeling, everything thrown into the same bag – the friends, the work, the bombs, the meals, the frightfulness and the enjoyment.

The trouble was that Tony read them differently, not in the thick of it as they were written, but alone and separate, in his camp or his mess. Her letter to him when she got back to London from Wales and Derby, for example, swings blithely through things any one of which would have stopped him in his tracks. She was exhausted from the journey, she says. Then a friend of Dolly's turns up – Dolly's 'rich Major', Zippa calls him. 'The Major is nice,' she writes, 'but rather Noel Cowardy and is very much in love with Dolly, but he has a wife and two children, so no good! She is just playing with him but he has fallen hard.' As it happened, Dolly was very beautiful and people were always falling hard. She herself was in love with an American artist, Garth Williams, also married with small children, who had gone back to America early in the war.*

Zippa goes on. After putting Rosalind to bed, they all went to the pub, 'The Town of Ramsgate', just behind the house, 'and the passage beside it leads to Wapping Old Stairs, past our back-yard ... Anyway I felt terribly tight though I'm supposed to have

---

* Dolly later married him. Garth Williams illustrated *Charlotte's Web*, *The Little House on the Prairie* and the rest of that series, and many other children's books.

behaved quite well!!' Then they trooped back to a 'huge supper cooked by Dolly', who must have stayed behind to babysit for Rosalind: 'And then the sirens went and there was quite a noisy raid – I brought Rosalind down and she won the Major's heart completely. Well, finally we got to bed and the next day I made my presence felt about the house and by the evening it looked delightful!!'

There's lots more. Franz, Dolly's brother, arrives on his way to something. Someone called Mona turns up with nowhere to live – 'she is still here till she gets a room'. And somewhere in between there's a party for Zippa's brother Denny and his wife, Molly: 'Dolly and I practically prepared a show … candles and flowers in the drawing-room and hidden lights on the shelves by the window behind the flowers and a lovely fire blazing'.

Zippa paints a wonderful picture – all warmth and friendship and the house itself, welcoming and hospitable. But in Tony's mind, something jarred. It was partly to do with Zippa exhausting herself. But also: 'I don't at all like the sound of Dolly and her Major round about our house. I don't see that it can lead to any good and he can't really be over nice. Any way, even if he is nice, Dolly should not play around with him.'

'Our house.' What Dolly should and shouldn't do. Tony sounds a little sour – the aggrieved householder, a little school masterish with a touch of Malvolio – though he contains himself heroically over the Major losing his heart to Rosalind. Zippa's reply is missing, but she was clearly irritated, for in his next he quotes her saying: 'Well, you don't like Dolly and I do', and that Dolly 'has a sense of the ridiculous and we laugh at the same things'. He also quotes her saying that 'Geraldine and Dolly have every intention of disappearing', when he comes back. The words sent a chill through him and he 'shut up the letter', he said, 'with an angry snap':

I do hope, Zippa darling, I am not going to find myself insen-
sibly spoiling the atmosphere you have built up in the house.

There was no quarrel, no rupture. All seems well in his next letter:
'Now I don't feel like that at all,' he says.

But what was it? Zippa had given him a glimpse of something
easy-going and irreverent, something a little cock-eyed, unsafe
even. It hadn't mattered when she had done the same thing about
their holiday in Wales – an unruly crowd of children, Zippa leaping from rock to rock with Rosalind clinging on, all their luggage
left behind on the platform. Wapping was different: a grown-
up place, their house and, one day, his home. In his reply, Tony
denied disliking Dolly, but admitted to not liking the sound of
her friend – 'slightly dangerous'. Did he in fact think that Dolly
herself was 'slightly dangerous'? Slightly dangerous for Zippa to
know? What did Zippa and Dolly laugh about together?

Tony sometimes asked Zippa about Dolly and Garth, whether
Garth intended to come back from America, and how she felt
about him. In fact she was miserable, fearing that Garth had
forgotten her. But Tony puts it the other way about: 'Has Dolly
forgotten Garth?' Was this his own lurking fear? 'Don't forget
me', he wrote to Zippa at about this time. It was over eighteen
months since he had kissed her last. It was every soldier's dread.

The whole exchange clearly knocked Tony off balance.
Like Zippa's letter about breast-feeding a gurgling and ecstatic
Rosalind on the train to Derby, her jolly letter about life in
Wapping withered in transmission. Reading it, Tony seems to
have felt suddenly out in the cold. 'I don't quite know if you can
realize or understand,' he wrote, 'just how my whole life and self
hangs on you.' It triggered a stream of self-castigating reflections –
about being not quite as he seemed, about being shy inside while
appearing easy and relaxed, about having 'tied-up ideas' beneath

the surface, 'little quirks that lie at the back and are a legacy of grandmother and the 19th century'. He was mysterious about these quirks, but perhaps he was trying to explain his reaction to Dolly and the Major, trying to make Zippa see that there was something inherently negative and critical about him, that he was less open and generous than he appeared, and certainly than she was. It was enough to revive all his old doubts about himself in general: his intellectual limitations, his lack of focus and authority.

Zippa had spoken a few weeks before about finding a new sense of authority in herself and had added that 'you get a very firm idea of what you want, or anyway what you don't want in this war'. She had imagined that the army had done the same for him. No, he says, 'the war … has been bad for me':

> It would have been best to have flung into the army with 100% energy, uncritically, to work hard, get all the experience it had to offer … Instead I have shrunk away instinctively … I am aside and apart from most of the other people without any justification of being better than them in any way. I cannot fling into it and am critical and impotent … So I don't really get on. Not that I get on badly at all, but there is always a bar.

That idea of a bar runs through all Tony's thoughts – whether it was a moral inhibition over Dolly, or an instinctive shrinking from the military, or a kind of timidity of intellect and will. He knew the world didn't see him like that, but it was precisely because it didn't that he thought of himself as a fraud. One of the things he constantly said about Zippa – and he says it definitively in this letter – was that she had 'unblemished the qualities which in me I feel are a little tarnished, complete honesty and genuineness'. That was 'what made her such a wonder', he said, 'at making other people happy'. She was, he said, 'in a different class from me':

> *And so Zippa, it has always seemed to me a little odd that you should love me and I have often wondered whether you quite knew all about me.*

What he hoped was, that 'you will be able to change me and I shall grow into your lovely atmosphere'. In short, he laid himself at her feet.

'Zippa what a fearful letter this is I have written.' It was: keen self-awareness on one side and a kind of abdication on the other. As though he were playing hide and seek with himself – and knew it.

~

That winter, friends of Zippa, actors in a small London theatre company called the Masque Theatre, invited her to join them. These were John and Anne Crockett. Anne had been a member of the Margaret Barr dance-drama company which Zippa and Alured had belonged to before the war, and John was an artist-designer and actor-director – pretty well a one-man theatre company in himself. During the war, there were a number of shoe-string theatre cooperatives heroically criss-crossing the country in all weathers – actors, props and costumes jammed together in old trucks and vans, with the scenery tied on top. Their aim was to bring high quality theatre to people who would otherwise have no experience of it, and they were supported in this by the Council for the Encouragement of Music and the Arts (C.E.M.A.) – the precursor to the Arts Council. They would perform anywhere – sometimes in big houses, more often in schools, churches, village halls and Nissen huts. These little companies

– the Century Theatre, the Adelphi Players, the Pilgrim Players, the Oxford Pilgrims, the Canterbury Pilgrims and others – sometimes consisted of no more than three or four actors, each playing many parts. They would form, split, re-form, grow and sometimes collapse. John Crockett had belonged to the Adelphi Players and would go on to form the Compass Players.[1]

For now, their little company had a programme and some venues booked in east London, which was convenient for Zippa. With Rosalind weaned and a houseful of babysitters, rehearsals and performances were just about feasible. She wasn't sure what Tony would think, whether he would be as excited as she was. 'I am delighted to think of you acting,' he assured her, 'and do really want you to.' He didn't know about C.E.M.A. yet, but was pleased to discover that Maynard Keynes, fellow of his old college, King's, had been an inspiration in its formation.* At the same time he couldn't help hating the thought that she would be 'so stretched'. Her letter describing how she fitted everything in that winter is lost, but from Tony's reply it's just possible to guess at it – dashed down in one of her slapstick flights:

> *My poor darling, your letter gave an impression of rather a dreadful time ... toothache and flying across London for rehearsals and cooking and Rosalind and nappies and dressmaking, my poor poor darling, you can't and mustn't do it all.*

The only things missing from this list are the bombs. One evening, towards Christmas, Pier Head was very nearly hit. Zippa's first night was approaching and she had to rush out that

---

* Keynes became the first chairman of the Arts Council when it was formed after the war.

same evening, pausing only to snatch a pencil and scribble a note on the back of an envelope to warn Dolly when she got in. 'Rosalind is asleep in the dining-room,' it says, 'Geraldine in drawing-room. There has been a very nasty raid – both shattered. Phosphorous incendiary on the P.L.A. clinic – Fire engines etc. – All lights went out & the house rocked! – Goodnight Dears – Lights still dim.' When Tony heard, he was appalled. If the raids continue, he said, 'you must at once get straight out, because Wapping would be a dangerous area and not just chance.'

Zippa worried him – bombs or no bombs. He knew how difficult it was to tell her anything, but she might at least try: 'You know if you go on for ever always doing too much, and sleeping too little, you will outdo your strength … and Rosalind must have taken a lot out of you.' She told him about her rough hands and the lines under her eyes. 'I would adore you whatever you had,' he wrote back, 'but Zippa, please, please, for my sake, do look after yourself. You must must rest and not run yourself to death or you will get lines under your eyes that won't go so quickly.'

He himself felt old now, he said. It was one of his worries about getting a job in the Foreign Service – too old for it. In 1939 he had been too young to know what he wanted. Now, in 1944, he was suddenly – 26! He writes it like that, with an exclamation mark. 'And I look older too, I think!!' They were warning each other, preparing one another for the shock of meeting again. But it wasn't an equal business. Time, in Tony's mind, was crueller to women. Some months later, when he was at last in Italy, he described a family he was billeted with. They were attractive, friendly, and the children could sing all the operas, with gestures. But, he says,

> it is an awful shame the way all the women grow old and
> ugly so early here. I suppose it is from work and babies.

202

Work and babies – that was Zippa now. And if he was 26! in 1944, there was no avoiding the fact that in May she would be 30!

The rehearsals Zippa spoke of were for Chekhov's one-act comedy, *The Bear*, paired with a dance-drama, *A Merry Death*, by a younger contemporary of Chekhov, Nikolai Evreinov. The first night was in early January 1944 at Charlton House, a grand Jacobean building in Greenwich. Alured was on leave and he and Betty came to stay during the run. Veronica joined them, though it was hard for her to get away from her agricultural course in Shropshire. Franz also stayed, and his girlfriend.* From Zippa's (missing) description of it, Tony thought *The Bear* sounded 'charming', in spite of what she felt about the director, Eileen Thorndike.† It got better as they went on. After Charlton House they performed a few nights for the YWCA (Young Women's Christian Association) where, Tony was thrilled to hear, they had a great success. They had another hit at a girl's school in Edmonton, where a Columbine and Pierrot sequence in Evreinov's dance-drama got the girls giggling. Veronica had had to go back to Shropshire by then, and Zippa wrote to her in one of the rare letters between them to survive the war years, describing the performance: 'One flower from my wreath as Columbine got loose and dangled just between my eyes while I was swearing at Pierrot, and got such a roar of laughter, that we were all reduced to pulp and couldn't go on!!' But outside, the bombs were still falling – 'terrifying' wrote Zippa, 'like the big raids of 1940' – and after a few more performances at the Garrison Theatre in Woolwich, she decided to call it a day.

---

* I don't know who this was. But through my parents, Franz came to know the Crichton family and eventually married Sheila, Aleck's sister (see footnote on page 100).
† Sister of Sybil Thorndike.

It was a wrench. She was in the middle of rehearsals for a new dance-mime with John Crockett, a 'Harlequinade' she calls it, and someone had written them the music for it. But with Rosalind to think of, she couldn't stay. By early March she was with Betty at Hilton Lodge again and Tony heaved a sigh of relief: 'it is maddening to have all your plans put out and you can never know when the raids will start or stop'. But he was glad. At least she would be safe. Privately, he might have hoped that, with a little rest, some of those lines might smooth themselves out.

Chapter 12

'She looks like you'

One of the things that distressed Tony during 1943 and '44 was that he had no decent photographs of Zippa. Soon after the fall of Tunis, he lost his wallet with all his snaps of her, as well as a scrap of handkerchief with her scent on it – 'which used to make you seem very close if I shut my eyes and sniffed it!!' It was May and very hot, but without her photographs or her handkerchief, he was reduced, he said, to wearing her woollen gloves, the ones she had knitted for him before he came out. He begged her to send more pictures. Nothing came. In August he was still asking. Zippa was in Wales, and said she couldn't send him anything nice until she got back and had a proper one taken.

> Don't wait till you get back to London … That means I shall
> have to wait till Christmas. Don't you realize I have nothing
> at all of you to look at.

It turned out she didn't think she looked slim enough. 'I don't mind', he answered, 'please send something soon!!!' She was feeding Rosalind still, and didn't feel neat and smart enough for Tony yet. Especially now that he was thinking of the Foreign Office and what a wonderful ambassadress she'd make. Perhaps the whole idea of the Foreign Office had begun to alarm her.

Tony quotes her saying that she thinks he should have 'a smart on-the-spot sort of girl who would push for me in a career'. 'My Zippa darling,' he replied, 'I should have no possible sort of wife but you. ... I shall be much happier and live a much nicer life with you than with an ambitious girl.'

Finally, at the end of September, some photos arrived. 'I was so so excited to see you again.' But on closer inspection, they weren't very good. Could she send more? 'I have so much hated not having them.' Again she was slow. By November she thought she was presentable enough to have some taken: 'Get your roll of film developed and printed, I want very much to see them and as soon as possible.'

And so it went on, into the New Year and beyond. In February she went to a professional theatrical photographer in Shaftesbury Avenue. She and her brothers and sisters had inherited a little money from their mother. She had bought some smart clothes and was experimenting with her hair: 'I sometimes wear it up with my best black dress and the fox fur and look no end of a lady, so they all say, but I can imagine you thinking me too sophisticated like that!'

She was right. At least about the hair. He liked to think of her as he had known her, with her hair down to her shoulders. In March she sent some of herself and Rosalind. He liked the ones of Rosalind, but was otherwise 'disappointed completely':

I hate photographs of you which don't give any feeling of you. The nice one of Rosalind smiling is horrid of you, and the rather stagey one of you smiling has been played about with round the mouth.

Nothing worked. Nothing could bring her to life. Really, he needed Zippa herself, in person – 'close and vivid', he wrote,

Studio portrait of Zippa

'filling my mind and thoughts all day and every day'. If only he could get to England, 'even if it were only for one week-end just to see you and touch you and be sure that you really are there just the same ... sometimes it seems so long that I can hardly think you are real'.

And so he sat and pored over whatever she sent him. By August he had almost given up:

> *Somehow, I don't know why, I never ever get any good photographs of you. You go to photographers and one thing and another, but nothing remotely reminiscent of you ever reaches me!*

He was losing her.

Tony was a man clutching at straws. Photographs couldn't save him. The truth was, he was drowning, and had been since at least the spring. What had happened – as my mother told me later – was that he had fallen in love with another woman. She was called Simone, the 'charming French girl' he had told Zippa of, whom he had met at a regimental dance before Christmas 1943. It didn't mean he had ceased to love Zippa. Nothing so simple. But Zippa wasn't there, and Simone was.

Tony never hid the fact of Simone. At least not initially. In early February, he told Zippa he had taken her out to lunch twice and had found her 'quite delightful', 'so perfectly French'. He had discovered a little more about her. Her family was from Brittany, and her father, now dead, had been a school master. She was 'extremely well educated ... full of the right ideas and outlook'. 'Her boy,' he said, 'is conscripted in Germany for work', and she was now a French military officer in Algiers – though 'most unmilitary'. The striking thing about her, he said, was 'how she looks like you, the same long face and high set eyes, grey green'. And he closes his letter in his old familiar way – 'oh my darling darling, nobody anywhere in the world is utterly lovely and satisfying as you'.

Here was food for thought. There had been many families with wives and daughters in Tony's letters: the Polish family in Palestine, the French family in Tunis, the beautiful Austrian in Cairo. But never before had any woman reminded Tony of Zippa. There is no knowing whether she stopped a moment to mull this over. Maybe Tony's openness about Simone was reassuring. He tells Zippa that he had told Simone about Rosalind, and had suggested sending her to stay with Simone after the war, 'when she is old enough to learn French!! She was delighted and said she would retaliate with her own children.' Of course Simone was not married – and, incidentally, there is never any further mention of her 'boy' in Germany. But still – some time, in that magical after-the-war world, she would have a family, and they would all know each other and be friends.

At the end of March, Tony writes about her again. It was a beautiful spring, the swallows arriving, the wild roses out, and 'the corn a foot high really like England in June'. He had had a wonderful time just the day before, a Sunday, spent with Simone and her cousin Victor, 'a very nice French naval officer'. He had got hold of a car, and they had driven along the coast to a lovely place, 'hills dropping down to a rocky shore with a cove', which he said was like Cornwall, and they said was like Brittany. Tony had bathed, while Victor 'cut open sea urchins, scooped out their insides and eat them with relish'. Had Zippa ever seen sea urchins? 'All spikey, rather like a chestnut in its case, only dark red'. Then they had gone on to 'a charming village, little houses arranged round the quayside', where they had eaten a delicious fish supper. But Simone's mother was waiting up, so he had had to drive them home at breakneck speed to get Simone back by 'the early hour required by her maman!' No doubt 'maman' had become wise to something, and had organised Victor, as chaperone.

March was a dangerous month, it seems. Warmer days, seaside expeditions. It was in this letter that Tony spoke so desperately of needing to see Zippa, to touch her, to make sure she was really there. And from then on, Simone disappears from the letters. She's there, for anyone reading with hindsight, but in the shadows – though occasionally she seems on the point of stepping forward. In August, for example, he describes another day by the sea. 'I wandered about among pools in the rocks and discovered all sorts of lovely brilliant coloured seaweed, and starfish and nasty spiky sea urchins. It was so lovely. All afternoon by the sea and then a delicious dinner with crevettes at a black market restaurant.'

On his own?

~

To anyone judging the situation from the outside, Simone – or someone like her – seems inevitable. It's almost more surprising that Zippa didn't see her coming and spot her immediately. But from what I learned later, she didn't. She had no inkling, not even a suspicion.

Perhaps what masked the truth from Zippa was what masked it, or half-masked it, from Tony himself. Tony idolised her and went on doing so, Simone notwithstanding. He believed he loved her, and in his worshipping way, he did. Again and again, he tells her how much he longs for her, how much he thinks about her, how much he needs her, 'both to make me realize again what is worthwhile but above all to hold close and lovely in my arms.'

I don't believe he was lying. But he was struggling to remember her.* Tony had a collection of mental pictures of Zippa, each one a memory of a time they had spent together. Those moments were his photographs. Zippa wearing her long red dress in Oakley Street; Zippa at Stansted, Christmas 1939; Zippa on their honeymoon, riding in Dorset, 1941; Zippa riding again near Marlborough in 1942, and lying on the bed in the hotel – each picture set against its background: the same Christmas goose, the same crackling fire, the same Dorset or Wiltshire downs. They flickered across his mind like an old film played in an endless loop, gradually growing grainier until they became almost symbolic. The one of her on the bed in Marlborough returns obsessively: sometimes her face is flushed, sometimes her hair is spread out around her, sometimes she's in her riding things. And always she is lovely. Perhaps Zippa became as hypnotised as he was.

---

* It reminds me of myself as a child at boarding school, suddenly realising I couldn't quite remember the faces of my parents.

The only thing that might have alerted Zippa was a rising note of panic. In April 1944 someone steals his wallet – another wallet. 'A terribly sad thing happened yesterday and I am so upset about it':

> Oh Zippa, my lovely wallet that you gave me, that I have kept all the time and worn every day since you gave it me, 3 years now.

It was a piece of her. Without it, he was bereft. And the letter ends with a desperate cry: 'I have nothing nothing nothing in the world except lovely things to remember about you. I don't deserve you, my sweet.' Then in May, on the anniversary of their wedding, he suddenly writes this:

> Oh Zippa it is lucky that you are such a lovely darling, but sometimes I do wonder if you should have married me! … You are going to have a lot to do to improve me … when I come back.

Thoughts like these were familiar to her, but they take on a new urgency during the spring and summer of 1944. Why? Why didn't he deserve her, what was it all about? She must have wondered.

At the same time, there was so much else in the world that was crazy. Perhaps, in Zippa's mind, the war itself was to blame. They were all in its mad grip. In the same letter, Tony speaks of a deep sense of fracture. Looking back, life had 'sense and proportion', he says. Now it was 'ridiculous and topsy turvy'. For months now their conversations had pondered the big questions of war. In January 1944, the area bombing of German cities by the Allies was on Zippa's mind. She hated it and feared the lasting consequences of it. She was not alone. The diarist Hermione Ranfurly felt equally grim: 'Our target is peace on earth', she wrote, 'but we must do most ghastly things to achieve this ... we have all become murderers.'[1] Tony too was full of anxious foreboding:

Oh Zippa, yes, I do agree about the war and bombing. It is too terrible to realize if one remembers London in 1940 and this is far far worse. I too feel that what is dreadful is the bitterness it will leave and the thousands of broken people there will be afterwards, people with families killed, lives suddenly shattered with no further interest in the world. It is a long way since the days before 1914 when everyone accepted automatically that the world was getting better and better. Now there is this terrible lack of security and the scepticism which is the curse of our generation.

He was thinking just then about Berlin* – 'this bombing now, with all pretence of bombing factories gone, is dreadful' – and he goes on, in a kind of manifesto, to reiterate the principles of his pacifism in 1939–40. It's as though, after more than four years, the time had come to remember and to say it all again:

It was because of all this that I was a pacifist. I always knew that if war came, and I thought it must come ever since I was about 15, that it would be like this, that there would be no rules and no limits, that there would be mass bombing. Moreover, I firmly believe that it is only because it is not

---

* Between November 1943 and January 1944 alone, 4,000 Berliners were killed, 10,000 injured and 450,000 made homeless. *Wikipedia*, 'Bombing of Berlin in World War 2'.

very practical that gas has not been used. The reason for my
pacifism was really just that feeling that war created such an
exhaustion of the spirit and such a sea of bitterness that after
a war there could never be a foundation on which to build a
new world. It was only because I was too much of the world
we live in, of society, and not a philosopher on a mountain
that I had to give it up. Maybe it is right and one would
lose even more by giving in and hoping that the conquering
tyranny would become civilised. Still it is sometimes hard to
see what the Western Civilisation for which one is fighting
is. I feel now that I have gone into a sort of chrysalis. I rarely
think or discuss things. I only hope that when I come out of
it, which will be when I join you again, I shall not have lost
all power to do so. The world is going to be a more terribly
complicated place than one can realize. Europe will be full
of disillusion. France terribly touchy and unhappy. Central
Europe bitter and revengeful. A thousand thousand young
people with no roots or homes.

The only comfort he could see was that, 'this war just must
<u>must</u> come to an end, and soon. The horror of it is inconceivable
and cannot go on.' He hoped the Allied landings behind the
German lines at Anzio, about 30 miles south of Rome, would
lead to the taking of Rome* – but really he felt so numbed that
he could scarcely grasp it:

One is so inured to war news now that one does not picture
what it really means when one hears a river crossing being
gained or 2,000 tons of bombs on Berlin.

---

* The landings succeeded in surprising the Germans, but the operation
became bogged down and it was another six months before Rome was taken.

Maybe the bombings would shorten the war; maybe Anzio would be successful; but then again, maybe not: 'the tragedy is that there is nobody in Germany to make peace'. And even supposing there were, then what? War trials? Zippa said she dreaded them. A 'dangerous policy', he agreed, 'so hard to stop and it leads to private vengeance. So easy to say "Off with his head."'

Sometimes in these exchanges they spoke of Europe and sometimes they spoke of themselves. 'I am a little worried,' he wrote, 'how we shall steer ourselves through the shifting wilderness after the war. There will be no signposts.' But he wasn't as worried as he should be, he added, because, 'I have the most terrific faith and reliance on you my darling to make us live rightly … You can't imagine how lovely it is for me to think of you and Rosalind.' There was one comfort: 'in spite of the war, we in England are terribly terribly lucky'. England had been bombed but not smashed to smithereens like Dortmund or Berlin. And it had never been occupied.

By March, Zippa was looking ahead and trying to work out the practicalities of Tony's return. She was thinking about Wapping. Dolly and Geraldine had said they would leave when Tony got back. But that would mean no more help with Rosalind. She and Tony would be tied. No dancing the night away. Could he be happy like that? And would Wapping be convenient for him anyway? Should they find somewhere else, and let Dolly and Geraldine stay? She was reluctant to lose the place altogether. Whatever happened she didn't want (and he agreed) to move in with his mother in Oakley Gardens.

Tony waved it all away: 'I realize we must keep other people in Wapping till after the war.' And as for us, 'it will be so lovely just to be near you, that I shan't want to go out, but just stay at home with you and Rosalind.' Besides, he might not be demobbed for a while, he said, might not be in London, nor even in England:

'Maybe for some months after the war I shall be occupying a lot of Europe and you might come out ... Please, please ... don't fuss about us. You are my darling treasure and so right and lovely, and of course we shall be happy.' He couldn't think of the details. It was enough simply to come home to Zippa's arms. That was happiness. 'It will be a very difficult world, we must be happy by ourselves' he writes, almost as though he were pulling the bedclothes over their heads.

All this was written just as Tony was falling in love with Simone. He was beginning to clutch at Zippa. Zippa would save the situation. A couple of months later, when it was virtually irretrievable, she had become something like a magic wand: 'As soon as we are together, everything will be blotted out, and it will be as if I had never gone away at all.' The subject lapsed, for the time being.

Meanwhile, Zippa was left hanging. Whatever they decided, something would be lost. From her point of view, Wapping was home. Even when bombs were falling there, and she was at Hilton (which she was during the spring and summer of 1944), Wapping was still home. As Tony had said, she had built up something there. He had called it an atmosphere, and had said he didn't want to spoil it. But it was more than an atmosphere. The war had taken the men away, and between them, she and Dolly and Geraldine had coped. They had made a sort of co-operative, a community of women, with Rosalind and everything else shared between them. Tony's return would undo all that. A married couple was a different kind of set-up. What kind of life was he holding out to her? The three of them alone together in army quarters near a base somewhere in England? Or in Germany, with the occupying forces? On the other hand, he could scarcely be expected not to want to live with his wife.

Chapter 13

'To sustain and stimulate guerilla warfare'

'May 1944: I left the 1st Battalion 60th and joined a military organisation in N. Africa under the control of the War Office.' So wrote Tony in a memo to himself listing various dates, scribbled on the back of an old letter. Just a few months before, he had resigned himself to drifting on in the battalion until he could get out of the army. Now, at last his fortunes changed.

The military organisation under the control of the War Office was SOE – Special Operations Executive. It had been set up early in the war to conduct espionage, sabotage and reconnaissance operations in occupied Europe. Its headquarters were in London, there was a branch in Cairo, and at the time of the American landings in North Africa at the end of 1942, another branch was established just outside Algiers. It was code-named 'Massingham' and was run jointly by SOE and the American Office of Strategic Services (OSS), the precursor to the CIA. Tony had heard in December 1943, that Montgomery was leaving the Mediterranean theatre to take command of all Allied ground forces in England. He guessed then that 'something must be going to happen come the spring'. Presumably he was part of a new intake at Massingham in advance of Operation Overlord – the Normandy landings.

The move was a big step for him, and it brought him much relief. He had told Zippa he didn't know how to find a new job, but in fact, as he now admitted, 'I had been trying to get this job for some time and have now succeeded. I think it should be extremely interesting and more like the kind of thing I might do after the war.'*

Within the week he wrote to say that indeed 'the work is extremely interesting' – though 'complicated', and it would take him a while to understand it all. On 9 June, three days after D-Day, came an excited letter apologising for a longish silence. Such a lot had happened. He'd been so busy, 'frequently I don't stop until half past 12 or 1 in the morning'. The second front, 'that you were so sceptical about', has started, 'and really I do feel optimistic about its success'. 'I'm sure we were right to wait so long': 'The size and scope of the whole operation is tremendous, 4000 ships and practically no losses. I can't really write about my job, but one day you will be interested.'

He was also delighted that, just a few days before, the Allies had taken Rome, and without a battle: 'From the speed of the German retreat it looks as though they intend to go right back to the Pisa-Rimini line. Everything is so exciting and I really feel that anything might happen now.' Altogether, he thought that it would probably now be safe for her and Rosalind to go back to London: 'I do not myself feel that the Germans will ever again be able to carry out any heavy attacks on London. I think they will have far more urgent things to do with their comparatively small supply of bombers.'

One of the things Tony liked about his work was that it was 'mixed American and British' – though a little later he calls it a

---

* I don't know what Tony meant by this, except in a very general way. As far as I know, he never worked for MI6.

'triple organisation', with the French included. In fact, it's possible that Simone, a 'military officer', as Tony had described her, was working for the Free French within the same organisation. Tony himself gives nothing away – neither about that, nor about the nature of the work. But his phrase 'triple organisation' accords with the tripartite missions that were being organised by SOE and OSS with the Free French Central Bureau of Intelligence and Operations (Bureau Central de Renseignements et d'Action).

These missions were carried out by what were known as Jedburgh teams, parachuted into France behind the lines, each consisting of three people – one always French, and the other two either British or American, or one of each. Of the 93 such missions sent into France from D-Day onwards, 25 were organised from Massingham, many of those around the middle of August when there was a second invasion of France in the south known as Operation Dragoon.[1]

There's a buzz now about Tony's letters – 'really I'm extremely glad to be doing a job which means doing some work':

We live in American tents with concrete floors with electric light, though the electric light does not work yet. Our offices are those semi-circular corrugated iron huts [i.e. Nissen huts] and the mess is a long wooden hut on stilts … I am in my office now and so are six other people though it is half past ten [pm] … Truly I never get time to think, I never read or do anything outside my work!

In July, he was promoted to captain. The only cloud was that he felt 'somewhat guilty working in an office when so much is going on' – 'ashamed' even, he said a few weeks later, 'of being in a terribly safe job'. Still, 'I do think I am doing something useful as well as interesting'.

A sample of these Massingham operations, taken from the National Archives catalogue, gives an idea of what they were up to:

> Purpose: Mission from Massingham base; assist developments in the Pyrenees area … harass enemy lines of communication and organise reception for daylight troop landings.
>
> Massingham team, to harass German communications on the left bank of the Rhone and roads and railway transport, Lyon/Vienne area.
>
> Purpose: Massingham mission, to sustain and stimulate guerrilla warfare, Basses-Alpes area.[2]

The only glimpse offered by Tony himself is a description of 'dealings with loading and despatching … a two-master sailing ship', whose captain used to be 'a smuggler in a fairly big way'. He was 'absolutely like a 16th century pirate', wrote Tony, and his crew were 'the dirtiest looking cut-throats you can imagine'. But the most terrifying thing about the captain was his Alsatian dog, which 'stands on the top of the wheelhouse, and is prepared to tear anyone to bits on the slightest word from his master.'

Perhaps the man was running guns 'to sustain and stimulate guerilla warfare', somewhere in the Pyrenees or the Basses-Alpes.

~

On 13 June, four days after Tony had assured Zippa that London was safe from bombers, the first German pilotless aircraft fell on the city. It was the beginning of a campaign of raids which, at its height, dropped more than a hundred bombs a day on London and the southeast. People called these aircraft doodle bugs because of the droning noise they made as they came over.

They would cut out before the explosion, and the silence that followed was horribly ominous. If Zippa had been thinking of returning to Wapping she wasn't now – and a few weeks later, towards the middle of July, Pier Head was hit. Luckily neither Dolly nor Geraldine was hurt, but they had to move out – Dolly to friends in west London, while Geraldine and her two children joined Zippa at Hilton. Tony was 'shocked ... terribly sorry' that all her hard work at Wapping had come to this. The worst of it was that the Port of London Authority wouldn't repair the house because it was just about habitable, and there was an acute short-age of labour in London.

Not surprisingly, Zippa begins now to sound less buoyant. From Hilton, she tells Tony about not being able to sleep, and of creeping out of the house at dawn into the dewy, misty fields, where 'the corn looked as though it was reeds in a lake'. She col-lects a pocketful of mushrooms and 'for the first time in months', 'felt that old magic feeling of being in the country – just a sad, longing feeling.' In passing, she says something about having fun together when he comes home, but the picture she paints is of evenings sewing peacefully while he reads aloud to her. It was a thing Alured used to do and which Tony was never very good at, but she missed it anyway. At the very end of her letter, before signing off she says she 'can't think this war will go on very much longer', and adds: 'I'm very nervous of the peace – it doesn't look as though anything will be settled.'

Of the two of them, it was usually Tony who felt dispir-ited. But for the moment he was relatively cheerful. The Italian campaign was going faster than expected. Rome had fallen in June, and the Allies were pushing north into Tuscany. Assisi was taken on 17 June; Arezzo on 16 July, and at the end of the month, Florence itself. Everything was suddenly opening up, the lights were coming on, he could feel a breeze. He wanted to be there, among the terraced slopes and hilltop towns. Or in France: 'Europe more than England somehow. I should like us to go for a long holiday in France, Switzerland and Italy. I have a longing for mountains and would love to ski.'

It was in these weeks that Tony's love affair with France seemed to deepen. He had always made a point of finding friends among the French of North Africa, but now it was as though the second front were revealing France itself again, her true face. The second front, and – of course – Simone. If France had a face, it was Simone's.

'It's odd', he wrote, 'how the Battle of France is proving just like the Battle of 1940.' He meant, I think, the special intensity of feeling with which people followed both battles. Mollie Panter-Downes, the London correspondent for the *New Yorker* who had described London's stunned silence when France surrendered in 1940, noticed the same thing now – 'a queer hush' in the streets immediately after D-Day:

> *Everybody seemed to be existing wholly in a preoccupied silence of his own … one could sense the strain of a city trying to project itself across the intervening English orchards and cornfields across the strip of water to the men already beginning to die in the French orchards and cornfields.*

Tony was doing just that from Algiers, across a much wider stretch of water. Dormant memories were springing to life. Chartres, for example: 'I am so delighted that Chartres is free', Tony wrote in August: 'Somehow Chartres is for me the place I remember most … the cathedral rising straight from a flat plain … the loveliest building I have ever been in. I wish I were in France now.' And he goes on, in the same breath: 'Very sad, I heard the other day one Humphrey Woods who was with my Bn [battalion] in the desert and had been ever since 1939 was killed in France ... He was a most charming person.'

As for the fall of Paris on 23 August, it was a moment of wild celebration everywhere. Algiers erupted: 'flags, dancing in the streets, ships madly blaring sirens', says Tony. Would he and Simone have gone dancing too? Surely yes. But Tony is almost comically reticent:

Truly I am delighted and especially that it was so largely done by the French themselves. It is wonderful to think that if one happened to be there one could walk peacefully down the Champs-Elysées.

During these months after the Normandy landings, Tony's enthusiasm for France becomes charged, explosive even, and Tony himself curiously touchy and emotional. France was a delicate subject in any case. 'The average British soldier', wrote Alan Moorehead, 'had been taught to believe that the French had "let us down" in 1940', and that they were 'a weak and venal people'.[3] It infuriated Tony:

People are horribly smug and talk about the decadent French. They forget that if France was weak, as she was, it was because she had twice as many casualties as we had in the last war and that she was utterly exhausted. They don't remember that the British Army was as utterly defeated in 1940 as the French, and that it was the Channel which saved us.

He was particularly incensed by the Allies' treatment of de Gaulle. It was a week since D-Day and 'he ought to be in France and recognised. It is the Americans who are holding it up.'

And then Zippa put her foot in it. 'I can't think who you have been talking to,' he replied, 'or what propaganda you have been reading. What on earth makes you write "I think de Gaulle should be shot" with no added comment. I couldn't agree with you less.' I don't know what Zippa was referring to, but it might have been de Gaulle's refusal to throw his full weight behind the Allies on D-Day.

It was a long story, with much back history which Zippa may not have known. The point was that de Gaulle believed he had been insulted. Relations between the General – a stiff and prickly man – and his allies, Churchill and Roosevelt, had never been easy. But he was the President of the French Provisional Government and his famous BBC broadcasts to the French Resistance had meant that, in Moorehead's words, his name had come to stand, 'for the ideals of anti-Fascism, of democracy, of the willingness to fight on for principles … It had become a sort of trademark for liberty.'[4]

The problem over D-Day was that the Allies had left it until two days beforehand to tell him they were about to invade his country. What's more, General Eisenhower's speech, broadcast to the people of France and the other occupied countries, made no mention of him, nor of his provisional government. 'Americans think,' wrote Tony, 'because of their vulgar wealth and the fact that they do admittedly supply the arms, that they can treat France like a 3rd rate power!!' As a result, de Gaulle refused (though he later relented) to broadcast a speech of his own, and he withdrew 200 French liaison officers from the operation – on the grounds that there had been no discussion as to their political function.*

---

* Though he relented in the end on both points. See Simon Berthon, *Allies at War* (HarperCollins, 2001). There is a summary at: www.bbc.co.uk/history/worldwars/wwtwo/allies_at_war_01.shtml.

No doubt there were things to be said on the other side, but Tony would have none of it:

I think the Americans have behaved atrociously to him and us slightly less badly … Personally I think de Gaulle has done wonders for four years. With no strength to bargain with, he has never given way in his convictions as to France's position and he has contrived to keep alive the idea of a strong France.

And he ends his letter with an apology of sorts:

I love France and hate the idea of people being superior about her!! This outburst isn't at you but at stupid people. Where did you get your idea from?

How Tony and Zippa resolved the question of de Gaulle, I don't know. But a few weeks later, Zippa did it again, blithely passing on something else she had heard. It was from a colonel she knew who had been involved in the landings and who told her that half the Normandy villages he had passed through had been pro-German, not welcoming. Tony replied with a curt list: A, her colonel was just one person, maybe prejudiced; B, Normandy was a small part of France, and the Normans, like the English, were undemonstrative by nature; C, the colonel's account didn't agree with what he, Tony, had heard; and D, 'you will always find girls who marry occupying enemies, you would in England. Four years is a very long time, and look at the Americans in England, or what I hear of them!!'

Heavens! she replied, surely he must realise that she was only saying what she'd heard, and the colonel was only saying what he'd seen:

He just said it was interesting to find about fifty per cent of the villages <u>he</u> and his regiment passed through, definitely pro-German – the other fifty per cent hailed us as demonstratively as the papers said they did! But I expect now the pro-German elements will be completely reversed in the excitement of victory. The French are the most practical race in the world!

And anyway, 'I have always loved them.'

It was an odd spat – untypical of Tony in some ways, willing as he usually was to see things from different angles. But France was different. Tony's opinions were his own, but Simone would have made him especially sensitive. De Gaulle would have been her hero, the man who had kept the Resistance alive when all had seemed lost.

There may have been something else, though. It seems that, privately, Tony wasn't as completely convinced by France as he made out. He once mentioned meeting the chief of staff of General Leclerc, the commander of the Free French force that fought alongside the Eighth Army at the Mareth Line. He admired him, he said, and he admired his general too. But 'for all that, it is fine individuals who stand out, not a solidly fine people'. Just recently, he had persuaded the French writer and biographer of Disraeli, André Maurois, to come and give a lecture to the battalion. It had not been a success. Not many had turned up. Tony himself had been disappointed. 'He obviously has a great grasp and understanding of English thinking', he wrote, 'but he is a snob':

I feel so sad about the whole business of France … there is, no doubt there is, little real love for them … I suppose there is sadly a certain amount of truth in public opinion, but it always seems such bad taste to express it.

~

Tony was now thoroughly fed up with the Americans. It wasn't just their condescension towards the French. It was their attitude to Europe in general, and to Russia too – 'far more anti-Russian than we are'. He feared their isolationism, which stemmed, he thought, from a basically provincial and materialistic outlook:

> *I'm afraid it is very likely they will say again 'To hell with all these too clever intriguing Europeans, let them get on with it, we have all we need, and let's get on with our life of motor cars and refrigerators' – and so will lose interest in Europe.* *

And as if that weren't bad enough, 'an enormous influx of Americans' had just arrived – 'mostly rather stupid, and I get driven mad trying to explain to them how to work'. The trouble, he thought, was that 'they are not really at war'. It didn't mean the same thing to them, so they didn't have the same sense of duty. What they had was money and equipment: 'They can produce such terrific results without being all out, that they have not yet got round to being all out.'

Besides, he didn't like their food. Slops.

---

* Alan Moorehead made the same point: 'to the average American, France was simply another untidy foreign country … He compared France to his own sane and much-desired world where there was decent plumbing and ice cream and movies and a language you could understand.' *Eclipse*, p. 98.

Chapter 14

'The mechanics of it'

A t the end of the first week of July 1944, Tony wrote:

It does look as though something is really happening in the war. Wild rumours flash round here but I'm sure there is a very real basis of trouble in Germany and that it will have an effect on the armies. Nothing would surprise me if it were over tomorrow and I definitely think it will be over this year in Europe.

I don't know for certain what he was referring to, but it sounds as though the wild rumours were about the 20 July plot to assassinate Hitler. Not that the British were involved in it. The Allies' insistence on unconditional surrender meant that they weren't active in internal German opposition. But the plot was known to SOE before it happened,[1] and it would have lifted hopes, even when, in the event, it failed. Three days after it, on 23 July, the correspondent for the *New Yorker* wrote that it was 'everybody's absorbing topic of conversation',[2] and in a speech to the Commons a week or so later, Churchill himself spoke of 'tremendous events':

The highest personalities in the German Reich are murdering one another, or trying to, while the avenging Armies of the Allies close upon the doomed and ever-narrowing circle of their power.[3]

Halfway through August, on the eve of Operation Dragoon (the Allied invasion of southern France) Tony too was writing about 'tremendous things' – though in the next breath he admits to a certain flatness: 'I suppose one is not excited,' he said, because, 'everything is now clear and finished. The war is now over and decided but the mechanics of it are still going on.' Retreating Germans 'packed on the roads' were being bombed. It was '1940 in reverse with no Dunkirk'. The machine 'was going on its own now'. It horrified him, as it did Zippa, who feared that the Allies might 'have to fight all through Germany before we get peace'. Tremendous things were happening, but what was this tremendousness compared to the harm?

And then there was the question of peace, the longed for peace. It seemed imminent again – as it had in January at the time of the Berlin bombardment. But what would it bring? Revenge and punishment, Zippa feared. It was a common cry, and had been since the beginning. Mass Observation surveys of what people thought should happen to Germany after the war, showed consistently that about a third of respondents 'based their ideas on revenge'.[4] Thinking back to the interwar years, Zippa was full of foreboding: 'If we aren't very careful we'll just be sowing the seeds for another Hitler in a matter of time – probably fifty years instead of twenty this time.' Tony was worried too. 'It is depressing,' he wrote, 'to think of the arrogance and despair of the Germans. It is going to take a long time to heal Europe. If only we can have a period of peace and freedom from starvation … but it won't be done round any conference table.'

They began to talk again, as they had earlier, of Tony's return and civilian life. Could they even imagine it? Tony was nervous – more so, somehow, than before: 'I can't get myself adjusted to the idea of peace and what I am going to do. It has gone on for so long now it does not seem real I shall lead an ordinary life again.' All the old worries about where and how they were going to live came back. Last time, he had told Zippa not to fuss and that everything would be alright. Now nothing seemed so sure.

Once, just being with Zippa and Rosalind had been enough – 'You can't imagine how lovely it is for me to think of you and Rosalind,' he had said. Even England had seemed a lucky place to be – not as ravaged as Europe. He had thought then that he wouldn't be demobbed 'for some months'. Now those months stretched out indefinitely. 'If I have got to be in the army for a year or so after the war, I should like to be in France or Italy, and for you to come out and live with me. That, I think, might be rather fun.' Meanwhile: 'I don't think it'll be worthwhile our settling down to anything too elaborate or expensive in the way of a house for a year or so, everything will be in such an uncertain state.' They would have a lovely time though, take a holiday and travel somewhere – 'I don't quite know how we shall manage with Rosalind, but we will somehow.'

It was all very vague. England is scarcely mentioned, and he says nothing about a job – though in one of his next letters he makes a sudden swerve away from the Foreign Office: 'I sometimes hark back to my old idea of teaching, not in England, but in Europe and America mostly ...I don't know if I could have the energy to do the social whirl of the Foreign Office.'

Zippa must have puzzled over these letters. What was he thinking of? She had never spoken of anything 'elaborate or expensive'. And why this sudden distaste for the Foreign Office?

The social whirl seems a singularly lame reason. As for his year or so of uncertain times – he had done something like it before, in 1941, with his vague and convoluted argument against marrying in the present unsettled state of everything. At that time, it seemed that all of postwar Europe had to be fixed before the banns could be read. Now, here he was again, shying and prevaricating.

Of course, the reason was Simone. She was, I think, the big question in his mind. He didn't know what to do. The end of the war would mean having to decide. He didn't want to decide; probably didn't even want to think about it. But in the mean time he didn't want to put down roots in England. A house and family and a government job were all solid English roots. Teaching, on the other hand, was a looser, freer kind of profession, or so he thought. He could do it anywhere, and the holidays would allow time for travel. Somehow, I can imagine him thinking, it offered a way of life in which there might be room for Simone.

Tony

As with Rosalind, he wasn't sure how, exactly. But something would turn up.

~

Meanwhile, Zippa was trying to understand and be helpful. Yes, she wrote, let's have a holiday. The Lake District would be nice. She was writing on the train from Derby just then, on her way to stay with a friend in Edinburgh, having left Rosalind with Betty. They were passing through 'lovely mountainous country, little streams dashing over stones and the heather out on the hills'. She wished she 'could be helpful about a job' for him too. She had talked it over with his mother, who knew of someone willing to pull strings, and there was someone else, a friend in business. Perhaps 'you ought to be a brilliant international commercial traveller!' she suggests brightly.

Zippa was putting a brave face on things. She had been living at Hilton Lodge since early March when she had fled the bombing in London with Rosalind. In July, when Pier Head was hit, her sister Geraldine and her two children had joined her. With Betty's two as well, she was beginning to feel overwhelmed. 'I never seem to manage to escape to write to you properly', she wrote:

Even now there is a swarming mass of children round me. Rosalind is a little pest now that she is half walking. She can climb onto sofas and chairs by herself and absolutely nothing is safe from her. I just managed to stop her drinking a bottle of ink this morning.

Zippa was feeling restless generally. Hilton was a haven, but – children apart – it was dull. Betty had married into a desperately respectable family. She could turn a cartwheel in the road under the moon in Wales, but not really at Hilton. There were servants, set meals, the in-laws, visitors and invitations from the surrounding big houses. The life of the rich went on much as it always had – though petrol rationing made a bit of a dent. Zippa describes a birthday party for one of Betty's boys, with mothers and nannies and children 'arriving by pony trap and taxi and very smart'. She had baked a cake and they had managed a spread. It had been fun.

But really, she was out of her element. She longed to turn a cartwheel – to act and dance and join the theatre world again. This little visit to Edinburgh had an ulterior purpose. While she was there, she tried to wangle an introduction to the director of the Edinburgh repertory company, and she made a dash to the Perth rep too, to see if there were any openings. 'I don't quite know how I'll take it if I get a job!!' she told Tony: 'I'll have to come and live here for the winter – then what'll I do if you come back?! Well, I can't think. All I know is I must work again, or bust.' Then she had an idea: 'By the way, I heard last night, from a magazine Editress, that journalism in Scotland was going to be vastly expanded, and they're looking out for young men.' Tony made no comment. In the event, nothing came of Edinburgh or Perth – nor of Scottish journalism either. Her commercial traveller idea dropped like a stone.

Zippa was casting around, desperately stabbing at possibilities for them both. She takes another little break from Hilton, this time to friends in Leamington Spa. The house there, she told Tony, 'is rather like ours used to be':

Full of people who have asked themselves for a night or two – every bedroom and the drawing-room sofa full up.

It was like old times. She talks about everyone, in particular an architect she knew. He loved Rosalind – though 'it seems so out of place', she said, that he should meet her before Tony did. And she goes on to describe a wonderful sunset walk they all took by the river. Then suddenly, at the bottom of the page, comes this: 'Darling, how long do you think the interval will be before you get back after peace is signed?' It's an abrupt transition – as though she were suddenly catching herself. After all, this was her world, something like Wapping – crowds of old friends, people sleeping all over the house – not Tony's. Especially if they were all cooing over Rosalind.

A little later she had a dream. In it, she was at Hilton, and Elsie, one of the servants, 'came rushing up to me during the morning and said "I believe Mr Moore is coming up the drive", so I dashed to the window and there you were – then I gave one look at myself in the glass and nearly screamed.' She looked awful, she said, clothes, hair, face, and she couldn't find Rosalind. 'Then you arrived at the door and I flew away to hide, and you came dashing up the stairs and shouted "Zippa" and banged into all the rooms and I just evaded you all the time.' She thought if she could only get into Betty's room and lock the door she could at least brush her hair. But she hears him coming, 'and then I was in your arms and you had a sweater on and no horrid buttons and it was absolutely alright – but mind you, I woke up before you had seen my dirty face!'

And before she could find Rosalind, either. Poor Zippa – so torn, so unsure of herself, so worried about where Rosalind was in their marriage, how she fitted in. And then the whole business of beauty. Many women would have been dreaming such dreams just then, but not many would have had to live up to Tony's ideal of beauty. I don't know whether she looked as awful as she thought, but by 1944 a lot of people did. One London observer described 'shadowed faces' everywhere, some 'pinched', some 'puffy', all sapped of vitality from a diet of starch and little else.[5]

Tony's food parcels – another one, of butter, sugar and raisins arrived at the end of September – had been treats, little shots of luxury, but not enough to counteract the years of general skint.

∼

At the end of September Zippa travelled down to London to inspect Pier Head and see about repairs. It was a joyful homecoming and Tony wrote back, delighted 'to think of you being greeted rapturously by the "Prospect of Whitby"* and the Dockers. Zippa darling, you have got a genius for making people like you.'

But Zippa was not entirely happy. On her train journey down she had written to Tony to say that she hadn't heard from him for three weeks. She didn't know whether he was 'well or ill or moved or what'. Then, rather sharply, she says: 'I swore I wouldn't write again till I heard, and I've not done so for a week, and now I break my promise because the journey's long and boring.' Tony was shocked. He had never left it as long as that before. 'Please forgive me', 'I am in rather a miserable listless sort of state, waiting for something to turn up and fed up completely with this country … [I] somehow feel as though I just have not got any virtue in me at all.'†

Partly, it was Massingham. Nothing much of interest was going on there. Italy was where the action was and staff were gradually moving across to new headquarters near Bari, on the Adriatic.‡ Tony too was waiting for a transfer and kicking his heels as interesting jobs for him were proposed only to melt away. There was one good moment while his colonel was away

---

* A Wapping riverside pub close by, like 'The Town of Ramsgate'.

† By 'virtue' he means 'spirit' or 'essential energy' – though, in the circumstances, the term is a little ambiguous.

‡ In an operation known as 'Maryland'. See *The Secret History of SOE*, p. 549.

in London, and he found himself, 'acting more or less entirely for him which means deciding a lot of things I don't really know very much about ... everyone comes to me and solemnly does whatever I say. It makes me laugh. One day I shall have a lot of interesting things to talk about to you.'

But his colonel returned and he found himself unemployed again – 'except that, thank goodness, one's pay goes on!':

So the result is that for the moment I am feeling considerably depressed ... It is absurd to think one can have nothing to do.

Then his brigadier – that's to say the officer senior to his colonel – offered him 'what would have been a good job in India, might even have been a major (!) but I refused it. I don't know, perhaps I was foolish ... What decided me was a fear of being kept in the army after the time I would normally have been demobilised in Europe.'* What also might have decided him was the impossible thought of being so far from Simone.

Tony was stuck. He was 'fed up completely' with the place, but it was where Simone was. 'Considerably depressed', is like him. 'On the point of breakdown' would have been closer: 'half asleep', he told Zippa, 'lost and uncertain about everything ... dead and devoid of ideas'. It was a kind of inner paralysis. In the end, on 23 October, something did turn up and Tony flew out, bound for Sicily and eventually Italy.

It must have been an unbearable farewell. From the story that emerged later, Tony begged Simone not to marry for a year. What exactly he had in mind would become clearer in time, but

---

* Some time later, his father ran into Tony's brigadier in India and heard about his son's refusal: 'he gave me a grossly eulogistic account of you', wrote Arthur, and said 'he tried to get you to come with him but you wouldn't come!'

for the moment he was probably trying not to see, crossing his fingers. To Zippa he said only that he was 'rather excited' about going to Sicily, though he feared he would be 'very much at the wrong end of the war'. He wanted to be in France – of course – 'or in the North of Europe somewhere'.

Chapter 15

The soldier's return

Soon letters from Tony were arriving from 'H.Q. No I Special Force, C.M.F.' [Central Mediterranean Force] – that's to say from Bari. Naturally, he says nothing about his job, beyond the fact that he was working a twelve-hour day. It was probably like Massingham all over again, liaising with, supporting and supplying resistance groups, Italian this time, in acts of sabotage behind the German lines.[1] First though, he took a week's leave.

Ever since its liberation in early June, Tony had wanted to go to Rome. Now he seized his chance, and it bowled him over. Perhaps it even distracted him a little from his sorrow at leaving Simone. He spent his time walking, city walking, miles in every direction, developing blisters on his feet and a crick in his neck as he craned and marvelled. There was a special exhibition in the Palazzo Venezia where he gazed his fill of Titians, Raphaels and Botticellis, paintings he had only ever known as reproductions. He heard the 'Barber of Seville' at the opera house, and promised himself another visit the next night. He ate an apple which he hadn't done since arriving in Egypt. And, perhaps in homage to Zippa, he went to the ballet, faithfully reporting on the baller- ina (as good as Fonteyn) and on the male lead (modelled on Robert Helpman). Prices everywhere were fantastic, he said, but he managed to buy a doll for Rosalind, and stockings and gloves for Zippa, which he sent off.

As for private houses, he had one or two introductions, but was faintly disgusted by 'the usual contessas and duchessas' and their 'good time parties': 'They are charming and amusing but somehow quite rootless and also amoral I imagine, popping in and out of everyone's beds.' Tony had seen something of the rich – most recently in Cairo. But he had never spoken of them quite like that. Perhaps in Rome he sniffed a particular taint, left behind by decades of Mussolini and the years of Nazi collaboration.

Otherwise, what struck him about Italy was its wretched poverty, its miserable, filthy little villages where exhausted women carried enormous loads on their heads and their daughters couldn't even pretend – as they had in Tunis – to put on a cheerful face. One other thing shocked him – the ruins of Monte Cassino, the town spread out below an ancient hilltop monastery which had been occupied by the Germans and which the Allies had bombed flat in February 1944 after the Anzio landings: 'an astonishing sight. Not one single building has more than four ruined walls.'*

As for Bari, where he was based, there wasn't much to be said for it. Though he liked the family he was billeted with – the one that made him lament the effects of work and babies on the beauty of women. He describes them all, especially their operatic children: Diana, thirteen, flashing her eyes; and Pierino, eleven. When Pierino sang a tragic aria, tears poured down his cheeks.

---

* 'According to General Maitland Wilson's report to the Combined Chiefs of Staff, 142 Fortress bombers dropped 287 tons of 500lb general purpose bombs, and 66½ tons of 100lb incendiaries, followed by 47 B. 25s and 40 B. 26s, which dropped another 100 tons of high explosive bombs'. Alan Moorehead, *The Villa Diana* (Hamish Hamilton, 1951), p. 88.

~

In November 1944, John and Anne Crockett asked Zippa to join their newly formed Compass Players – a chance at last to return to what she loved. She then did a strange thing. She said yes, but only as an understudy. Tony, when he heard, thought she was mad:

Why say to John and Anne you will understudy a part but that they must try to get someone also? … I should like you to get a really good part with a good company!! of course. But … I hate the thought of you rushing about getting tired and helping John and Anne out, and yet not getting any real chance or experience for yourself.

Did she or did she not want to work in the theatre, and if she did, what was she doing about it?

The truth was that Zippa was in an impossible position. When it came to it, there was too much to juggle. Tony was encouraging, but he knew nothing about it. He had seen her looking charming as Cinderella in 1940, and he had heard her reading Shakespeare. To him she was lovely – just as Fred Astaire was, or Sonja Henie, the ice skater. Sweat and tears, long hours and late nights weren't part of his picture. But if Zippa were to make a career for herself, she would be rehearsing, practising, out in the evenings, on tour maybe, not at home. The coming peace, the soldiers' return, was scarcely the moment for that. Tony had once cast her as the person who would point the way for him through the fearful postwar wilderness. How could she do that if she was pushing – as she would have to push – for herself? And in any case, how was a life in the theatre compatible with a diplomatic career for him? Or with anything else – travel, teaching – he might think of?

Besides, there was Rosalind to consider. With Wapping gone and her circle of friends dispersed, she had nothing to fall back on. Tony hadn't a clue, as he admitted himself, about Rosalind and her care. 'You tell me about it,' he had written recently, 'but still, as I have never done it with you, I can't properly imagine it all.' In fact, for him, there was only ever one question to be asked about Rosalind. Not whether she would stop Zippa from working, but whether she would stop the two of them from having fun. He was 'appalled', he had written, 'at the thought of the constant problem Rosalind will present. Somehow we must get away and have a good time and dance and ski and drink champagne! Just a bit. Some solution must be found so we don't always have to take her with us.'

They had talked about employing someone, a 'treasure', as Tony put it, but they had never felt they could afford it. Perhaps once Rosalind was 'house-trained', he suggested, she could be 'parked' with people from time to time. But, that was no career solution for Zippa. Anyway, at eighteen months, Rosalind was difficult to 'park'. Tony's mother wrote to say she had a terrible temper. Zippa wrote about having to hold her hand all night once, to stop her crying. It horrified him. The whole subject was exhausting – almost as exhausting as Rosalind herself.

In the middle of November, the question of Zippa and the Compass Players was taken out of her hands by a bomb. Pier Head was hit again, by a doodle bug.* I don't know how badly, or how far the earlier repairs had got. But the Port of London Authority must have redoubled its efforts for by early December, a letter to Zippa from Tony's father, found her at Wapping. It had

---

* The word had possibilities. A letter from Tony's father, Arthur, commiserated with her about the house being 'doodlebuggered up'.

been addressed to Hilton Lodge, but was redirected to Pier Head. So there she must have been, preparing for her third Christmas without Tony.

At which point, abruptly, everything falls silent. The letters stop. The next thing was Tony's father again, writing to Zippa in the New Year of 1945, and referring to the fact that Tony was now in England. Perhaps, hearing of the bombing, Tony had managed at last to get home leave in time for Christmas. Perhaps it was all done at the last minute, by telegram. However it came about, I can imagine Zippa frantically making the house beautiful again – and herself too. Looking in the mirror, putting on his face cream, powder and lipstick and searching for an unladdered pair of his silk stockings.

As for Tony, the strangeness of returning – not only to Zippa and Rosalind, but to England – must have been overwhelming. Shocking too. Tony had known the Blitz, but this was three years on and many bombings later. The doodlebugs alone had done huge damage and as soon as their launching pads in France had been overrun by the Allies, they had been replaced by the V2s, rockets launched from further away in Holland – faster, stealthier, more frightening than anything that had gone before. England was battered, London especially, and people were exhausted – 'tired to the bone', wrote one observer in December 1944. Tony would have seen it from the train windows, and observed it in the faces of the people in the seats around him:

> Civilians as well as service men and women fall asleep almost as soon as they sit down in the train. Doctors say they are kept busy dishing out tonics to workers who really need the unprocurable prescription of a long rest from blackout, bombs and worry.[2]

Rosalind in Wapping

And when they finally met, did Rosalind look at the strange man and say: 'Don't like you'? Were Tony and Zippa speechless? Did they search each other's faces for new lines and changes? Had they remembered each other right? It is impossible to imagine the moment. From North Africa, Tony used to say in different ways again and again, how bad it was to have had, 'so much experience … without being able to share it … to have a great chunk of separate life like 2 years and more'. Could they blot it all out, as he had imagined, as though it had never happened? And did he take her dancing at the nearest Palais de Danse?

~

As far as Tony, Zippa and Rosalind are concerned, a curtain falls over the next eight months and the great events of their lives: the advance of the Allied armies on Berlin; Victory in Europe in May 1945; the elections in July and the landslide victory for Labour. The curtain over the rest of the family lifts a little in December

1944 with news from Alured in Belgium, where his battalion landed by glider for what was known as the Battle of the Bulge against an unexpected German counter-attack. It lifts again when their gliders crossed the Rhine on the morning of 24 March 1945 and the battalion continued on towards Berlin. A week before the Germans surrendered, Alured's commanding officer sent a report to his men about that landing and the subsequent battle, with a note attached. 'These have been great days,' it said:

> We have had the satisfaction of seeing the 'Master Race' in defeat trudging back through their own villages, ready to give themselves up, and the smiling faces of our liberated allies.

～

Alured has been missing from this story ever since Zippa's marriage in 1941. Veronica too has faded from it, last glimpsed in early 1944, dashing up to London from Shropshire to see Zippa in Chekhov's *The Bear* and Evreinov's *A Merry Death*. The reason in Veronica's case is that so little war correspondence between the two sisters has survived. In Alured's case, there may be more to it.

Towards the end of 1942, Zippa wrote to Tony about something Alured had said which had upset her. He had spoken about a glass wall that now stood between them, and Tony had written back sympathising:

> *Darling, I do hope you get rid of Alured's glass wall ... it is so hard when you are in the army and in a different world, and now you are in a different world of being married. Have you read a very remarkable and beautiful book called* Howards End *by E.M. Forster? That is where he gets*

the phrase. E.M. speaks of the glass shade that falls between
people and the rest of the world when they marry.

Alured's reference to *Howards End*, was apt. At the risk of
reading too much into it, there is something suggestive about it.
In the book, the shade comes down between two sisters, Helen
and Margaret Schlegel – but the rhyme, as it were, between the
Schlegel and the Weigall siblings goes further. There is an uncanny
kinship between these families, fictional and real, in the things
they thought important. Forster labelled these things 'personal
relations' – by which he meant an inner world of feeling and
intuition and their representation in literature and art.

Howards End contrasts this inner world of feeling with the
outer world of material success, progress, and commerce, all of
which it represents in another family, the Wilcoxes. But there was
a difficulty: the book argues for the mutual interdependence of
the two halves of this contrast. The cultivation of the inner life
is enabled by the material security of the outer. So – to put it
crudely – in order to reconcile inner with outer, Forster marries
one of his heroines, Margaret Schlegel, to one of the Wilcoxes.
Her sister, Helen, romantic and idealistic, is dismayed – and so
'the astonishing glass shade' in Forster's words, 'that interposes
between married couples and the world', becomes (temporarily)
a barrier between them.

More than anyone, Alured knew what dancing and acting
and poetry meant to Zippa. Like Helen, he was dismayed by
her marriage. Tony was no Henry Wilcox, but he was not an
artist. Perhaps I make too much of this. Perhaps Alured was simply jealous – as Aunt Jane thought when Zippa told her that
he didn't like Tony. Alured was a complicated character, as was
the relationship between him and Zippa. His very rejection of the
world made it difficult for him to judge or understand it. Tony,

for all that he was more engaged in it, was not as at home there as Alured supposed. And after all, he did align himself with Forster – 'a remarkable and beautiful book', he said.

The war was as bad for Alured as it was for Tony. Worse probably in that he spent most of it in a limbo of training and waiting. Between Dunkirk in 1940 and Operation Overlord in 1944, unless a soldier was involved in campaigns in the Far East or the Mediterranean, there was no action. In fact, the Battle of the Bulge in December 1944 was Alured's first engagement of the war. There are very few surviving wartime letters between Alured and Zippa, but from odd glimpses of him here and there, he appears tired, sometimes haggard and generally listless. 'Very irritable', Aunt Jane pronounced after one of his leaves, 'and inclined to yawn and scratch'.

Of course his leaves would have helped. He and Zippa would have seen each other quite often. But with Tony between them, it wouldn't have been the same. They would have been more careful – Zippa a little defensive, perhaps, and Alured not wishing to offend. One thing would have drawn them together – and that was Rosalind. Alured was at ease with children. As the eldest of five siblings, he had grown up with them; there had always been a baby or a toddler around. He was the one who told them stories, made them toy theatres and sang silly songs. In later years, he and Rosalind were especially close, something I imagine starting here. It would have been odd, though, for Zippa to watch the two of them now, getting to know each other before Tony had even set eyes on the child.

Chapter 16

'My despair is indescribable'

On 11 August 1945, Zippa sent a letter to Alured that broke the glass wall between them. 'I have had a shock that I don't seem to be able to surmount,' she wrote. She had discovered 'a desperate letter' written by Tony to a young woman in Algiers. It was a love letter describing 'every detail of his feelings like a wild cry from a desperate soul in the desert'.

Tony, not yet de-mobbed, was about to take up an appointment in the British zone in Germany,* and was due to leave in two days' time. 'I told Tony what I had done', Zippa wrote, and he had poured out the whole story. The girl was called Simone, and he had been in love with her since the spring of 1944. Before leaving Algiers in October, he had made her promise not to marry for a year. This, he told Zippa, had been because 'he wanted to see if he could forget her and make a success of his marriage to me'. Had he told Simone that? perhaps not quite so brutally.

Then in May, Zippa continued, Simone had sent a letter to say that she was engaged to be married, but that she 'was marrying the other chap out of desperation and loved him [Tony]

---

* He was first at Bad Oeynhausen and then Minden in the Economic Division of the Control Commission, British Element – that's to say, the British part of the Allied military government of occupied Germany.

still'. It arrived at the very moment when Tony had 'just about decided he couldn't bear it any more'. So he immediately sent her a cable 'to break it off and marry him as soon as he was free'. Too late. His cable was opened by Simone's mother, who replied that Simone was on her honeymoon. It appears that 'maman' – so vigilant and strict the summer before – had discovered the situation and had hurried her daughter into marriage to avoid a family scandal. As Tony explained it to Zippa: 'Divorce is a more terrible thing in France than here and it would have meant Simone cutting with her whole family if she had decided to marry him.'

'The last seven months here have been torture to him', wrote Zippa. The agonised letter she had found had been written only a fortnight before, at the end of July. Those months had been torture to Zippa too. She had been dismayed at his return, she told Alured, by 'how dull and even callous and how selfish, he was'. It had baffled her. She had begun 'to grow bitter and thought with hard defiance' that she would leave him. Now she was ashamed of herself for not understanding, 'and I feel humble as I've never felt before':

> *I have begged him to let me have it all, every little detail and he has told it to me … and each word is almost worse pain. I have seen her pictures and O my God she is charming – very very slight with a face a little the shape of mine but much finer – a sad and pensive look with a degree of refinement that I haven't got. She is apparently utterly sweet in everything, and has a wonderful understanding and intellect.*

Knowing all this, she said, had brought her face to face with the truth of her own feelings:

It has been forced into me with knives that I am in love with him and my despair is indescribable. Even when I don't think about it, the physical pain in my guts cuts me almost in half ... I cannot sleep and can hardly eat and a violent hunger gnaws at me and then makes me sick.

Why hadn't Tony told her? Would he have? Why had he not sent the letter she found? Come to that, why had he written it – in July, when Simone had married in May? If he had changed his mind about sending it, why hadn't he destroyed it? Did he mean Zippa to find it? In fact, had it been written expressly for her to find? And was it a coincidence that she discovered it just as he was about to leave? When she told him that she'd read it, 'he was relieved', she told Alured, 'so relieved that he is almost happy'. And she goes on to describe how they talked about it, the whole extraordinary situation, its history and growth and unresolvable contradictions:

He begs me to believe that he never fell out of love with me – that he fell in love with this girl with a bang after not having seen me for 18 months – that even while he loved her he never ceased to care about me and that was why he couldn't write and finish it with me before he came home or even soon after he came back ... He begs me to believe that it is possible to love two people even though one has the stronger pull. Now he repeats over and over that he has found me again and that he can begin to think of Simone without the raw edge of pain.

'All that is balm,' says Zippa, 'but the pain is still too new to be touched except in moments held tight in his arms.'

That was the curious thing about it, she says. Physically they were still close, and at those times she could feel – more than feel, know – that he did still truly love her. In a way it would have been easier had it not been so – though she does not say that. She looks back over the last months and remembers a little holiday they took by the sea in Ireland. He told her that Simone

loved the sea and the sun and they spent all their free time
on the rocky coast and in the hills around Algiers. He tells
me what agony he suffered bathing with me those few hot
days in the west coast of Ireland. And yet he assures me all
the time that he never compared us in his mind and if only
I can bear it would like to reconcile us both in his heart.

Reading this cold, it is hard not to think cutting things, or to wish Zippa could have said them. But she was infinitely forgiving. Besides, she was trapped. She loved him. What could she say?

At one point in her letter, Zippa says a curious thing. When she asked him to tell her everything about Simone, every little detail, he did so, she says, 'like a boy clinging on to his last hope'. The image is striking – though which of them was his 'last hope' isn't clear. Perhaps that's the point. If not one, then the other, or both at once. What did he mean by reconciling them in his heart? What were either of them to make of the idea? Simone too must have been infinitely forgiving. There was something about Tony that prevented women from saying the obvious thing – 'Choose!' Perhaps it was that he hurt himself as much as he hurt them. 'I have given him all the sympathy I could', wrote Zippa, for all the world as if he were the wounded one:

And he has cried and said I was the only thing that now
made life bearable to him. I can understand it, but my

*despair seems to intensify rather than diminish … I can't
describe to you the agony of the whole thing. When I think
of the last 18 months and the way my thoughts have turned
to him and then realize that all the time I was not there for
him, I want to die.*

Did she go back and read his letters from those last months
again? Not yet, perhaps. But if ever she did, she would have realised, on the contrary, how much she had been there for him. She
was all over those desperate pages – the person he needed to see,
'close and vivid'; the person who was his standard, to tell him
what was right; the one without whom everything was 'broken
and unsatisfactory', and about whom he had 'nothing nothing
nothing in the world except lovely things to remember'.

And behind those words, if she had read them again, Zippa
would have seen clearly enough, as I saw when I read them, the
ghost of Simone – a kind of 'get-thee-behind-me' Simone. When
Tony told Zippa again and again that he didn't deserve her, that
he was so lucky to have her, that she would have to work to
improve him – even when he said, ambiguously, that there was
no virtue in him – it was as though he were secretly confessing.

Before her wedding, Zippa had told Alured that she half
wanted to die. Now she completely wanted to die. There was
just one consolation. Alured had leave and had suggested a little
holiday. Yes, she said,

*I must come away with you to the Scilly Isles. At least I must
get pretty again – it is wonderful he is not revolted by me – I
don't even understand it, having seen her picture … I feel
better after writing to you.*

~

Tony left for Germany a couple of days later, and Zippa took stock. Not that there was much peace in which to think. Her letters to Tony were written, as they had been from Hilton, from the middle of a scrum of children and family. This time she was staying with her sister Geraldine who, after Wapping was bombed, had settled in Chelsea again. Betty with her two children had come down to visit, and to complete the circle, Dolly lived not far away. So, despite her aching heart, Zippa wrote heroically of children's outings and picnics in the park, of Kensington Gardens and Rosalind losing her head with delight over the statue of Peter Pan. She 'tried to take the mice and the birds home with her, and shrieked when she couldn't pull them off and other children touched them. I was dead beat at the end of the day!'

All the same, she had managed to talk to Dolly and Betty about the situation. Both of them had suffered similar problems, one with a returning husband and the other with a non-returning lover – in fact there must have been conversations like this all over the country at that time. Gradually, it seems, Zippa was beginning to see things more clearly. For in one of her next letters, hardly breaking her stride amidst all her easy, friendly, domestic descriptions, she puts to Tony the devastating question:

> *Tell me, Tony, have you thought – quite apart from Simone*
> *– that perhaps we should part?*

The only hint that her voice might have been breaking comes at the point before 'we should part'. Until that moment, her letter is in pen; after it, in pencil. She had needed a moment. She had put her pen down. Perhaps she had gone for a walk. When she came back, it was gone – or Rosalind had drunk her bottle of ink. So she found a pencil and finished the sentence.

As for herself, 'I don't think I'll know for a year – till I know what I shall make of my life – I can imagine you feeling the same way. I know I love you, but in loving you I only want you to be happy and free, and I know I can't give you anything of myself unless I'm free and happy too.' She speaks of making something of her life – her life in the theatre, I think she means. At first glance, she seems to be saying that they could go on together if they were both doing the things that made them happy and free. It sounds good. But there was a contradiction at the heart of it. Acting and dancing made her happy and free. For him it was work and travel. Maybe that was the point. Was she in fact saying that their paths were bound to fork? I think so, though she hesitated. 'Tell me what you think, darling,' she says:

> *I feel I am a lot to blame for what has happened – I have been so very undecided – I too need your forgiveness.*

Zippa once told me that, although she always wanted to act and dance, she was never single-minded enough to make it happen. One half of her always turned towards home and family. That, I think, was what she meant by being 'so very undecided'. If Tony couldn't choose, nor could she. She couldn't bring herself to sacrifice either one or the other. But what had that to do with Simone? The answer, possibly, is that the Simone affair sent her mind casting back over the whole story of Tony and herself. What she saw was a sequence of ambivalences. From the very beginning, even in those golden Stansted days, she had been equivocal. 'I feel very tenderly towards him,' she had said to Alured, 'and so hope I never hurt him.' Her very tenderness had come with a sense of ill omen. But it hadn't stopped her. She had allowed the spell to work. She had both known and not known. That letter again, the one to Alured about marrying Tony and living 'happy ever after'. 'I could too', she had said, 'but then comes something in dancing, in poetry or trying a part that gives me such joy, that is more vital to me than anything else, and I know I shall have to do it.' For some reason that she doesn't explain, she had put the two things in opposition. She had felt that she couldn't dedicate herself both to Tony and to Art.

I don't think Zippa meant that she could never marry. It was more this particular marriage. I think she had known, as Alured had, that Tony belonged in a different world and that, however much they loved each other, they wanted incompatible things. In marrying him, she had fudged the question. Now, four years later, she seems to be inviting him – gently, for both their sakes – to unfudge them. Getting married had been a mistake. And in laying at least part of it at her own door, she was, in effect, pre-empting Simone. She was asking his forgiveness for never having loved him completely enough.

There had been a chance in 1941. It would have been hard but, as she had explained to Alured, 'I could have borne it, if he had agreed'. But Tony hadn't agreed. He had been distraught. And she had been too caught up in him herself to be rational and ruthless. And now? Could she have borne it?

The years had passed. There was Rosalind. Nothing was the same. She may not have been wholly in love with him before, but she knew she was now – knives had forced it into her. And yet the slow, considered manner of her question – 'Tell me Tony, have you thought – quite apart from Simone – that perhaps we should part?' – suggests that she thought she could have borne it. But she was reckoning without Tony. History was about to repeat itself, almost exactly. He had been unable to let go of her in 1941, and so it was now. Looking back and putting it all together, it seems that Tony lived in mortal fear of ever letting go. But Zippa was more cautious now, less inclined to say, as she had said then,

'Better not think'. She didn't quite trust him and she told him so. He had to woo her.

~

Over the next weeks and months, Tony broke down her defences. It wasn't easy. Her letters are missing, but he refers to them – one in particular, a 'sad letter' in which she speaks of feeling 'closed up and dead'. He was 'so terribly unhappy' he replied, 'to think of all the misery I have brought'. He begged her to allow him to earn her trust again. He always knew she was the better, richer person – but, still, they could help each other. They had both been hurt, and 'I do believe with all my heart … that for both of us our best hope of happiness and contentment is in each other, and I do completely believe it can grow again, because for me at any rate it has never died.'

Without her letters it is difficult to know how persuaded she was. But his words would have been 'balm' to her. He said he knew it would take time, and he knew it would be easier for him than for her, but he begged her to try, because she was his only hope. He was not strong, he said, and 'without you, anything might become of me'. What was Zippa to do? When they had first spoken about Simone, he had seemed to her 'like a boy clinging on to his last hope'. Whether that hope was herself or Simone had been unclear. Now it was as clear as day. She was the one, he said. She could not spurn him. 'I honestly don't think,' he wrote, 'that it has been anything inevitably in me that made this happen, but just quite extraordinary, really quite extraordinary circumstances, with which I was not strong enough to deal.' There was no more to say. Except perhaps one last thing.

In her letter to Alured about Simone, Zippa had said that, whatever else, she must now work. It was her only remedy – like her 'work or bust' moment at Hilton, though much more urgent now. In one of her next letters to Tony, she told him about a moment when she had been able to overcome her low spirits. It had happened one evening when she had suddenly decided to roll up the carpet and put on the gramophone: 'I danced till midnight,' she said, 'and happily all thought but exhilaration in working well, left me.' But the fact remained, that if she were ever to do anything more than dance to herself in the drawing room, something had to be decided, practically speaking.

It is astonishing how rarely, in all his letters from North Africa about teaching or the Foreign Service, about living abroad and travelling, Tony mentioned the implications for Zippa's work. Equally, how quiet she kept on the subject. Now at last they must have discussed it, for that winter, from Germany, Tony made a promise: 'Not to make any domestic demands at all and not to interfere in any way with any chances of work and theatre that you may be able to fix. I will be happy to live just wherever and however you like.' It was Zippa's last attempt to stake a claim for herself.

In the event it was more symbolic than real. Zippa's career in the theatre was slipping away. It had always been a tenuous thing. As a dancer, she was really too late. Long before, in 1941, she had consulted a dancer friend who had complimented her and said she had talent and promise.* But she lacked technique, he said. It would take at least three years hard training in ballet – not to turn her into a ballet dancer; she would never be that – but to give her a technical foundation. Meanwhile (as she wrote to Tony at the time), 'he couldn't recommend any group I could join or

---

* This was Rupert Doone, the last premier danseur engaged by Diaghilev for the Ballets Russes. He was also an actor and theatre director of left-wing and avant garde plays.

even anybody who would teach me cheaply – or even a room to practise in in London'.

In other words, dancing professionally had been a dead duck even then. Now, at 31 with a small child in tow, she couldn't realistically hope for anything beyond rolled up carpets and the gramophone.* As for acting – her best chance had also been years before, when she had been a student at the Old Vic. If she had continued then, if the fees had been found, if she had been determined, something might have come of it. She had done things since, but not enough.

Now it was December 1945, and Tony was about to fulfil another promise. He had said they must have fun and drink champagne after the war, and he was arranging just that. He would whirl Zippa off for a New Year's holiday. In Paris! Without Rosalind!! He was wildly excited: 'Oh darling, I do hope you are as happy and excited at the thought of Paris as I am. It will be such fun. I have got a lot of food fixed to bring – I hope <u>goose</u>!' Goose! Underlined and with an exclamation mark. What a word! It was their code, their signal. It was Stansted again, that glorious first Christmas. He would take her back to it. Everything would be blotted out – the war, North Africa, even Simone, all as if they had never been.

And there the letters stop.

At some point after Paris, Tony came back to England. His letters had talked about wanting to transfer to the London end of the Control Commission as soon as possible. He hadn't wanted to wait until he was de-mobbed in July or August 1946 before coming home. He and Zippa must then have discussed the future, what he was to do and how she would fit herself in with it. The Foreign Service was the likeliest thing, and Zippa must have been

---

* My own earliest memories are of prancing at her heels in various drawing-rooms to the *Nutcracker Suite* on the old wind-up gramophone.

encouraging. With her own prospects fading, she couldn't have held him to his promise. I don't know when exactly he was de-mobbed (something that seems to have coincided with the award of a medal*), or when he made his Foreign Office move, but at some point he took the exam, went through the interview, and was successful. By the end of that year, or in early 1947, they were in their first foreign posting.

Tony receiving a medal from American General John C.H. Lee, Acting Supreme Commander, Mediterranean, 1946

It was Rome. What a joy, my mother always remembered, after the shabbiness of London. 'A most wonderful city', Tony had written in 1944 when he took his leave there, 'it would be such fun if you were here.' Well, now she was, and he could show

---

* He never spoke of his medal.

her not just St Peter's and the great palaces and churches, but his out-of-the-way discoveries: the staircase somewhere with its 'odd landing with a lovely little ceiling', and 'beautifully carved window'; a little painted Cupid somewhere; the unexpected piazzas, like 'sudden clearings in the narrow streets'. They found a flat on the Via Gregoriana near the Spanish Steps, and there towards the end of 1947, in one of the coldest winters anyone could remember, a second daughter was born, Juliet – or, as I came to be known, Julie.

~

Tony and Zippa

How they weathered the interval is anyone's guess. They must have had fun in Italy that first year. They visited Siena in the summer for the Palio,* and in the autumn, someone lent them

---

* The annual bareback horse race round the Piazza Pubblico.

a beautiful, frescoed palazzo outside Venice for a holiday. They also found a weekend retreat outside Rome, on a hillside looking across to the little town of Tivoli, which they shared with friends from the embassy. But it was not easy. Zippa felt sick and nauseous throughout her pregnancy, which made the diplomatic round of cocktail parties and dinners hard to bear. It was difficult for Tony too, his first experience of what he had found so baffling in Zippa's letters when he was in North Africa. When the moment came, in late November, he was thrown in at the deep end. Zippa's labour was so short, and the birth itself so sudden, that 'Tony practically delivered me', she told his father, Arthur. And that was just the beginning. The baby turned out to be a screamer. For the next two months, I screamed all evening, every evening and half the night. They were both exhausted. 'A miserable little baby,' Zippa continued, 'although she looks fine and healthy.' Altogether 'no introduction to a baby could have been more beastly for Tony'.

Zippa was writing some three months after my birth, from Tivoli, where she had gone to rest and recover her health. From her tone – open, frank, confiding – it is clear that, somewhere along the line, she and Arthur had become firm friends. Zippa was in desperate comic-horror mode, cheering herself up, as always, by writing about it. Things were now beginning to get a little easier, she admitted, but the drama of it was recent enough for her to get a decent performance out of it for his entertainment.

The villain of the piece was my nurse – a Russian woman, always referred to as Signorina, ridden with superstition and old wives tales, 'wonderful' with the baby and Rosalind, but a terrible tyrant with Zippa. Signorina thought I was starving, and that Zippa's milk was all wrong. 'Butter!' she said, 'Cheese!' she said, 'Whipped Cream!' It would give the baby a 'vile crust on its

Signorina and Julie

face', she said. Zippa must drink more, eat more, and walk with her arms swinging, so! Signorina would tap on their bedroom door at intervals through the night, to say I needed feeding. Tony would groan, and Zippa would fall out of bed and run shivering to the nursery.

To make matters worse, Zippa had invited Tony's mother Eileen to stay over Christmas, just when everything was most fraught. And of course, there was also Rosalind:

At 7:30 just as we're in our first proper sleep, Rosalind bursts in with a book – 'Tell [i.e. read] me this' she says, and Tony and I dive to the bottom of the bed. Then, clatter, bang, crash! – breakfast being brought into the dining room. Eileen arrives – says brightly 'May I come in?' – looks obviously shocked at the scene of disarray and Tony dressing Rosalind in a fury – me too exhausted to move – ... the cook and maid can't take on Rosalind as they've quarrelled with Signorina – Tony, having turned the room upside down, flung his pyjamas to the winds, and left every single door and drawer gaping, is ready for breakfast … Eileen says she'll take Rosalind to school, Rosalind sits on the floor and says she won't go.

Zippa had never lived with Tony and Eileen together, and she was dismayed to discover that he was constantly irritated by his mother who in turn was offended by him. So she found herself forever smoothing things over between them. It was surprising of her to be so frank about these two with Arthur, but it sounds as though she had found a comrade-in-arms. She could trust him – like Dolly – to see the funny side.

Half the problem for Zippa was the servants. The diplomatic way of life required them, entertaining being part of the job: lunches, teas, drinks and dinners for colleagues at the embassy, for counterparts from the other embassies, for members of the host government and for anyone else of interest. When a diplomatic wife wasn't herself attending these things, her (unpaid) role was to plan and create them. In fact, directly and indirectly, everything about a diplomatic wife – her parties, her house, her clothes, her social talents – counted towards her husband's success or otherwise. And none of it could be done without, at the least, a cook, a maid and, if there were children, a nurse.

Zippa sometimes softened towards Signorina – an 'entertaining old witch', she called her. But the old witch set everyone else by the ears. 'The kitchen loathes her', she told Arthur. They thought she gave herself airs. The cook called her a 'pup of a bitch from the Siberian steppes'. All over the house, colossal rows would break out:

> Up and down stairs – doors are banged and then locked. The
> fire is out. I call for the maid or the cook. They are talking
> so loud and so fast behind closed doors that they can't hear.
> I burst in. Furious silence. Then both set on me and tell me
> their stories at one and the same time. I say 'yes, yes – but
> the fire – lunch'.

No one worked properly, nothing got done, Zippa did the household accounts and found she was being robbed left and right, and when the cook wanted to know the menu for the day, her Italian vanished and she couldn't think of any food at all.

The effect of all this on Tony was disastrous, she said: 'He loathes the fuss of domesticity and was swamped by it and he loathes not being free to do exactly what he wants when he wants.' There might have been a way out of the situation, Zippa thought. 'If anybody had been able to laugh … I wouldn't have found it so bad':

> but Tony and Eileen were angered and as a result I was
> humiliated and nervous and also was in no strong state of
> health to deal with all the difficulties. So six weeks of Hell
> were passed, with Tony depressed and irritable, me wretched,
> and Eileen … shocked at what she felt to be a change in
> Tony … The thing they both lack is a fundamental sense
> of humour – a sense of the ridiculous. A sense of fun is not
> the same thing.

For all her ebullience, Zippa was clearly feeling bleak. 'This second baby is perhaps a mistake', she says. She was also coming to conclusions about herself and Tony. Tony, she realised, was 'terrifically ambitious, without really knowing it'. That being so, 'I am just the wrong woman for him', she says. He is

full of vitality and he's clever and popular, and all set, I
think, to go far; but he needs someone of great character and
great charm and wit, who can speak at least French very
well, who is well-read and has plenty to say, to help him. I
am very slow, very lazy and completely uneducated, and
I forget everything. It drives him crazy.

All the same, she was surprised he minded quite so much, and
she wished she could take it all more lightly. But Tony's criticism
and any doubt she had of his affection were enough, she said,
to 'stamp out the only attraction I ever had, which was a
certain gaiety!':

And without being myself, I know I am absolutely no use to
Tony, and when I am no use, he makes me less so, so we are
in a vicious circle. I'll let you know when we get out of it, if
we haven't blown up!

I don't know what it was about Zippa that drove Tony crazy.
True, she hadn't had a formal education, but that wasn't so
unusual for women then, and she was no fool. Perhaps it was
her directness and simplicity. But Tony knew – people always
loved her. It was why they loved her. When he had first considered the Foreign Service, just after Tunis in 1943, he had said to
her – laughing a little at his presumption – 'you would make a
lovely ambassadress!' He was right. She was naturally gracious
– if that was what he meant. And the wives of diplomats, even
the wives of ambassadors, were not always so. Soon after arriving in Rome, he wrote to his father about two ambassadresses
he had just met, one current, the other retired. The first, he said,
was 'very brisk and business-like … rather like a schoolmistress',
and the other was 'somewhat devastating'. They had had her to

dinner: 'there was no possibility of anyone else talking at the same time', he said. She was 'obviously used to much larger rooms'. Lady Catherine de Bourgh comes to mind. Zippa wouldn't, I think, have found it difficult to shine.

Were it not, that is, for Simone. The 'someone' of charm and wit who spoke French, who was well-read and had plenty to say – this 'someone' was, of course, Simone. In her shadow, Zippa's sparkle dimmed and her light went out. Whatever she did, Simone stood behind her – her great advantage now being the reverse of what it had once been: she was not there. By the time Tony had established himself, with a career, a wife and two children, Simone had joined the impossible dreams that he'd always kept somewhere separate in his mind – the special, inviolable place that Zippa had first occupied when he had sailed for North Africa in 1942.

~

These were the worst days. I remember my mother telling me that, between them, Tony and Signorina made her so nervous that her milk dried up, and I was weaned at three months. But things did get better. She grew stronger, she got the house under control, Signorina departed, and the children became a pleasure. By the summer of 1948, she could report to Alured that the baby was 'quite captivating', with 'an excited, happy, amused little laugh' and, at eight months, almost walking. Rosalind too was 'entertaining' with the Italian she was learning. There were some wonderful times. One of the wives, Cécile Howard, 'a most beautiful French woman' said Zippa (another one!), was a brilliant pianist, and the first secretary at the embassy, Henry Hankey, was also an accomplished player.* Cécile and her husband, Mondi, were the

---

* Years later, Henry's son, Peri, became my husband.

Rosalind with Julie

couple with whom they shared the house near Tivoli. There was a piano there and friends would come out and join them – with the chance, always, of hearing some fine music-making. Zippa describes one particular gathering which included the war correspondent Alan Moorehead, and Peter Ustinov – Ustinov visiting Rome just then to shoot his film *Private Angelo*: 'He was brilliant and kept us long into the night in fits of laughter. When he isn't acting he is quiet and very natural, even retiring – looks rather a goof with his floppy figure, longish hair and too long upper lip.'

That Christmas had something of the old enchantment. 'This house looked wonderful' wrote Zippa to her sister Geraldine, 'with masses of ivy and holly', and a tree which she made beautiful 'with rather little decoration and that long straight icicle tinsel'. There is a hint of Stansted in her description. They gave Rosalind a doll's house, built like an Italian villa by the gardener out of old packing cases, and dressed with curtains and furniture made by Zippa. And Julie, 'tottering and shrieking, delighted with herself', was 'entranced with the tree'. She 'adores a party', said Zippa.

Two days later, Zippa went to a party herself. It was the Christmas dance at the Embassy and, Tony being unwell, she went on her own. She had a wonderful time, dancing into the small hours, with no shortage of partners. 'I enjoyed myself very much,' she wrote, 'and came back at three.'

Julie and Tony

Chapter 17

Dreams and shadows

When the Allies entered Rome on 5 June 1944, riding in the first jeep was Tony and Zippa's friend Mondi Howard, at that time an intelligence officer on the staff of General Eisenhower. Many decades later, Mondi described that moment to my husband, Peri, whose father Henry had been the musical first secretary at the embassy in Rome, when he was a small boy. It was just before sunrise when the column entered the city, Mondi said, no sight nor sound of anyone stirring. No one could be sure of what awaited them, whether the Germans had left entirely or whether danger lay ahead. As they rolled through the streets, the sun began to rise, and they noticed a window going up here, another there, someone stepping out onto a balcony further along. Little by little, the people of Rome came out of their houses and began to clap, the sound spreading as the sun rose. It was very moving, he said.

By the end of the war, Italy was suffering. After two decades of fascism under Mussolini, and a war in which it had fought first on one side and then on the other, the country was politically riven and bitter with vengeance and score settling. It was also desperately poor. Prices for everything were sky high and there was a thriving black market. That winter the Communist party called a General Strike in Rome. Zippa's Christmas shopping for the family in England was cloak and dagger: 'It was only by chance that I found a toy shop open at all and I had to creep in under half-lowered iron shutters to make my purchases in the dark, so that the shop-owner wouldn't be caught selling things!' And it was cold. Zippa didn't have enough blankets. The cheapest were £5 each – a huge sum then. 'I suppose no one has any extra blankets or eiderdowns (however old)', she asked her sister Geraldine, 'or by chance Tony's sleeping bag … as we are freezing here.'

All the same, Zippa and Tony always looked back on their years in Rome with nostalgia. It was an extraordinary time, and nothing subsequently could match the sense of possibility and goodwill that Mondi Howard conjured in his description of that first day. Zippa spoke of ambition in Tony. In a way, it was the moment for ambition. Tony was 30 in 1948, and for the first time since Cambridge, everything came together – place, time and work. The delay of war had exacerbated the frustration of a naturally impatient man, and now Rome made him feel like a champagne cork popping. Uncomfortable perhaps for those closest to him, but Zippa too felt the fizz, once the first dire months of my newborn life had faded.

~

After Rome, there was less sparkle. Tony once said that it would take years for Europe to heal, but that he wasn't as worried as he should be because Zippa would make everything right – for them at least. But face to face and day to day was a different matter. Tony's Algerian affair had driven deep. For Zippa nothing now could reverse that. Simone was such a close competitor, so like herself in many ways, so much the kind of person she might have hoped to be. Like a better educated sister – Veronica, say. Veronica, after all, had been given more of an education, and a

French one at that. In fact Zippa once told me that Tony had likened Simone to Veronica. Simone-Zippa-Veronica – whoever this composite person was – continued to haunt Zippa over the next decades, silent and unmentioned, but there. Like Europe, it would take a long time for her to heal.

And for Tony too. It was many years before he overcame the shadow of Simone. Simone and her husband emigrated to America, and much later, in the late 1950s, when Tony was posted to the United Nations in New York, he did an extraordinary thing. He took Zippa and me (I don't remember Rosalind being with us) to visit her and her husband at their home. I was about ten at the time, and I remember that day. I have no recollection of Simone, and I imagine that the four grown-ups discreetly arranged for Simone's husband to take me off, leaving the other three to themselves. At any rate, what I do remember is his study, and being with him, a kind and gentle man, who showed me how to make a fly for a fly-fishing rod. I never thought to wonder what had become of the others.

I mention this visit because a couple of years later, in 1960, Zippa brought it up in a letter to Alured. The marriage at that time was in another unhappy period, and Dolly – who had also emigrated to the States – was staying with them in New York. As an old friend, she was a natural confidante to both of them – and, as Zippa explained to Alured, Tony 'confirmed to Dolly what I know' –

That the image of Simone was always in the background, right up to 2½ years ago, when seeing her again laid her ghost (in a happy way).

Sadly, the exorcism did nothing to help the marriage. In fact, the present crisis, in 1960, was to be the last. It led in the end to divorce and, for Tony, to re-marriage and another child, a son. It is a painful story – more knives, driving deeper now – but it goes beyond the scope of this wartime tale. Only this last American inch of Simone's long Algerian shadow belongs. The irony and the pity of it, as it appeared to Zippa at the time, was that the end of her marriage to Tony arose ultimately from what might have been its saving. Namely, from the laying of Simone's ghost.

I used to think that my mother was a dreamer and my father was a man of the world. I'm not so sure now. Zippa described Tony in Rome as clever and ambitious. Later, in New York, she told Alured of conversations she had had with 'all sorts of heads of Foreign Delegations' at the U.N. who had come up to her and told her that Tony 'is quite outstandingly brilliant as a diplomat and that he will go very far'. And yet, beneath the career, Tony had always been wrapped in dreams. He had been born in the last year of the First World War and had come of age in the first year of the next war. In between, he had grown up with the pacifist, socialist and anti-imperialist views held by many at the time, including his father. And alongside the politics had run a certain aesthetic ideal, a love of beauty, elegance, charm, and a horror of ugliness. In 1939, at the very moment when horror and ugliness seemed to have won, his imagination had been lighted up by Zippa. The years of separation that followed had only heightened the flame, and all his idealism and love of beauty had come to rest on her. She had carried the burden of his dreams – and when ordinary life returned, they had crushed her.

For who could carry such a load? Could it have been Simone? What was it about that visit to her in America that laid her ghost? One or two things suggest themselves. Tony in New York might have thought of himself at a turning point. He was approaching

40; his U.N. posting was a significant step in his career; and at about that time, his mother Eileen died. The future beckoned. Now was his moment. His visit to Simone was a pilgrimage to the past, to the war, to the whole entanglement of feelings that had wound the three of them – Tony, Zippa and Simone – into an impossible knot. He had once thought he could reconcile Zippa and Simone in his heart – whatever that meant. I suspect that what Simone now showed him was that life had moved on. They may have had a delightful afternoon, but practically speaking the matter was closed. It woke him from his dream, and in that moment the knot unravelled and both women fell away. It's impossible to guess. My mother spoke to me about the Simone of Algeria but never the Simone she met. My father never spoke to me of her at all.

~

The war was over. It had done its worst. For Tony and Zippa, their parting was its last breath – and with it, comes the end of this story. The rest is coda. My parents lived on until the turn of the century, smoothing over the past and, perhaps for the sake of their daughters, remaining friends. War had driven them together and it had driven them apart. But it had also driven the birth of their children. Tony had had misgivings with both of us, but he had been pleased with Rosalind in the end, and even I – as Zippa told Arthur – had seemed a good idea: to 'patch up our marriage and be a companion to Rosalind'.

It worked for a while. But I am left with a sense of sadness and futility. There would have been no wounds to patch, or only small ones, if they had loved and never married. Zippa used to say 'at least I have you two', and it seems a little extravagant to reply that it would have been better not to have been born. But Tony had suspected almost from the first that Zippa needed someone older and more fulfilled, with more to give than he had. Then, as always, he had shut his eyes tight – and she had too. If only they had had time. Of all the things war robbed them of, time was the most valuable. I remember Zippa's remarks on the 60s generation – how sensible we were, she would say, to live together, to take our time, to let marriage wait. How progressive she was, we thought. She was – but I realise now that she envied us, and that she was remembering herself and Tony.

And yet something remains: the intensity of the whole thing, their romance and the desperation of the times they lived through. Reading the letters was a surprise to me. Not so much Zippa's, in which her voice was instantly recognisable. But Tony's: his reflections on books, the freshness of his language, above all his diffidence and self-doubt. I remember him as expansive, solid, oak-like. The language always mattered to him, but when I went to university in the 60s to read English Literature, it was the *Shorter Oxford English Dictionary* he gave me, and *Fowler's Modern English Usage* – not Shakespeare or the poets. Accuracy, clarity, pith – these were his virtues. The letters he wrote to us from his travels were interesting, full of information, but they rarely took flight. Something, it seems, went underground. Perhaps it was inevitable. The feeling of those wartime letters belonged just there. They sprang from extraordinary circumstances. What was laid bare then, was likely in ordinary times to become more or less skinned over.

I don't suppose, in all their later encounters, that Tony and Zippa talked much about the past. But I don't think they forgot it either. It was their peculiar possession, and they kept hold of it, if only in their letters. When they parted, Tony took her letters with him, and she kept his. In the following 40 years there were several foreign postings and house moves and the question must have arisen – what to do with them? Some did go missing, especially Zippa's. In fact it's surprising how many survived the hurry and violence of North Africa, the sudden stuffings away and flinging of rucksacks into trucks and jeeps. But enough remained to tell their story. I doubt they re-read them much, if at all. My mother's family were notorious for keeping letters, and in later life Zippa re-read those, sometimes annotating the envelopes. There are no annotations on her letters from Tony. But, re-read or not, they stood for something: youth, love, war, history. Who knows – perhaps, in some corner of their minds, they meant them to be found. And so they were, by his three children, at different times, as their houses were cleared – our half-brother kindly delivering Tony's packet, the letters from Zippa, into my hands.

~

In his second marriage, particularly in his retirement, Tony achieved the kind of life he had dreamt of during the war – more travel, for pleasure now, and a generous, hospitable house in the country. My mother never re-married. And yet, in spite of everything, she recovered. Like a daisy, my sister once said, irrepressible. Her siblings healed her and over the years, her old gaiety returned. It's preserved now in her letters to them. Her children and grandchildren became part of her material now, and it's odd to see ourselves in these letters, shaped, as I have shaped her, into characters in her special world, trailing a history we knew nothing about. I can see my mother now, better than I did then. It was with them, her brothers and sisters, that she was happiest and most alive, and I realise why those summers spent with them back in England, remain my own most vivid memories: Zippa, Veronica, Betty and the rest, all talking and laughing while I sat goggling, ears flapping, unobserved.

As for Alured, he never married, and Zippa made a home for him in the half-basement of her house in London. They grew old together. He would join her for supper from time to time and they would entertain together. They loved the garden and they made it in their particular way – with just a touch, in miniature, of their old garden in Mitcham. Zippa's grandchildren got muddled and sometimes thought they were husband and wife. I too remember an aura of coupledom about them. Once in particular, when we were playing some kind of acting game – charades perhaps – and they made an entrance together as Alfred Lunt and his wife Lynn Fontanne, famous American actors of their youth. Just for a moment, I saw them as a stunningly elegant pair – just that. There was a gaiety and naturalness about the way they walked in, arm in arm, that was utterly captivating. No ambassador and ambassadress at a British Embassy ball could have done it better.

One last glimpse: my mother, in her 60s, writing to her sister Veronica in the hot summer of 1976:

I am sitting in the drawing-room on a sunny afternoon where it is cooler than in the garden. The sunlight plays all about the room, dancing with the moving shadows of the trees … I am quiet and alone, listening to Arthur Rubinstein playing Chopin's nocturnes. Suddenly I want to dance, with the same lift and passion as I had years ago. And now my body is old … Well, that hovering lift is just below the surface and something wonderful could come if only it could soar and be free. So strange to look about the room, and feel it in my heart, just there.

Zippa, years later, in her London garden

Notes

Chapter 1

1. Anne Olivier Bell (ed.), *The Diary of Virginia Woolf* (Hogarth Press, 1984), V, p. 242.

2. Frances Faviell, *A Chelsea Concerto* (Cassell and Co. Ltd, 1959; reprinted by Dean Street Press, 2016), p. 17.

3. Norman Longmate, *How We Lived Then: A History of Everyday Life during the Second World War* (Hutchinson, 1971), p. 11.

4. *A Chelsea Concerto*, p. 7.

5. Ibid., p. 11.

6. Ibid., pp. 14–15.

7. See: https://www.cooksinfo.com/british-wartime-food/.

8. W.E. Shewell-Cooper, *Land Girl: A Manual for Volunteers in the Women's Land Army* (1941; Amberley 2011).

9. Ibid., p.iv.

Chapter 2

1. Elizabeth Bowen, *The Heat of the Day* (1949; Vintage, 1998), p. 59.

2. Quoted in Juliet Gardiner, *Wartime: Britain 1939–1945* (Headline Book publishing, 2004; pbk 2005), p. 189.

3. Mollie Panter-Downes, *London War Notes: 1939–1945* (Farrar, Straus & Giroux, 1971), pp. 69–70.

4. *A Chelsea Concerto*, 'Prologue', p. 1.

5. Ibid, p. 98. For her description of the raid on the surrounding streets, see pp. 96–98.

6. See Angus Calder, *The People's War, Britain 1939–1945* (1969; Pimlico, 1994), p. 248. For class snobbery in the army generally see pp. 247–48.

Chapter 3

1. See *A Chelsea Concerto*, p. 120.

2. 'After a Raid', *This Our War* (Statesman Press, Calcutta, 1942), p. 13.

3. *A Chelsea Concerto*, pp. 211–20.

4. *This Our War*, 'After a Raid', p. 12; 'Impressions of Wartime England', p.ii; '"Blitz" Scare in London', p. 11; 'London's Changing Face', p. 30.

5. *A Chelsea Concerto*, p. 92.

6. Bernard Kops, quoted in *Wartime: Britain 1939–1945*, p. 377.

7. See *The People's War*, p. 184.

8. *The People's War*, p. 186.

9. See Paul Sangster, *Doctor Sangster* (The Epworth Press, 1962), p. 189.

10. Ibid., see Chapter XII.

11. *Wartime: Britain 1939-1945*, p. 171.

12. See Mollie Panter-Downes, *London War Notes, 1939–1945* (Farrar, Straus & Giroux, 1971), p. 213.

13. See *Wartime: Britain 1939–1945*, p. 183.

14. See *Wartime: Britain 1939–1945*, pp. 168–169.

15. Quoted in Pamela Dellar (ed.), *Plays without Theatres: Recollections of The Compass Players, Travelling Theatre (1944–52)* (Highgate Publications, [Beverley] Ltd, 1989), p. 1.

Chapter 4

1. *How We Lived Then*, p. 275.

2. February 1942. Quoted in ed. Penelope Middelboe et al, *We Shall Never Surrender: Wartime Diaries 1939–1945* (Macmillan 2011; pbk 2012), p. 159.

3. *London War Notes, 1939–1945*, p. 213.

Chapter 6

1. John Bierman and Colin Smith, *Alamein: War Without Hate* (Viking, 2002; Penguin Books. 2003), p. 255.

2. *The Desert War*, p. 9; p. 3.

3. H.S. Gear, M.D., D.P.H., 'Hygiene Aspects of the El Alamein Victory 1942', *British Medical Journal*, 18 March 1944.

4. Col. Ronald F. Bellamy, MD, U.S. Army and Col. Craig H. Llewellyn, MD, U.S. Army, Retired, 'Preventable Casualties: Rommel's Flaw, Slim's Edge', *Military Review*, May–June, 2020. The authors refer to *The German Army 1933–1945* by Matthew Cooper, who quotes Sir Sheldon F. Dudley: 'Montgomery says the Eighth Army won, but Rommel claimed the victory for dysentery.'

5. 'Hygiene Aspects of the El Alamein Victory 1942'

6. Hermione Ranfurly, *To War with Whitaker: The Wartime Diaries of the Countess of Ranfurly 1939–1945* (William Heinemann 1994; Mandarin Paperbacks, 1996), p. 134.

7. *To War with Whitaker*, p. 105.

8. See *Alamein: War Without Hate*, pp. 328 and 334.

9. See Ken Ford, *The Mareth Line 1943: The End in Africa* (Osprey Publishing, 2012), pp. 28–9.

10. *London War Notes, 1939–1945*, p. 5.

11. *A Chelsea Concerto*, p. 111.

12. Quoted in *We Shall Never Surrender: Wartime Diaries 1939–1945*, p. 213.

13. Quoted in *The Desert War*, p. 454.

14. *The Desert War*, p. 196.

15. *Alamein: War Without Hate*, p. 348.

Chapter 7

1. *The King's Royal Rifle Corps Chronicle, 1943* (Warren and Son, 1944), p. 85.

2. Ibid., p. 89.

3. Quoted in *Alamein: War Without Hate*, p. 395. The description of the fighting at enemy machine-gun nests by the Gurkhas serving with the Indian Division is particularly bloodcurdling, pp. 391–2.

Chapter 8

1. https://www.cvce.eu/en/obj/address_given_by_winston_churchill_
   on_post_war_21_march_1943-en-831b4069-27e5-4cd7-a607-
   57d31278584d.html.

2. *The Desert War*, p. 196.

3. *The King's Royal Rifle Corps Chronicle*, p. 93.

4. See Philip Jordan, *Jordan's Tunis Diary* (Collins, 1943), p. 235.
   Jordan tells of sudden optimism in military circles that Tunis would
   fall by 27 April, making Africa 'clear' by 4 May.

5. Ken Ford, *The Mareth Line 1943: The End in Africa* (Osprey
   Publishing, 2012), p. 92.

6. *The King's Royal Rifle Corps Chronicle*, p. 90 and p. 91.

7. *Jordan's Tunis Diary*. These five quotes can be found variously on
   pp. 220–21 and 244.

8. *The King's Royal Rifle Corps Chronicle*, p. 96.

9. Ibid., p. 100.

10. Ibid., p. 108.

11. Alan Moorehead, *A Late Education* (Hamish Hamilton, 1970),
    pp. 134–5.

12. *The King's Royal Rifle Corps Chronicle*, p. 102.

Chapter 9

1. See *London War Notes, 1939–1945*, p. 275.

2. *The Daily Sketch*, 25 May 1943.

Chapter 10

1. https://api.parliament.uk/historic-hansard/commons/1943/mar/18/
   foreign-service-reform.

2. *To War with Whitaker*, p. 224.

Chapter 11

1. See Pamela Dellar (ed.), *Plays Without Theatres: Recollections of The
   Compass Players, Travelling Theatre 1944–52* (Highgate Publications
   (Beverley), 1989).

Chapter 12

1. *To War with Whitaker*, p. 204.

Chapter 13

1. See W.J.M. Mackenzie, *The Secret History of SOE: The Special Operations Executive 1940–1945* (St Ermin's Press, 2000), pp. 604–5.

2. National Archives, Kew, catalogue numbers in order: HS6/490, 501 and 517. For a list of the Jedburgh teams, missions and summary descriptions, see: http://www.ampltd.co.uk.

3. Alan Moorehead, *Eclipse* (Hamish Hamilton, 1945), p. 98.

4. *The Desert War*, p. 445.

Chapter 14

1. See *The Secret History of SOE*, pp. 688–89.

2. *London War Notes, 1939–1945*, p. 335.

3. https://api.parliament.uk/historic-hansard/commons/1944/aug/02/war-situation#S5CV0402P0_19440802_HOC_380.

4. *The People's War*, pp. 490–91.

5. *Wartime: Britain 1939–1945*, p. 175.

Chapter 15

1. See http://www.ampltd.co.uk/collections_az/SOE-1-5/description.aspx. Part 5: Italy, 1941–48 (Public Record Office Class HS 6/775-908).

2. *London War Notes, 1939–1945*, p. 350.

Bibliography

John Bierman and Colin Smith, *Alamein: War Without Hate*, Viking, 2002.

Angus Calder, *The People's War: Britain 1939–1945*, Pimlico, 1969.

Pamela Dellar (ed.), *Plays Without Theatres: Recollections of the Compass Players, Travelling Theatre (1944–1952)*, Highgate Publications [Beverley] Ltd., 1989.

Frances Faviell, *A Chelsea Concerto*, Cassell and Co. Ltd., 1959.

Ken Ford, *The Mareth Line 1943: The End in Africa*, Osprey Publishing, 2012.

Juliet Gardiner, *Wartime: Britain 1939–1945*, Headline Book Publishing, 2004.

H.S. Gear, M.D., D.P.H., 'Hygiene Aspects of the El Alamein Victory 1942', *British Medical Journal*, 18 March 1944.

Philip Jordan, *Jordan's Tunis Diary*, Collins, 1943.

Norman Longmate, *How We Lived Than: A History of Everyday Life During the Second World War*, Hutchinson, 1971.

W.J.M. Mackenzie, *The Secret History of SOE: The Special Operations Executive 1940–1945*, St Ermin's Press, 2000.

Penelope Middelboe et al. (eds), *We Shall Never Surrender: Wartime Diaries 1939–1945*, Macmillan, 2012.

Arthur Moore, *This Our War* (Statesman Press, Calcutta, 1942)

Alan Moorehead, *The Desert War*, Hamish Hamilton, 2009.

Alan Moorehead, *Eclipse*, Hamish Hamilton, 1945.

Alan Moorehead, *A Late Education*, Hamish Hamilton, 1970.

Mollie Panter-Downes, *London War Notes: 1939–1945*, Farrar, Straus & Giroux, 1971.

Hermione Ranfurly, *To War with Whitaker: The Wartime Diaries of the Countess Ranfurly 1939–1945*, William Heinemann, 1994.

Paul Sangster, *Doctor Sangster*, The Epworth Press, 1962.

W.E. Shewell-Cooper, *Land Girl: A Manual for Volunteers in the Women's Land Army* (1941; Amberley 2011).

The King's Royal Rifle Corps Chronicle 1943, Warren and Son, 1944.

Acknowledgements

All those who knew my parents during the war, when most of this book is set, died long before I began to write it. My sister Rosalind, to whom I would most naturally have turned, has for many years been unwell with dementia. I am grateful, therefore, to my oldest childhood friends who knew my parents in the aftermath of these events: Natalia and Margarita Jimenez, and Katharine Urquhart, all of whom read an early draft and gave me heart at a time when I had little idea whether the story was worth telling outside the family.

A stiffer test lay with friends who scarcely knew my parents, and I must thank Lindsay and Henry Herford for the encouragement they gave me at that same early stage.

The stiffest test of all came with friends who never knew my parents: Penelope Middelboe, one of the editors of *We Shall Never Surrender: Wartime Diaries 1939–1945*, and the historian Jon Rosebank. Both were able to see the letters my parents wrote not just as personal expressions but as historical documents, and both helped me to understand them in that light too. Jon in particular gave me the impetus to do more with my material, to widen the perspective and to paint a fuller picture of what it was like to live through the war in those particular places. Whether I have succeeded is another matter, but I am very grateful for his insights.

I am also grateful to my agent, Peter Buckman of The Ampersand Agency, for believing in the book and responding to it so generously. Equally, my thanks to my editor at Icon Books, Ellen Conlon, not only for her enthusiasm, but for her keen textual eye.

Finally, I thank my family for putting up with this story as it evolved, for listening at odd and inconvenient times to bits of it being read out, and generally for taking an interest. The person closest to all this was, of course, Peri, my husband, who has always been unfailingly patient and kind. The peculiar coincidence of our shared family backgrounds – not only in the diplomatic world, but in Rome itself – has been invaluable. To have been able to talk to someone whose parents were close to mine, to discover in him memories of Rome just after the war, memories even of me and Rosalind, has been an amazing piece of luck. Looking back now, I realise how much it served to connect me with a past that lies just out of my reach.